Questions & Answers
Remedies

Carolina Academic Press Questions & Answers Series

Questions & Answers: Administrative Law, Third Edition
Linda D. Jellum, Karen A. Jordan

Questions & Answers: Antitrust
Shubha Ghosh

Questions & Answers: Bankruptcy, Second Edition
Mary Jo Wiggins

Questions & Answers: Business Associations, Second Edition
Douglas M. Branson

Questions & Answers: Civil Procedure, Fifth Edition
William V. Dorsaneo, III, Elizabeth Thornburg, and Brooke D. Coleman

Questions & Answers: Constitutional Law, Third Edition
Paul E. McGreal, Linda S. Eads, Charles W. Rhodes

Questions & Answers: Contracts, Third Edition
Scott J. Burnham

Questions & Answers: Copyright Law, Second Edition
Dave Fagundes, Robert C. Lind

Questions & Answers: Criminal Law, Fourth Edition
Emily Marcus Levine, Paul Marcus

Questions & Answers: Criminal Procedure — Police Investigation, Fourth Edition
Wayne A. Logan

Questions & Answers: Criminal Procedure — Prosecution and Adjudication, Fourth Edition
Wayne A. Logan

Questions & Answers: Environmental Law
Dru Stevenson

Questions & Answers: Evidence, Fourth Edition
Paul C. Giannelli

Questions & Answers: Family Law, Third Edition
Mark Strasser

Questions & Answers: Federal Estate & Gift Taxation, Third Edition
James M. Delaney, Elaine Hightower Gagliardi

Questions & Answers: Federal Income Tax, Second Edition
James M. Delaney

Questions & Answers: Intellectual Property, Third Edition
Gary Myers, Lee Ann Wheelis Lockridge

Questions & Answers: International Law
Rebecca Bratspies

Questions & Answers: Patent Law
Cynthia M. Ho

Questions & Answers: Payment Systems, Second Edition
Timothy R. Zinnecker

Questions & Answers: Professional Responsibility, Fourth Edition
Patrick Emery Longan

Questions & Answers: Property, Second Edition
John Copeland Nagle

Questions & Answers: Remedies, Second Edition
Rachel M. Janutis, Thomas O. Main

Questions & Answers: Secured Transactions, Fourth Edition
Bruce A. Markell, Timothy R. Zinnecker

Questions & Answers: The First Amendment, Fourth Edition
Russell L. Weaver, William D. Araiza

Questions & Answers: Torts, Fourth Edition
Anita Bernstein

Questions & Answers: Trademark and Unfair Competition
Vince F. Chiappetta

Questions & Answers: Wills, Trusts, and Estates, Third Edition
Thomas M. Featherston, Jr.

Questions & Answers
Remedies

Multiple-Choice and Short-Answer Questions and Answers

SECOND EDITION

Rachel M. Janutis
PROFESSOR OF LAW
CAPITAL UNIVERSITY LAW SCHOOL

Thomas Orin Main
WILLIAM S. BOYD PROFESSOR OF LAW
UNIVERSITY OF NEVADA, LAS VEGAS, WILLIAM S. BOYD SCHOOL OF LAW

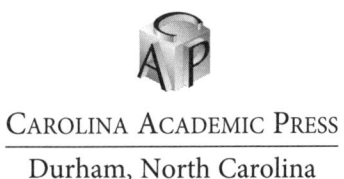

CAROLINA ACADEMIC PRESS
Durham, North Carolina

Copyright © 2022
Carolina Academic Press, LLC
All Rights Reserved

ISBN 978-1-5310-2319-5
e-ISBN 978-1-5310-2320-1
LCCN 2021055534

Carolina Academic Press, LLC
700 Kent Street
Durham, North Carolina 27701
Telephone (919) 489-7486
Fax (919) 493-5668
www.cap-press.com

Printed in the United States of America

Contents

Preface	vii
About the Authors	ix
Questions	1
Topic 1: Introduction to Remedies	3
Topic 2: Compensatory Damages	5
Topic 3: Contract Damages	9
Topic 4: Damages for Bodily Injury and Death	17
Topic 5: Property Damages	25
Topic 6: Punitive Damages	29
Topic 7: Qualifying for Injunctions	33
Topic 8: Injunctions	37
Topic 9: Temporary and Preliminary Injunctions	41
Topic 10: Contempt	47
Topic 11: Unjust Enrichment	51
Topic 12: Equitable Restitution	55
Topic 13: Declaratory Judgment	59
Topic 14: Remedial Defenses	63
Topic 15: Attorney Fees	67
Topic 16: Right to Jury Trial	71
Practice Final Exam: Questions	73
Answers	95
Topic 1: Introduction to Remedies	97
Topic 2: Compensatory Damages	101
Topic 3: Contract Damages	107
Topic 4: Damages for Bodily Injury and Death	115
Topic 5: Property Damages	123
Topic 6: Punitive Damages	129

Topic 7: Qualifying for Injunctions	133
Topic 8: Injunctions	137
Topic 9: Temporary and Preliminary Injunctions	141
Topic 10: Contempt	147
Topic 11: Unjust Enrichment	151
Topic 12: Equitable Restitution	157
Topic 13: Declaratory Judgment	161
Topic 14: Remedial Defenses	165
Topic 15: Attorney Fees	169
Topic 16: Right to Jury Trial	173
Practice Final Exam: Answers	175
Index	199

Preface

Most courses in law school focus on one substantive area of law—tort law or contract law—and explore how that body of law applies to various factual settings. The study of Remedies provides students with a unique opportunity to study the law from a trans-substantive perspective. By integrating the various substantive areas of law, Remedies allows students to focus on the commonalities of judicial relief across the board. In Remedies, students also consider how legal theories from several substantive areas of law can apply to a single transaction or dispute and how those differing legal theories may produce different outcomes in a given case. Remedies also provides students with an opportunity to observe how the law impacts the everyday lives of the parties to litigation by focusing on what relief the parties will take from the case—the "bottom line." Finally, through the study of Remedies, students can gain insight into the value that society places on various personal rights and interests. Remedies explores questions about which losses we choose to compensate as well as the manner in which we compensate and value those losses. The answers to these questions reflect on the value we place on the underlying rights and interests that have been harmed.

This book is designed to guide students through the study of this multi-faceted area of the law. It can be used to assist in preparation for a final exam. However, students will also find it useful to assist in understanding core topics and issues during the course of the semester.

To this end, the first part of the book is divided into separate chapters. Each chapter concerns one specific Remedies topic. The topics covered in these chapters represent the core topics covered by most leading Remedies casebooks. Each of these chapters provides multiple choice and short answer questions covering the main issues surrounding the specified topic. The questions are designed to highlight common areas of misunderstanding. The corresponding answers and explanations are intended to dispel common misconceptions and strengthen understanding and comprehension of troublesome areas.

The second part of the book consists of a practice final exam. The practice final exam, like the individual chapters, consists of multiple choice and short answer questions. It also includes sample essay questions. However, unlike the first part of the book, the topic or topics covered by a question are not expressly identified. Additionally, the questions are not organized by topic but rather appear in a randomly selected order. Finally, some of the questions raise issues pertaining to multiple topics.

We hope that students will find this book to be useful and that students will find the study of Remedies to be both fascinating and thought-provoking. Finally, we wish to thank the numerous students who have inspired us to write this book and our families for their support and patience during the completion of this project.

Rachel M. Janutis
Thomas Orin Main
October 2021

About the Authors

Rachel M. Janutis is Professor of Law at Capital University Law School. She teaches courses in Remedies, Torts, Civil Procedure, and Complex Litigation. Professor Janutis is a co-author with Professors Murray Tabb and Thomas Main of *Cases and Problems on Remedies*. She also has authored several articles on remedies and civil procedure. She is a member of the United States Supreme Court Bar, the State Bar of Illinois, the American Bar Association, the Illinois State Bar Association, the Ohio State Bar Association and the Columbus Bar Association. Professor Janutis previously served on the executive committee and as chair of the Remedies section of the American Association of Law Schools.

Thomas Orin Main is William S. Boyd Professor of Law at the University of Nevada, Las Vegas William S. Boyd School of Law. Professor Main teaches Remedies, Civil Procedure, and Conflict of Laws. Professor Main is a co-author with Professors Murray Tabb and Rachel Janutis of *Cases and Problems on Remedies*. He has authored books and numerous articles on civil procedure, remedies and conflict of laws. He is a member of the American Law Institute and the International Association of Procedural Law. Professor Main previously served on the executive committee and as chair of the Civil Procedure section of the American Association of Law Schools.

Questions

Topic 1   Questions

Introduction to Remedies

1. Which of the following are remedies at law?

    (A) Replevin.

    (B) Specific Performance.

    (C) Constructive Trust.

    (D) Backpay.

2. What is the difference between substitutional and specific remedies?

    ANSWER:

3. Plaintiff, a former employee, sued Employer in federal court. Plaintiff alleged that Employer wrongfully fired Plaintiff for engaging in political conduct. Plaintiff initially sought reinstatement and backpay. Plaintiff filed an amended complaint, seeking front pay in lieu of reinstatement and adding a jury demand. Employer moved to strike Plaintiff's jury demand. Assuming that Plaintiff's jury demand is timely, how should the court rule on Employer's motion?

    (A) The court should grant the motion because Plaintiff seeks both legal and equitable relief.

    (B) The court should grant the motion because Plaintiff seeks only equitable relief.

    (C) The court should deny the motion because Plaintiff seeks only monetary relief.

    (D) The court should deny the motion because Plaintiff seeks both legal and equitable relief.

4. Plaintiff, a former employee, sued Employer in New Colorado state court. Plaintiff alleges that Employer wrongfully fired her for reporting misconduct in violation of New Colorado law. Plaintiff seeks compensatory damages for emotional distress, reinstatement and backpay. Plaintiff's Complaint includes a jury demand. Employer moved to strike Plaintiff's jury demand. Assuming New Colorado follows the equitable clean-up doctrine, how should the court rule on the motion?

    (A) The court must deny the motion because Plaintiff seeks both legal and equitable relief.

    (B) The court must grant the motion because Plaintiff seeks both legal and equitable relief.

(C) The court should grant the motion if it concludes that the legal claims significantly overlap with the equitable claims.

(D) The court should deny the motion if it concludes that the legal claims significantly overlap with the equitable claims.

5. Calibraska state law makes it illegal for an employer to inquire into an employee's credit history or perform a credit check on an employee as a condition of employment. The statute provides that:

> An employee who is aggrieved by a violation of this Act is entitled to recover from the violating employer $500 per violation and attorney fees incurred in maintaining an action against the employer.

Until recently, Potter was employed by Darko Industries in its Calibraska office. Unbeknownst to Potter, a Darko supervisor obtained a copy of Potter's credit report from a consumer reporting agency. As a result of the information contained in the credit report, Darko fired Potter. Despite reasonable efforts, Potter has been unable to find another job. Potter brought an action against Darko under the statute. In the lawsuit, Potter seeks reinstatement and backpay. Assuming that Potter can show that Darko violated the Act, what are the best arguments in favor of granting Potter reinstatement and backpay? What are the best arguments in favor of limiting Potter's recovery to $500 and attorney fees?

ANSWER:

6. Publisher entered into a contract with Producer under which Producer granted Publisher the exclusive right to publish a series of graphic novels based on Producer's successful television show. After Publisher began production of the series, Producer informed Publisher that Producer would be granting licensing rights to a competing publisher as well. Publisher sued Producer for breach of contract. Publisher seeks an order of specific performance compelling Producer to honor the exclusivity clause and compensatory damages for lost profits as a result of the loss of exclusivity. If Publisher prevails in its lawsuit, which of the following is true?

(A) The court cannot award specific performance and compensatory damages because that would constitute a double recovery under any circumstances.

(B) The court cannot award specific performance and compensatory damages because an award of compensatory damages would be inconsistent with a finding that Publisher's remedy at law was inadequate.

(C) The court may award specific performance and compensatory damages only if the compensatory damages are limited to an amount that is necessary to compensate for profits Publisher has already lost.

(D) The court should award specific performance and compensatory damages if Producer acted in bad faith.

Topic 2   Questions

Compensatory Damages

[handwritten: CL   benefit of bargain]

7. Contractor entered into a contract to construct an office building according to Owner's specifications. The specifications called for the front door of the building to face south. Contractor constructed the building with the door facing west. Owner sued Contractor for breach of contract. Under which of the following circumstances, if any, is ==Owner likely to recover the cost to remedy the error?==

    (A) The building must be razed and rebuilt with the front door facing south. *[circled A]*

    (B) A building with a front door facing south is more aesthetically pleasing than a building with a front door facing west.

    (C) The specifications called for the front door to face south so that Owner could capitalize on prevailing winds to cool the building. *[circled C]* *[handwritten: defect frustrates the purpose → that's when you'd get the money to rebuild]*

    (D) Owner will not be entitled to recover the cost to remedy the defect under any circumstances.

8. After retiring from a successful career as an attorney, Benson entered into an agreement to open and operate a Pizza Pal franchise restaurant. Under the terms of the franchise agreement, Pizza Pal agreed to permit Benson to use its trademarks and name. Pizza Pal also agreed to provide Benson with its secret recipe. In exchange, Benson agreed to use reasonable efforts to promote the franchise and to pay Pizza Pal a certain percentage of the profits. ==Benson spent $10,000 to advertise the opening of the franchise.== Two days before the mutually agreed upon opening date, Pizza Pal repudiated the contract. If Benson sues Pizza Pal for breach of contract, what will be the likely measure of Benson's recovery?

    (A) Benson will be entitled to recover lost profits because Benson's success as an attorney demonstrates that Benson would have operated a successful franchise.

    (B) Benson will be entitled to recover the money expended to advertise the restaurant because Benson expended the money in essential reliance under the contract. *[circled B]*

    (C) Benson will be entitled to recover both the lost profits and the money expended on advertising.

    (D) Benson will be entitled to no damages because Benson cannot prove any losses with reasonable certainty.

9. After retiring from a successful career as an attorney, Benson decided to open a restaurant. Benson entered into an agreement with Contractor to renovate a commercial building for use as the restaurant. Pursuant to the agreement, Contractor was to complete construction by a

specified date. While construction was taking place, Benson spent $10,000 advertising the date for the opening of the restaurant. Contractor failed to complete construction on time, and Benson could not open as advertised. If Benson sues Contractor for breach of the contract, what will be the likely measure of Benson's recovery?

(A) Benson will be entitled to recover the money expended to advertise the restaurant opening because Benson expended the money in essential reliance under the contract.

(B) Benson will be entitled to recover the money expended to advertise the restaurant opening only if Contractor could reasonably foresee that Benson would incur these expenses.

(C) Benson will not be entitled to recover the money expended to advertise the restaurant opening because Benson cannot prove cost of the advertising with reasonable certainty.

(D) Benson will not be entitled to recover the money expended to advertise the restaurant opening unless Benson can prove that the anticipated profits exceeded the cost of the advertising.

10. Which of the following is not an example of special or consequential damages?

(A) Medical expenses in a personal injury action.

(B) Damages for lost use in an action for damage to an automobile.

(C) Lost earnings in an action for defamation.

(D) None of the above.

11. Under which of the following circumstances will the buyer be most likely to recover lost profits?

(A) A finished goods manufacturer produces contracted-for component parts in-house at a cost that exceeds the market value of substitute component parts.

(B) A sole proprietor fails to purchase a replacement delivery truck when a comparable truck is available at the same price in a different state.

(C) A farmer is unable to find a replacement tractor at the start of the planting season when the seller repudiated the contract three months before the start of the planting season.

(D) None of the above.

12. Distinguish conduct which constitutes comparative or contributory negligence from conduct which constitutes a failure to mitigate damages.

ANSWER:

QUESTIONS · TOPIC 2: COMPENSATORY DAMAGES

13. Owner entered into a contract with Rancher to board and care for Owner's healthy cows. Owner intended to breed the cows and sell the calves when the cows reached maturity. Rancher failed to properly care for and feed the cows. As a result, the cows became sickly and were unable to breed. Owner purchased medicine and supplements and hired a veterinarian in an attempt to nurse the cows back to health. Owner's efforts were unsuccessful. If Owner sues Rancher for breach of contract, which of the following will be true?

    (A) Owner will not be entitled to recover the cost to nurse the cows back to health because Owner's efforts were unsuccessful.

    (B) Owner will not be entitled to recover the cost to nurse the cows back to health because Owner failed to notify Rancher of its intent to nurse the cows back to health before Owner undertook the efforts.

    (C) Owner will be entitled to recover the cost to nurse the cows back to health only if Rancher acted in bad faith.

    (D) Owner will be entitled to recover the cost to nurse the cows back to health as long as Owner's efforts were reasonable at the time the Owner undertook them.

14. Corporation hired Executive to serve as President and Chief Executive Officer of Corporation. Executive's employment contract prohibited Corporation from terminating Executive's employment except for cause. Corporation wrongfully discharged Executive. After the discharge, Executive searched for a new job. Executive received only one offer. A smaller corporation offered Executive a position as one of six executive vice presidents. Executive declined the offer. If Executive sues for breach of contract, which of the following will be true?

    (A) Executive will be entitled to the remaining salary Executive would have earned under the employment contract less any expenses Executive saves as a result of the breach.

    (B) Executive will be entitled to the difference between the salary Executive would have earned on the remainder of the employment contract with Corporation and the salary Executive would have earned under the offer from the smaller corporation.

    (C) Executive will be entitled to the amount Executive would have earned under the offer from smaller Corporation.

    (D) Executive will not be entitled to damages because Executive failed to mitigate.

15. Parker bought a used car from Fast Eddie's Used Car Lot. The Fast Eddie's sales person represented that the car had been driven for fewer than 3000 miles. In reality, the car had been driven for more than 5000 miles. If Parker brings a fraud action against Fast Eddie's, which of the following will be true?

    (A) Parker will not be entitled to pre-judgment interest because Parker is bringing a tort claim.

    (B) Parker will be entitled to pre-judgment interest only if Fast Eddie's concedes liability.

(C) Parker will be entitled to pre-judgment interest only if Parker's damages are determined by the difference in fair market value between the car as represented and the car as delivered.

(D) Parker will be entitled to pre-judgment interest under any circumstances.

16. Potter and Davis got into a fight in a bar. Potter suffered serious injuries in the fight. Potter sued Davis for battery. If Potter seeks damages for pain and suffering as well as medical expenses in the lawsuit, which of the following is true?

(A) Potter will not be entitled to post-judgment interest because Potter is bringing a tort claim.

(B) Potter will not be entitled to post-judgment interest on any damages for pain and suffering because pain and suffering damages are committed to the discretion of the jury.

(C) Potter will be entitled to post-judgment interest only if Davis concedes liability.

(D) Potter will be entitled to post-judgment interest under any circumstances.

Topic 3

Questions

Contract Damages

17. Buyer and Seller entered into a contract for the sale of 5000 widgets at a price of $1.00 per widget. At the time and place for delivery, Seller delivered only 3000 widgets. Buyer paid Seller for the 3000 widgets. Buyer did not seek to obtain substitute widgets. The fair market price of widgets at the time and place for delivery was $4.00 per widget. In an action for breach of contract, Buyer will be entitled to recover which of the following?

    (A) $2000.

    (B) $6000.

    (C) $8000.

    (D) Buyer will not be entitled to recover damages because Buyer did not make reasonable efforts to cover.

Questions 18 and 19 are based on the following fact pattern.

Bombay Bicycle Company and Super Sprockets Inc. entered into a contract for the sale of 10,000 sprocket wheels. Bombay agreed to pay $1.00 per wheel for a total of $10,000. Unbeknownst to Super Sprockets, Bombay intended to install the sprocket wheels as component parts on Bombay's finished bicycles. Super Sprockets delivered to Bombay 10,000 bicycle sprocket wheels. However, the sprocket wheels were not the size called for in the contract specifications and did not fit in Bombay's finished bikes. Bombay rejected the sprocket wheels, then purchased 10,000 replacement sprocket wheels from Sprockets International.

18. The replacement sprocket wheels conformed to the specifications under the original contract. Bombay paid Sprockets International $3.00 per wheel. In an action for breach of contract, Bombay will be entitled to recover which of the following as general damages?

    (A) $20,000.

    (B) $30,000.

    (C) Bombay will not be entitled to recover damages. Because the replacement sprocket wheels cost more than the original sprocket wheels, they were not commercially reasonable substitute goods.

    (D) Bombay will not be entitled to recover damages because Bombay did not inform Super Sprockets at the time of contracting of Bombay's intent to use the sprocket wheels in finished bicycles.

19. Bombay incurred $500 in shipping costs to have the replacement sprocket wheels shipped to it. In an action for breach of contract, which of the following is true?

    (A) Bombay is entitled to recover the shipping costs as reasonable incidental costs.

    (B) Bombay is entitled to recover the shipping costs only if Bombay is a merchant.

    (C) Bombay is not entitled to recover the shipping costs because they were not foreseeable at the time of contracting.

    (D) Bombay is not entitled to recover the shipping costs because Bombay received nonconforming sprockets from Super Sprockets.

20. Buyer purchased a used tractor from Seller. Seller warranted that the tractor would be in good working order. When Seller delivered the tractor, Buyer discovered that the oxygen sensor was failing and preventing the exhaust system from working properly. Buyer had the oxygen sensor replaced. Buyer sued Seller for breach of contract. What will be the measure of Buyer's damages?

    (A) Buyer is not entitled to damages because replacing the oxygen sensor was not reasonable mitigation.

    (B) Buyer is entitled to recover the difference between the market price of the tractor as warranted and the contract price.

    (C) Buyer will be entitled to recover the cost to replace the oxygen sensor because the faulty oxygen sensor prevented the tractor from working properly.

    (D) Buyer is not entitled to recover damages if Seller did not provide any express warranty.

21. Betty contracted to purchase a used van from Stan for $10,000. At the time and place for delivery, Stan informed Betty that he would not sell the van to Betty. Betty protested that she needed the van so that she could open her delivery business. Stan refused again to sell the van. Betty searched for a comparable van, but none was available. In an action for breach of contract, which of the following is true?

    (A) Betty will be entitled to recover any lost profits from the operation of her delivery business because the lost profits were foreseeable at the time of the breach and Betty's lost profits were unavoidable.

    (B) Betty will not be entitled to recover her lost profits even though they were unavoidable because Betty's lost profits were not foreseeable at the time of contracting.

    (C) Betty will not be entitled to recover her lost profits even though they were foreseeable at the time of breach because she did not mitigate her damages by purchasing a comparable van.

    (D) Betty will not be entitled to recover her lost profits because her lost profits were not foreseeable at the time of contracting and because Betty failed to mitigate her damages.

QUESTIONS · TOPIC 3: CONTRACT DAMAGES

Questions 22 and 23 are based on the following fact pattern.

Electric Company entered into a contract to manufacturer and install an electric transformer in Metals Company's production facility. The contract contained a clause excluding recovery for consequential damages. Electric Company delivered a conforming transformer but improperly installed the transformer. The errors in installation caused the transformer to overheat when used, resulting in extensive harm to the transformer. The harm to the transformer forced Metals Company to close its production facility for several days while the transformer was being repaired. Metals Company sued Electric Company for breach of contract and negligence.

22. If Metals Company seeks to recover the cost to repair the transformer, which of the following will be true?

    (A) Metals Company will be entitled to recover the cost to repair the transformer.

    (B) Metals Company will be entitled to recover the lesser of the cost to repair the transformer or the diminution in the fair market value of the transformer.

    (C) Metals Company will be entitled to recover the difference in value between the installation service as contracted for and the installation service as received.

    (D) Metals Company will be entitled to recover both the difference in value in the installation service and lesser of the cost to repair or the diminution in value.

23. If Metals Company seeks to recover lost profits for the time the production facility was closed, which of the following are true?

    (A) Metals Company will be entitled to recover its lost profits because Electric Company reasonably should have known that Metals Company might have to close its production facility if Electric Company failed to install the transformer properly.

    (B) Metals Company will be entitled to recover its lost profits because the improper installation damaged the transformer.

    (C) Metals Company will not be entitled to recover its lost profits because Metals Company did not seek to purchase a substitute transformer.

    (D) Metals Company will not be entitled to recover its lost profits because the improper installation only damaged the transformer and did not damage any other part of the production facility.

24. Simon agreed to sell Barbara 500,000 bricks at a price of $0.10 per brick. At the time and place for delivery, Barbara accepted only 300,000 bricks and wrongfully rejected the remaining 200,000. At the time and place for delivery, the market price of the bricks was $0.08 per brick. If Simon does not resell the remaining 200,000 bricks, what will be the measure of his damages?

    ANSWER:

Questions 25 and 26 are based on the following fact pattern.

Stone agreed to sell Brown 5,000 Valentine's Day theme greeting cards for retail sale at a price of $2.00 per card. The contract called for delivery on January 27, Y01. When Stone attempted to deliver the greeting cards, Brown wrongfully rejected them. From January 27, Y01 until February 14, Y01, Stone attempted to find another buyer for the cards but was unable to do so. Stone stored the greeting cards until January 15, Y02 at which time Stone again sought out another buyer. On January 15, Y02, Stone notified Brown that Stone intended to sell the greeting cards to Thomas for $1.00 per card.

25. In an action by Stone against Brown, what will be the likely measure of Stone's damages?

    (A) Stone will be entitled to recover the contract price of $2.00 per card because the goods were not capable of immediate resale.

    (B) Stone will be entitled to recover the difference between the resale price of $1.00 per card and the original contract price of $2.00 per card because Stone resold the goods in a commercially reasonable manner.

    (C) Stone will not be entitled to recover the difference between the contract price and the resale price because Stone unreasonably waited for 1 year to resell the greeting cards.

    (D) Stone will not be entitled to recover the difference between the resale price and the contract price because Stone resold the greeting cards at a private sale.

26. Stone rented the storage space where the greeting cards were stored. Stone paid $500 to rent the space for the year. Will Stone be entitled to recover the rental fee from Brown?

    (A) Stone will be entitled to recover the fee because Stone reasonably incurred the fee in attempting to mitigate the loss.

    (B) Stone will be entitled to recover the fee only because Stone was successful in reselling the greeting cards.

    (C) Stone will not be entitled to recover the fee because sellers are precluded from recovering consequential damages under the Uniform Commercial Code (UCC).

    (D) Stone will not be entitled to recover the fee because Stone did not inform Brown that Stone intended to store the greeting cards.

27. Big City Bakery ordered 50 laptop computers from Super Computers, Inc., a successful computer manufacturer. Big City Bakery agreed to purchase the 50 laptop computers at Super Computers' standard retail price. A month before the laptop computers were to be delivered, Big City Bakery cancelled its order. Super Computers resold the 50 laptops to New City Bakery. New City Bakery paid the same standard retail price. In an action for breach of contract against Big City Bakery, what will be the measure of Super Computers' damages?

QUESTIONS · TOPIC 3: CONTRACT DAMAGES

volume seller?

(A) Super Computers will only be able to recover damages if the standard retail price is greater than the fair market value of the laptop computers.

(B) Super Computers will not be entitled to recover damages because the resale price is equal to the contract price.

(C) Super Computers will be entitled to recover the profit it had expected to make on the sale of the laptop computers to Big City Bakery.

(D) Super Computers will be entitled to recover the price of the laptop computers.

28. Buyer entered into a contract with Seller to purchase a specially designed molding machine. The contract provided that Seller was to ship the molding machine via railroad to Buyer's manufacturing plant. In an action for breach of contract by Seller against Buyer, under which of the following circumstances will Seller be entitled to recover the contract price?

(A) Buyer wrongfully refuses to accept delivery of the molding machine and Seller is not able to resell the molding machine because it is designed for Buyer's specific uses.

(B) Buyer accepts delivery of the molding machine but refuses to pay for the molding machine.

(C) The molding machine is stolen from a railroad freight yard after Seller delivers the molding machine to the railroad and makes a contract for its shipment to Buyer.

(D) All of the above.

29. Benny's Best Ice Cream Producer entered into a contract with Super Salty's Nut Shoppe to purchase 500 pounds of processed nuts at a price of $5.00 per pound. Super Salty was to process the nuts according to Benny's unique secret recipe for use in Benny's new "nutty surprise" ice cream. Super Salty purchased 500 pounds of unprocessed nuts at a cost of $2.00 per pound. Super Salty also purchased the additional ingredients necessary to process the first 100 pounds of the nuts at a cost of $0.50 per pound. Super Salty estimated that the depreciation of its equipment and rent on its plant would cost $0.50 per pound. Super Salty completed and attempted to deliver 100 pounds of processed nuts to Benny's Best. However, Benny's Best rejected the 100 pounds of completed nuts and informed Super Salty that it was repudiating the contract because the nutty surprise ice cream had not been well received in consumer taste tests. Super Salty immediately halted processing of the nuts and was able to sell the remaining 400 pounds of unprocessed nuts for $1.00 per pound. Super Salty was unable to resell the 100 pounds of processed nuts. What will be the measure of Super Salty's recovery in an action for breach of contract against Benny's Best?

ANSWER:

expectation OR reliance

500 at $5/pound

30. Which of the following liquidated damage clauses is most likely to be upheld by a court?

   (A) A contract between Shipper and Merchant provides that Merchant agrees to ship a minimum quantity of goods within 3 years and that if Merchant fails to ship the minimum quantity of goods within 3 years, Merchant will pay the difference between the full contract price and the price paid for goods already shipped.

   (B) A lease for a term of years between Landlord and Tenant requires Tenant to pay the present value of all remaining rent due under the lease if Tenant vacates before the lease expires.

   (C) A contract between Contractor and School District specifies that Contractor will complete construction of a new school building by the start of the fall semester and provides that Contractor will pay the fair market monthly rental value for each month that performance is delayed.

   (D) An employment contract between Chief Executive Officer and Corporation expressly designates as an enforceable liquidated damages clause a provision that provides that Chief Executive Officer will pay Corporation an amount equal to the number of years remaining on her contract multiplied by her annual salary if Chief Executive Officer leaves before her contract expires.

31. Brown entered into a contract to purchase a condominium from Smith for $150,000 and paid Smith $15,000 as a down payment. The contract expressly provided that if Brown breached the contract, Smith would retain the $15,000 down payment as payment for the damages occasioned by Brown's breach. Before the closing date, Brown decided not to purchase the condominium and instead purchased a different condominium. Smith refused to return the down payment. In an action by Brown to recover the down payment, which of the following are true?

   (A) Brown will not be entitled to restitution of the down payment because a breaching party cannot maintain an action for restitution.

   (B) Brown will not be entitled to restitution of the down payment because Brown willfully breached the contract.

   (C) Brown will be entitled to restitution of the down payment if Brown can show that Smith could have resold the condominium for $175,000 at the time that Brown breached the contract.

   (D) Brown will be entitled to restitution of the down payment because down payment forfeiture clauses are per se illegal penalty clauses.

QUESTIONS · TOPIC 3: CONTRACT DAMAGES

32. Baker entered into a contract to purchase a house from Stone for $300,000. A title search revealed that a utility company has an easement through Stone's garage. As a result, Stone failed to deliver marketable title at the closing. In a breach of contract action by Baker, which of the following are true?

    (A) Baker's recovery may be limited to restitution of any purchase price paid if Stone was unaware of the easement.

    (B) Baker's recovery will not be limited to restitution of any purchase price paid even if Stone was unaware of the easement.

    (C) Baker's recovery will be limited to restitution of any purchase price paid even if Stone was aware of the easement but failed to disclose it.

    (D) Baker will be entitled to recover the profit that Stone would have made on the sale to Baker if Stone was aware of the easement but failed to disclose it.

33. Biggs entered into a contract to purchase a house from Stanton for $350,000. Biggs paid Stanton $35,000 in earnest money. Biggs intended to pay another $35,000 in cash at the closing. Biggs arranged for a 30-year loan secured by a mortgage on the house for the remaining $280,000. The interest rate on the loan was 6%. A day before the closing, Thompson offered to purchase the home from Stanton for $370,000. Stanton repudiated the contract with Biggs. A month later, Biggs purchased a comparable home for $340,000. Biggs paid $70,000 in cash and obtained a 30-year loan secured by a mortgage for the remaining $270,000. The interest rate on the second loan was 7.5%. In an action for breach of contract by Biggs, what will be the measure of Biggs' damages?

    (A) Biggs has no damages because Biggs purchased a comparable home for less money.

    (B) Biggs is entitled to a return of the $35,000 earnest money only.

    (C) Biggs is entitled to a return of the $35,000 earnest money and the value of interest on $270,000 over 30 years at 1.5% reduced to present value.

    (D) Biggs is entitled to a return of the $35,000 earnest money and the difference between the value of a 30-year $280,000 loan at 6% and a 30-year $270,000 at 7.5% reduced to present value.

Topic 4   Questions

Damages for Bodily Injury and Death

34. Penny suffered a broken leg in an auto accident in which Dan was at fault. Dr. Quinn examined, set and cast Penny's leg. After treatment was completed, Dr. Quinn tendered a bill for $5,000. Under which of the following circumstances will Penny be entitled to recover $5,000 from Dan as damages for her medical expenses?

    (A) Only if Penny has paid the $5,000 bill at the time of trial.

    (B) Only if $5,000 is the reasonable value of the medically necessary services that Dr. Quinn provided.

    (C) Only if Dr. Quinn is a licensed physician.

    (D) Only if Penny's own health insurance will not cover the treatment.

35. Which of the following circumstances will preclude an injured plaintiff from recovering damages for lost or diminished earning capacity?

    (A) The plaintiff was an unemployed child at the time of injury.

    (B) The plaintiff returned to her pre-injury job before trial.

    (C) The plaintiff was an adult who was not employed outside of the home at the time of injury but instead was a full-time caregiver for his young children.

    (D) None of the above.

36. What are some of the factors that a jury will consider in determining damages for lost earning capacity?

    ANSWER:

37. Peterman was severely injured in an automobile accident in which Davidson was at fault. As a result of his injuries, Peterman was unable to work for three months. Additionally, Peterman will require long-term nursing care to help him meet his daily living needs. In an action for negligence, Peterman will be entitled to recover several items of damages for personal injuries. Which of the following items of damages, if any, must be discounted to present value?

    (A) Damages for Peterman's pain and suffering.

    (B) Damages for wages lost before trial.

(C) Damages for long-term daily nursing care.

(D) Both (B) and (C).

38. Penny suffered leg and back injuries when the truck she was driving collided with a truck driven by Dasi. At the time of the accident, Penny was working as a short-haul truck driver. Penny sustained comminuted fractures to her upper and lower leg in the accident. As a result, she underwent several long surgical procedures and physical therapy. Penny was unable to work in any capacity for two months while she underwent treatment and physical therapy for her injuries. After she completed physical therapy, she was able to return to work. While she is able to continue driving short-haul routes, her leg injuries will permanently prevent her from driving long-haul truck routes. Assuming Dasi was at fault in the accident, which of the following is true?

(A) Penny will not be entitled to recover damages for lost wages or lost earning capacity because she was able to return to work.

(B) Penny will be entitled to recover damages for lost wages for the period of time during which she was unable to work in any capacity, but she will not be entitled to recover damages for lost earning capacity because she was able to return to work.

(C) Penny will be entitled to recover damages for lost wages for the period of time during which she was unable to work in any capacity, and she will be entitled to recover diminished earning capacity for the difference in her earning capacity as a long-haul and as a short-haul truck driver for the remainder of her worklife if she can show that but for the accident she would have become a long-haul truck driver.

(D) Penny will be entitled to recover damages for lost wages for the period of time during which she was unable to work in any capacity or diminished earning capacity for the difference in her earning capacity as a long-haul and as a short-haul truck driver for the remainder of her worklife at her election. However, she will not be entitled to recover both.

39. Patterson was injured in the course of his employment at Dockers Inc. As a result of his injuries, Patterson will not be able to return to his job at Dockers, nor will he be able to re-enter the workforce in any capacity. At the time of his injury, Patterson was earning $40,000 per year. At the time of trial, Patterson had a remaining worklife expectancy of 10 years. At trial, experts estimated that Patterson's salary would increase over the course of the remaining 10 years by 2% annually as a result of cost-of-living increases; 3% annually due to general increases in industry productivity; and 2% annually as a result of merit-based bonuses. In an action for personal injuries against Dockers Inc., what would be an appropriate method for discounting Patterson's damages for lost wages to present value?

(A) Include increases due to industry productivity and merit-based bonuses in an estimation of Patterson's total lost wages and discount by a discount rate based on the current yield for a junk bond.

(B) Include increases due to industry productivity and merit-based bonuses in an estimation of Patterson's total lost wages and discount by a discount rate based on the current yield for a triple-A rated corporate bond.

(C) Include increases due to cost-of-living, industry productivity and merit-based bonuses in an estimation of Patterson's total lost wages and discount by a discount rate based on the current yield for a junk bond.

(D) Include increases due to cost-of-living, industry productivity and merit-based bonuses in an estimation of Patterson's total lost wages and discount by a discount rate based on the current yield for a triple-A rated corporate bond.

40. What are some of the types of harms for which a plaintiff can recover noneconomic damages in a personal injury case?

ANSWER:

41. Patty slipped on an improperly maintained deck at a local pool and suffered a lacerated leg. Patty's Aunt Alice, a physician, treated Patty's injuries. Alice provided the medical services gratuitously. If Patty brings an action against the operator of the pool, what will be the measure of her recovery?

(A) Patty will be entitled to recover the reasonable value of the medical services that Alice provided.

(B) Patty will be entitled to recover only the costs of any supplies Alice used to treat her.

(C) Patty will be entitled to recover the reasonable value of the medical services that Alice provided only if the operator acted recklessly or intentionally.

(D) Patty will not be entitled to recover any damages for medical expenses because she did not incur any medical expenses.

42. Patton and Dixon collided on a ski trail. Patton suffered a broken leg in the collision and was treated at a local hospital. Patton's health insurance company paid Patton's medical expenses. The hospital billed Patton's insurance company for $30,000 in medical expenses. Pursuant to a previously negotiated agreement between the hospital and the health insurance company, the insurance company was required to pay only $10,000. Patton was required to pay a $1,000 co-pay. The hospital "wrote off" the remaining amount, meaning it did not and will not seek to recover the remaining amount. Assuming Dixon is at fault for the accident, which of the following are true?

(A) Under the common law collateral source rule, Patton's recovery will be reduced by $10,000 because the insurance company paid his medical expenses.

(B) Dixon may be permitted to offer evidence that Paxson's health insurance paid $10,000 for Patton's medical treatment as evidence of the reasonable value of the medical services Patton received.

(C) Patton will be entitled to recover only $1,000 for medical expenses because that is the amount Patton actually paid.

(D) Patton will be entitled to recover $30,000 in medical expenses only if Dixon acted intentionally.

43. Pierson injured her rotator cuff in an auto accident for which Davidson was at fault. As a result of her injuries, Pierson has lost some mobility in her arm and suffers from severe pain. All of the physicians who have examined Pierson have agreed that a corrective surgery would restore much of Pierson's mobility and alleviate her pain. However, Pierson has refused to have the corrective surgery. In an action for damages by Pierson against Davidson, which of the following will be true?

(A) Pierson will be entitled to recover damages for her pain and suffering as a result of the rotator cuff injury because a defendant must take an injured plaintiff as she finds her.

(B) Pierson will be entitled to recover damages for her pain and suffering if the surgery carries a real but slight risk of failure.

(C) Pierson will be entitled to recover damages for her pain and suffering if she lacks the means to pay for the surgery.

(D) Pierson will not be entitled to recover damages for pain and suffering under any circumstances.

44. Harrison is injured in the course of his employment at Electric Company. As a result of his injuries, Harrison will be unable to return to work for several years. If Harrison and his wife, Wilma, bring an action for damages against Electric Company, which of the following is true?

(A) Harrison will be entitled to recover damages for lost wages and pain and suffering, and Wilma will be entitled to recover damages for lost financial support and loss of companionship.

(B) Harrison will be entitled to recover damages for lost wages and pain and suffering, and Wilma will be entitled to recover damages for loss of companionship.

(C) Harrison will be entitled to recover damages for lost wages and pain and suffering, and Wilma will be entitled to recover damages for lost financial support.

(D) Harrison will be entitled to recover damages for lost wages and pain and suffering, but Wilma will not be entitled to recover any damages.

45. Assume the same facts as in Question 44. Harrison and his wife, Wilma, brought an action for damages against Electric Company in a comparative fault jurisdiction. If a jury determines that Harrison was 30% at fault for his injuries, which of the following will be true?

(A) Wilma will be barred from recovering damages for loss of consortium.

(B) Wilma's recovery will be reduced in proportion to Harrison's fault.

(C) Wilma will be entitled to recover 30% of her damages from Harrison and 70% of her damages from Electric Company.

(D) Wilma's recovery will be unaffected by Harrison's fault.

46. Industrial cleaning chemicals were spilled on Poppins during the course of her employment. Poppins suffered minor chemical burns from the spill. She also has an increased risk of developing certain cancers as a result of her exposure to the chemicals. If Poppins brings an action for damages presently, which of the following is true?

    (A) Poppins can collect damages for the injuries from her burns and damages for her increased fear of developing cancer if she demonstrates to a reasonable certainty that she will develop cancer in the future.

    (B) Poppins can collect damages for the injuries from her burns and damages for any future medical expenses relating to cancer treatment if she demonstrates to a reasonable certainty that she will develop cancer in the future.

    (C) Poppins can collect damages for the injuries from her burns but must file a second action to recover damages for her medical expenses relating to cancer if and when she develops cancer.

    (D) Poppins cannot collect damages for injuries relating to future cancer treatment because such damages are too speculative.

47. Passenger was struck by a large wave while standing on the deck of a ferry that Dillon was operating. Passenger narrowly avoided being washed overboard but suffered only minor physical injuries. Passenger fully recovered from the physical injuries but continues to suffer from post-traumatic stress disorder as a result of the accident. Assuming Dillon is at fault for the accident, which of the following is true?

    (A) Passenger will not be entitled to recover noneconomic damages for pain and suffering or post-traumatic stress disorder because Passenger suffered only minor physical injuries.

    (B) Passenger will not be entitled to recover noneconomic damages for pain and suffering associated with the physical injuries because Passenger fully recovered, but Passenger will be entitled to recover noneconomic damages for post-traumatic stress disorder.

    (C) Passenger will be entitled to recover noneconomic damages for pain and suffering associated with the physical injures but will not be entitled to recover damages for post-traumatic stress disorder because it is not related to Passenger's physical injuries.

    (D) Passenger will be entitled to recover noneconomic damages for both pain and suffering and post-traumatic stress disorder

48. Watson was severely injured in an auto accident for which Davis was at fault. Several months later, Watson died in an airplane crash. What potential claims against Davis exist?

    (A) Watson's Estate possesses a survival action against Davis.

    (B) Watson's Beneficiaries possess a wrongful death action against Davis.

(C) Watson's Estate possesses a survival action against Davis, and Watson's Beneficiaries possess a wrongful death action against Davis.

(D) No claims against Davis survive Watson's death.

49. Parker was severely injured in an auto accident for which Dickerson was at fault. Several months later, Parker died as a result of her injuries. If Parker's Representative brings both a survival and a wrongful death action against Dickerson, which of the following will be true?

(A) Parker's Estate can recover damages for the wages Parker would have earned over the course of her natural lifespan.

(B) Parker's Estate can recover damages for the wages Parker would have earned over the course of her natural lifespan, and Parker's beneficiaries can recover damages for the loss of financial support from Parker.

(C) Parker's Estate can recover damages for the wages Parker lost between the accident and her death, and Parker's beneficiaries can recover damages for the loss of financial support from Parker.

(D) Parker's Estate cannot recover damages for lost wages, but Parker's beneficiaries can recover damages for the loss of financial support from Parker.

50. Dr. Doolittle failed to properly perform a tubal ligation on Paulette Patterson. As a result, Paulette and her husband conceived a child. Paulette ultimately gave birth to the baby. Which of the following best describes the Pattersons' likely recovery in an action against Dr. Doolittle?

(A) The Pattersons are likely to recover the damages for the pregnancy itself, including pain and suffering during the delivery and labor, as well as damages for the cost of rearing the baby because the Pattersons have a claim for wrongful pregnancy rather than wrongful birth.

(B) The Pattersons are likely to recover the damages for the pregnancy itself as well as damages for the cost of rearing the baby if the baby is born disabled.

(C) The Pattersons' recovery likely will be limited to damages for the pregnancy itself regardless of the health of the baby.

(D) The Pattersons will not be entitled to any recovery because they failed to mitigate their damages by placing the baby up for adoption.

51. Recently, the state of Calizona passed the following statute:

In a tort action to recover damages for injury or loss to person or property, the amount of compensatory damages that represents damages for noneconomic loss shall not exceed the greater of $250,000 or an amount that is equal to three times the economic loss of the plaintiff in the tort action to a maximum of $350,000 for each plaintiff not to exceed a maximum of $500,000 for each occurrence that is the basis of that tort.

QUESTIONS · TOPIC 4: DAMAGES FOR BODILY INJURY AND DEATH   23

After the statute went into effect, Wendy was seriously injured while using a defective product at her home in Calizona. Wendy and her husband, Harold, filed an action against the manufacturer in Calizona state court. The jury awarded Wendy and Harold damages as follows:

Past and Future Medical Expenses	$500,000
Past and Future Lost Wages	$250,000
Pain and Suffering	$1 million
Loss of Consortium (loss of companionship only)	$500,000
	$2.25 million

If the manufacturer files a post-judgment motion for reduction of the verdict based on the new statute, how should the court rule?

(A) The court should grant the motion and remit the jury verdict to $1.25 million.

(B) The court should grant the motion and remit the jury verdict to $1.45 million.

(C) The court should grant the motion and remit the jury verdict to $1.6 million.

(D) The court should deny the motion because neither Wendy's nor Harold's damages for noneconomic losses are greater than three times Wendy's economic losses.

Topic 5

Property Damages

52. While failing to maintain a proper lookout, Bertie drove her car in reverse and collided with Hewlett's old jalopy. Hewlett was uninjured, but his jalopy suffered damage to the body of the car. Several mechanics estimated that it would cost $2800 to repair the jalopy. However, the mechanics also agreed that the body damage would not affect the drivability of the jalopy. Immediately before the accident, Hewlett's jalopy had a "bluebook" value of $560. After the accident, the jalopy had a bluebook value of $500. In an action by Hewlett against Bertie, what is the likely measure of Hewlett's recovery for the damage to the jalopy?

    ANSWER

53. While driving too fast for conditions, Door lost control of his car and collided with a car driven by Potter. Potter was uninjured, but Potter's car was destroyed. In an action by Potter against Door, which of the following is true?

    (A) Potter will be entitled to recover both the pre-tort market value of the car and damages for the loss of use of the car during the length of time reasonably necessary to obtain a replacement car.

    (B) Potter will be entitled to recover both the pre-tort market value of the car and damages for the loss of use of the car only if the car was used primarily for commercial purposes.

    (C) Potter will not be entitled to recover both the pre-tort value of the car and damages for the loss of use of the car because the pre-tort value of the car already encompasses the right to use the car.

    (D) Potter will not be entitled to recover both the pre-tort value of the car and damages for loss of use because Potter's recovery would exceed the pre-tort fair market value of the car.

54. Broker held 100 shares of stock in Company XYZ in an account for Client. On March 1, Broker sold the shares without Client's consent for the prevailing market price of $100 per share. On May 15, the market price rose to $120 per share. Client did not discover Broker's misconduct until Client ordered Broker to sell the shares on June 1. On June 1, the market price was $110 per share. The market price fell to $75 per share on July 1. Client eventually sued Broker for conversion of the shares. When the case went to trial on Dec. 1, the market price had risen to $125 per share. Which best describes Client's likely measure of recovery?

(A) Client's recovery will be limited to $100 per share because it was the market price at the time of conversion.

(B) Client will be entitled to recover $120 per share because a reasonable investor could not have replaced the stock before May 15.

(C) Client will be entitled to recover $110 per share because a reasonable investor could have replaced the stock by July 1.

(D) Client will be entitled to recover $125 per share because Client has no obligation to replace the stock until Client recovers damages from Broker.

Questions 55–57 are based on the following fact pattern.

A fire caused by the tenants of a neighboring apartment destroyed Palmer's apartment. All of Palmer's furniture, clothing and personal belongings were destroyed in the fire. One of the items destroyed in the fire was an autographed photograph of Palmer with his favorite rock star. The picture was a snapshot taken by a friend of Palmer's on the night that Palmer's band performed as the opening act for the rock star.

55. In an action by Palmer against the other tenants for damages, which of the following best describes the likely measure of recovery for Palmer's destroyed clothing?

(A) Palmer is likely to recover the pre-fire market value of the clothing.

(B) Palmer is likely to recover the cost to replace the clothing with new clothing.

(C) Palmer is likely to recover the original purchase price of the clothing.

(D) None of the above.

56. In which of the following ways may Palmer prove the value of the destroyed clothing?

(A) Palmer may offer his opinion as to the value of the clothing as long as he explains the basis for his opinion.

(B) Palmer may offer his opinion as to the value of the clothing only if he corroborates that opinion with supporting documents such as the original receipts.

(C) Palmer may offer his opinion as to the value of the clothing only if Palmer has professional experience in buying or selling clothing.

(D) Palmer must offer independent expert testimony to establish the value of the clothing.

57. Which of the following factors will the jury likely be permitted to consider in determining an award of damages for the destroyed photograph?

    i. The cost of developing the film.

    ii. Palmer's sentimental feelings about the photograph.

    iii. The cost of purchasing the film.

    iv. The rate paid by newspapers and magazines for photographs of the rock star.

(A) iv only.

(B) i and iii.

(C) i, iii and iv.

(D) All of the above.

58. Outdoor Advertising leased space in a building owned by LaSalle Realty. Outdoor Advertising installed a large advertising sign on the roof of the building in violation of the terms of the lease. When Outdoor Advertising removed the sign, portions of the roof were damaged. LaSalle Realty sued Outdoor Advertising to recover damages for the injury to the roof. At trial, experts estimated that the fair market value of the building immediately before Outdoor Advertising installed the sign was $2 million, and that after the sign was removed, the fair market value was $1.8 million. Experts also estimated that repairing the damage to the roof would cost $600,000. What are the best arguments for awarding LaSalle Realty the cost to repair the roof? What are the best arguments for limiting LaSalle Realty's recovery to the $200,000 diminution in value?

ANSWER:

59. Under which of the following circumstances is the landowner most likely to recover the cost to repair the injury to the land?

(A) The landowner seeks $5000 to repair a hole in a sand dune that served as a tide breaker when the property diminished in value by $10,000 as a result of the hole in the dune.

(B) The landowner seeks $300,000 to re-build a home on her property when the pre-tort value of the home was $198,000 and the landowner used the home as her primary residence.

(C) A non-profit organization seeks $800,000 to re-build an apartment building when the pre-tort value of the apartment building was $500,000 and the organization received a loan to purchase the building on the condition that the organization maintain it as low income rental housing.

(D) All of the above.

Questions 60 and 61 are based on the following fact pattern.

Bunyan entered Loud's land and chopped down 50 of Loud's walnut trees. Bunyan then used his trusty ox, Babe, to haul the walnut trees off of Loud's land. In the course of removing the walnut trees, Babe trampled some small shrubs surrounding the orchard. Loud sued Bunyan to recover damages for the removal of the walnut trees and for the destruction of the shrubs.

60. Which of the following best describes the likely measure of Loud's recovery for the lost walnut trees?

(A) Loud will be entitled to the market value of the walnut trees at the time of removal only if the walnut trees had reached commercial maturity at the time that Bunyan removed them.

(B) Loud will be entitled to the current market value of mature walnut trees discounted to present value if the trees had not yet reached commercial maturity when Bunyan removed them.

(C) Loud will be entitled to the cost to replace the walnut trees if they had not yet reached commercial maturity at the time that Bunyan removed them.

(D) Loud will be entitled to three times the market value of the walnut trees at the time of removal if Bunyan removed the trees in bad faith.

61. Which of the following best describes Loud's likely recovery for the destruction of the shrubs?

(A) Loud will be entitled to recover the difference in the market value of the property with and without the shrubs.

(B) Loud will be entitled to recover the cost to replace the shrubs.

(C) Loud will be entitled to recover the original purchase price for the shrubs.

(D) Loud will not be entitled to recover damages because the shrubs have no marketable use.

62. Parker owns land on top of a shale formation. Davis purchased the rights to extract natural gas from beneath the land adjacent to Parker's land. Davis is mistaken about the property lines and mistakenly drills the wellbore on Parker's land. Davis then uses the well to extract natural gas. Parker does not extract the natural gas on her land herself. Rather, she licenses the rights to third parties such as Davis. Assuming Parker prevails in a trespass action against Davis, which of the following is true?

(A) Parker will not be entitled to recover damages because she does not extract the natural gas under her property.

(B) Parker will be limited to only the cost to remove the well and restore the land because she did not intend to extract the natural gas herself.

(C) Parker will be entitled to recover the commercial value of the natural gas as measured by the royalty payments she would have received for licensing the right to extract the gas to a third party.

(D) Parker will be entitled to recover the market value of the gas less the cost of extraction.

63. Contractor working on a house in a residential neighborhood accidentally damaged the utility lines, causing an internet outage to adjacent homes. One of the affected Homeowners runs a small business out of her home. She sued Contractor for lost profits she suffered because of the disruption to her business during the internet outage. Which of the following is true?

(A) Plaintiff can maintain a claim because she was not in privity of contract with Contractor

(B) Plaintiff can maintain a claim because business profits are a form of property.

(C) Plaintiff can maintain a claim because Contractor has a special duty arising out of doing work in a residential neighborhood.

(D) The economic loss rule bars Plaintiff's claims.

Topic 6

Punitive Damages

64. Dirk drove his car over the curb and crashed the car into Peterson's house. In an action by Peterson against Dirk, which of the following facts would support an award of punitive damages?

    (A) Dirk was driving with a suspended driver's license at the time of the accident.

    (B) Dirk drove his car into Peterson's house as revenge because Peterson had beaten Dirk in a golf tournament.

    (C) Both (A) and (B).

    (D) Peterson will not be entitled to punitive damages because Peterson did not suffer any bodily injuries.

65. For what two purposes are punitive damages usually imposed?

    ANSWER: punish + deter

66. Palmer purchased a homeowner's insurance policy from Casualty Insurance Company. The policy purported to insure Palmer against any damage to or destruction of the home from fire. A faulty electrical outlet caused a fire in Palmer's home. Firefighters who were attempting to put out the fire sprayed water on Palmer's walls, causing damage to the walls and floor. Palmer filed a claim with Casualty. Casualty denied the claim on the ground that the damage was caused by water rather than fire even though controlling precedent clearly prohibited Casualty from denying the claim on this ground. In a lawsuit by Palmer against Casualty for breach of the insurance contract and bad faith denial of his claim, which of the following are true?

    (A) Palmer may be entitled to punitive damages only if Palmer succeeds on the breach of contract claim.

    (B) Palmer may be entitled to punitive damages only if Palmer succeeds on the bad faith claim.

    (C) Palmer may be entitled to punitive damages if Palmer succeeds on either the breach of contract or bad faith claim.

    (D) Palmer will not be entitled to punitive damages because both claims are essentially contract claims.

67. A Big-Mart employee stopped and searched Pullman on suspicion of shoplifting. The employee stopped Pullman because Pullman was African-American. The employee had no other basis to suspect Pullman of shoplifting, and Pullman had not, in fact, shoplifted. In an action by Pullman against Big-Mart, which of the following is true?

    (A) Big-Mart may be liable for punitive damages only if Big-Mart's managers were aware that Big-Mart employees had a practice of stopping African-American customers but failed to end the practice.

    (B) Big-Mart may be liable for punitive damages only if the Big-Mart employee who stopped Pullman exercised managerial responsibilities.

    (C) Big-Mart may be liable for punitive damages if Big-Mart's managers were aware that Big-Mart employees had a practice of stopping African-American customers or the Big-Mart employee who stopped Pullman exercised managerial responsibilities.

    (D) Big-Mart cannot be held vicariously liable for punitive damages based on the conduct of its employees.

68. Potter was seriously injured when the passenger-side airbag of the car in which she was riding failed to deploy during a high speed crash. Potter sued Neptune Motor Company, the company that manufactured the car for products liability, alleging that a design defect in the airbag caused it to fail. Which of the following is true?

    (A) Neptune will be liable for punitive damages only if it intentionally designed the airbag to fail.

    (B) Neptune will be liable for punitive damages if Neptune's internal testing data revealed that the airbag failed to deploy in one out of six crashes and Neptune decided to market the cars without correcting the defect.

    (C) Neptune will be liable for punitive damages if Neptune's internal testing failed to detect the defect but more extensive testing would have revealed the defect.

    (D) Neptune cannot be held liable for punitive damages because products liability is a strict liability claim.

69. Which of the following are appropriate factors for the jury to consider in determining an award of punitive damages?

    (A) The financial condition or wealth of the defendant.

    (B) The extent of harm to the plaintiff.

    (C) The plaintiff's litigation costs.

    (D) All of the above.

QUESTIONS · TOPIC 6: PUNITIVE DAMAGES

70. What "guideposts" did the Supreme Court identify in *BMW v. Gore* as indicators that an award of punitive damages is unconstitutionally excessive?

    ANSWER: 1) degree of reprehens 2) ratios 3) similar conduct issues

71. Pittman sued Hospitality Inn alleging that Hospitality Inn knowingly let him a room that was infested with bedbugs. A jury found for Pittman, awarding him $5,000 in compensatory damages and $200,000 in punitive damages. Under which of the following circumstances would an appeals court most likely uphold the award of punitive damages if Hospitality Inn challenges the award as unconstitutionally excessive?

    (A) The award cannot be upheld under any circumstances because the ratio of punitive to compensatory damages exceeds 9-to-1.

    (B) Pittman suffered only minor injuries because he discovered the bed bugs shortly after settling into the room, but other guests had suffered from severe pain and serious medical complications as a result of their exposure to bedbugs.

    (C) Pittman suffered only minor physical injuries because bedbug bites generally do not pose serious medical risks. However, several other guests also suffered minor physical injuries from bedbug bites.

    (D) Hospitality Inn's managers had failed to report to its corporate headquarters a previous $100,000 punitive damages award imposed in a discrimination lawsuit.

72. Peters sued Officer alleging that Officer conducted an unconstitutional search of Peters' home in violation of 28 U.S.C. § 1983. The jury found that Officer had knowingly and intentionally acted unconstitutionally but that Peters suffered no compensable damage. If the jury also awards Peters $1 in nominal damages, will Peters be entitled to punitive damages?

    ANSWER:

Topic 7   Questions

Qualifying for Injunctions

73. Poitier lives on a large parcel of land. His neighbor, Dunn Stables, is a horse-riding school. For approximately three months, Dunn's students frequently rode horses on a circuit path that crossed onto a small corner of Poitier's land. The area of Poitier's land where the horses trod is now an unsightly mess, especially compared to the rest of Poitier's beautiful estate. Upon noticing the destruction, Poitier approached Ms. Dunn, who admitted that her students' riding caused the damage. Dunn explained that the circuit was a temporary riding path because of now-completed renovation to her own property; she showed Poitier the new riding circuit to demonstrate that her students were no longer entering his property. Poitier demanded that Dunn Stables repair the damage to his lawn. When she refused to do the work, he sued Dunn Stables seeking an injunction that would order it to complete the repairs in a timely fashion. Will the court grant the requested relief?

    ANSWER:

74. Poitier lives on a large parcel of land. While Poitier was out of town, a protest-artist entered the property and installed a statue on Poitier's front lawn that offered a strong message about an upcoming election. Security camera footage unmistakably identifies the trespasser as Lewis, who has been sued by Poitier. Poitier seeks an injunction that would order Lewis to have the installation removed. If you represented Poitier and could make only one of the following facts true, which would you choose?

    (A) Lewis chose Poitier's property because he (Lewis) knew that Poitier would be especially offended by this expression.

    (B) Lewis waited to install the statue until he knew that Poitier was out of town so that the installation would not be interrupted.

    (C) Lewis has publicly announced his intention to perform similar protests on other rich people's estates.

    (D) The installation is heavy, and its disassembly and removal could be dangerous.

75. The Aquas are a professional soccer team that has operated in the City of Atlantis for thirty years. The City of Atlantis owned the stadium, Municipal Stadium, where the Aquas played and leased it to the team. Two years ago, the City entered into a ten-year lease with the team, which agreed to play all of its home games in the stadium. However, Pete Poseidon, the owner

of the Aquas, became discontented with soccer in Atlantis and announced that he would relocate the team to Treasure Island. He was disillusioned with the falling ticket sales in Atlantis, the lack of a modern stadium with luxury boxes, and the disrespect he felt the City exhibited toward him in not responding to his requests for a new stadium. In contrast, Treasure Island had agreed to build Poseidon a new stadium complete with luxury boxes and seat license fees for season tickets that would generate substantial income for the team. The State of Oceana in which Treasure Island is located also agreed to use lottery proceeds to fund the new stadium on Treasure Island. Most cities eagerly desire a professional sports team because of its positive impact on city pride and reputation, as well as the perceived economic benefits to the city. The City of Atlantis decided it would not let the Aquas leave without a fight. The City sued the Aquas for breach of the lease agreement and sought specific performance of the lease requiring the Aquas to abide by the contract and play its home soccer games in Municipal Stadium for the remaining term of the lease. Is the court likely to require specific performance?

(A) Yes, because the claim is one for breach of contract.

(B) Yes, because of the uniqueness of the team's contractual obligation.

(C) No, because of the supervisory burden on the court.

(D) No, because of the public policy in favor of efficient breaches of contract.

76. Assume the same facts as in the previous Question. What is the team's best argument against issuance of the injunction?

ANSWER:

77. Dugal Management, Inc. operates its business from the 24th floor of the Sun Life Building. On the last day of each of the previous three months, Torre Solutions Co., another tenant in the office building, has hacked into Dugal's computer servers. Torre does not interfere with any of Dugal's computer data or data operations, but temporarily uses Dugal's servers as excess storage capacity to streamline Torre's monthly backup storage operations. Dugal has objected to Torre's practice, yet Torre has continued to do it, saying "send me the bill for any expense I've caused you; that's easier for me." Dugal pays approximately $600/month for the terabytes of storage that Torre uses one day each month. Is a court likely to enjoin Torre from using Dugal's servers?

(A) Yes, because Dugal's legal remedies are inadequate.

(B) Yes, because Torre's interference with Dugal's servers could damage data or injure Dugal's business.

(C) No, because Dugal has an adequate remedy at law, namely damages.

(D) No, because there is no imminent harm.

78. Kelvin Cline Perfumes builds a new, state-of-the-art manufacturing plant near the outskirts of town. The plant owners made a $60 million capital investment in the factory and employ over 300 people. The plant's residential neighbors are irritated by the flowery perfume smells that constantly emanate from the plant. Although the smell is harmless, the neighbors complain that they are unable to open their windows, enjoy the summer breeze, or use their decks due to the sickeningly sweet smell. Assuming that the neighbors can prove the elements of a nuisance claim, is a court likely to issue an injunction ordering Kelvin Cline to close down the plant?

(A) No, because of the undue burden on Kelvin Cline.

(B) No, because of the supervisory burden on the court.

(C) Yes, because of the balance of hardships in plaintiffs' favor.

(D) Yes, because the neighborhood existed before Kelvin Cline built its plant.

79. The Oden family read in their local newspaper of a plan to build an apartment complex on their block. Although the street is zoned for multiple family dwellings, the Odens are concerned that an apartment complex will change the nature of their quiet residential neighborhood. Is a court likely to issue an injunction to prevent the building of the apartment complex?

(A) Yes, because of the need to prevent legal harm in advance.

(B) No, because of the lack of an imminent threat of harm.

(C) Yes, because of the irreversibility of building the complex.

(D) No, because the zoning code permits the land use.

80. Molly Woo is a DJ whose inventive dance music is in high demand. Two months after signing a lucrative one-year exclusive contract with the Omnium Nightclub in Las Vegas, Woo accepts an even-more-lucrative offer to perform exclusively for another club in another country. The Nightclub sues Woo, seeking an order of specific performance. What result?

(A) Injunction granted because of the uniqueness of Woo's contractual obligation.

(B) Injunction denied because of the policy against personal servitude.

(C) Injunction denied because of the adequacy of the legal remedy.

(D) Injunction granted because of the policy of enforcing written promises.

81. Byun wrote a song that his former roommate, Jisoo, pilfered and turned into a commercial success. When Byun discovered the theft, he sued for copyright infringement. Assuming he can prove the elements of the cause of action, could Byun recover damages *and* an injunction?

ANSWER:

82. Pingree is shocked to learn that his neighbor Carole, two doors down, houses several adult tigers in her backyard. Pingree fears that the tigers will escape and harm his children. Will the court issue an injunction requiring the neighbor to get rid of the tigers?

   (A) No, because the tigers are the neighbor's property.

   (B) No, because the tigers have not caused any harm.

   (C) Yes, because a tiger is an inherently dangerous object.

   (D) Yes, because the tigers pose a real threat of imminent harm.

83. An employment law statute provides that, upon proof of a violation of certain enumerated circumstances, equitable relief "must" issue. Prem has sued her employer for committing two of the proscribed acts. She seeks injunctive relief but also admits, in candor, that an award of monetary damages would make her whole. Does this concession disqualify her for the injunctive relief that she seeks?

   (A) Yes, because the legal remedies are adequate.

   (B) Yes, because of the supervisory burden on the court.

   (C) No, because the availability of equitable relief is an issue for the jury.

   (D) No, because the statute trumps the traditional test for equitable relief.

Topic 8

Injunctions

84. Macrocorp was found liable for monopolization in violation of the antitrust laws. The court found that Macrocorp engaged in illegal anticompetitive behavior through a series of contracts with its software licensees. If the court wants to issue a preventive injunction, which of the following provisions is appropriate?

    (A) Macrocorp must develop a new standard contract for software licensees.

    (B) Macrocorp must stop monopolizing the market through its software agreements.

    (C) Macrocorp must split into two separate companies.

    (D) Macrocorp must rewrite the existing contracts with its software licensees.

85. A prophylactic injunction:

    (A) is designed to stop the existing harm.

    (B) is designed to address the facilitators of harm with additional precautions.

    (C) is designed to correct the continuing consequences of past harm.

    (D) is not a valid type of injunction.

86. Operators of an animal research lab have sued an animal rights protest group that has repeatedly trespassed the lab and assaulted lab employees. The protest group has advertised another protest — "our biggest and best yet" — for Monday of next week. The court orders the protestors to stay 35 feet away from the perimeter of the lab grounds. What types of injunctive measures has the court issued against the protestors?

    (A) Reparative and preventive.

    (B) Structural and reparative.

    (C) Preventive and prophylactic.

    (D) Prophylactic and structural.

87. Susie Smith is an administrative assistant for a high-powered lawyer, Bob Grant, at a large law firm in Cleveland. Ever since she began work for Mr. Grant three months ago, she has been subjected to his constant harassment of jokes, requests for dates, and touching. He also added an adverse notation in her personnel file for being "uncooperative." When she complained to the office manager, the manager told her to stop being so sensitive and to get a sense of humor.

Since learning that two other employees had previously complained about Grant, Smith is prepared to sue the law firm for violations of federal employment laws. The prayer for relief in her complaint may include a request for injunctive relief. Give a specific example of what she might request if she seeks *preventive* relief. Then give an example of *reparative* relief that she might (also) request. Finally, given an example of a *prophylactic* measure that she might (also) request.

ANSWER:

88. Clarion College is an all-female teachers college with an excellent reputation run by the state of California. The college claims that its pedagogy of discussion and consensus building is uniquely suited to women, and that such a learning environment would be destroyed by a coed student population. A California court has found that the exclusion of male students (by a public school) violates the Equal Protection Clause. What is the appropriate measure of injunctive relief?

    (A) Order California to build a similar college for men.

    (B) Order California to close Clarion.

    (C) Order California to privatize Clarion and divest public funds.

    (D) Order California to allow men access to Clarion.

89. In the previous question, Answer (C) might be labeled (pejoratively) as "structural" relief. Structural injunctions are often claimed to be illegitimate forms of injunctive relief. What are the arguments against the validity of structural injunctions?

    ANSWER:

90. A class of prisoners brings suit claiming that their right of access to the courts was denied by the prison's failure to provide an adequate law library. The evidence at trial proves that one inmate was prevented from seeking access to the court due to his illiteracy. The trial court enters an injunction mandating extended law library hours, adequate lighting, legal materials for Spanish-speaking inmates, paralegals, an adequate number of typewriters, and quiet rooms with soundproofing. What result on appeal?

    (A) The injunction is upheld because the scope of relief matches the scope of the harm.

    (B) The injunction is upheld as necessary to prevent future harm.

    (C) The injunction is overturned because the scope of the injunction is overbroad.

    (D) The injunction is overturned because it provides for services not constitutionally required.

91. Read Bull enters into a contract with Spice Girlz for monthly installments of flavorings needed to manufacture its signature energy drink. After six months, Spice fails to deliver the contractual amount of flavoring. Apparently, Spice has found a more lucrative customer in Energy 100, which is willing to pay Spice twice as much as Read Bull. Read Bull is unable to find any other company that can provide the flavorings for its energy drink, because Spice is the only company with the distinctive combination of flavorings Read Bull needs. Read Bull sues Spice for breach of contract seeking specific performance. What result?

   (A) Spice does not have to perform the contract, but must pay for Read Bull's extra costs.

   (B) Spice does not have to perform the contract, but must pay for Read Bull's future lost profits.

   (C) Spice must perform the contract and pay for Read Bull's future lost profits.

   (D) Spice must perform the contract.

92. In resolution of a dispute over water rights, a judge ordered the defendant, Masterman, to remove a levee that he had erected on his land near a natural watercourse. Masterman's levee was interfering with his downstream neighbor's irrigation of his almond trees. Masterman promptly undertook the complicated project, but then suspended the work when he learned that all of the neighbor's almond trees were killed by a ferocious strain of bacteria. The partially-removed levee allows more water to flow downstream, but Masterman retains more water than he would have if the levee were fully removed. Which of the following is true?

   (A) Masterman can seek modification of the order based on changed factual circumstances.

   (B) Masterman can seek termination of the order based on changed factual circumstances.

   (C) Masterman can seek modification of the order based on his good faith compliance with a substantial part of the order.

   (D) Masterman can seek termination of the order based on his good faith compliance with a substantial part of the order.

93. Rocky Husband is arrested on domestic violence charges. He is sentenced to jail until completion of a court-approved counseling program, Batterers' Treatment Program. Rocky objects to the counseling program, which is run by a religious organization. If Rocky challenges the counseling program as a violation of the First Amendment, what remedies are available to Rocky?

   (A) An injunction.

   (B) An injunction, mandamus, and contempt.

   (C) An injunction, mandamus, and declaratory relief.

   (D) An injunction, contempt, and declaratory relief.

Topic 9   Questions

Temporary and Preliminary Injunctions

94. Shoe Co. sells a very popular basketball shoe that a competitor, Kix Inc., is about to mimic with a model of its own. The shoes are scheduled to appear on the shelves in Kix stores in the next few days. If you represented Shoe Co. and had a viable claim for trademark infringement, should you seek a temporary restraining order (to enjoin Kix from selling the offending shoe)?

    (A) No, because "the next few days" lacks the requisite specificity to justify injunctive relief.

    (B) No, because a request for a preliminary injunction is more appropriate under these circumstances.

    (C) Yes, because there may not be enough time to request a preliminary injunction.

    (D) Yes, because Shoe Co. is automatically entitled to equitable relief because it has a viable claim on the merits.

95. A school board decided to expel for the remainder of the school year a seventh grader who wrote, recorded, and distributed a violent song about her teachers. The child's mother sought and received from a federal court, without notice to the defendant school board, a temporary restraining order that prevented enforcement of the board's decision. There are fifty days remaining in the school year. Which of the following events is the most likely terminus of the temporary restraining order?

    (A) The end of the school year, when the equitable relief will be moot.

    (B) A ruling on either the plaintiff's motion to convert the temporary restraining order into a preliminary injunction or the defendant school board's motion to dissolve the order.

    (C) A final judgment in the underlying action, when a permanent injunction will issue, if appropriate.

    (D) The passage of 14 days, the maximum length of a temporary restraining order.

96. The City of Acadia has been swamped with protestors from a Save the Whales campaign. A tidal wave of protestors has caused damage to the town buildings and property and blocked traffic for miles. Yesterday, the protestors got out of hand and assaulted some of the local fishermen during a particularly violent protest. The Acadian police would like to obtain a temporary restraining order to stop the protest scheduled for today. The police file a complaint with the court, and make no attempts to contact the protestors prior to the *ex parte* hearing. Will the court issue the requested temporary injunction?

(A) No, because there is no immediate harm threatened.

(B) No, because there were no efforts to notify the defendants.

(C) Yes, because actual notice to the defendant is not required.

(D) Yes, because *ex parte* injunctions are authorized by the court.

97. "Hostile Hawks" is a puzzle video game developed and sold by Finite Gaming Co. Finite Gaming has filed a copyright and trademark infringement action against defendant Stuffies Inc. for intentionally selling infringing and unauthorized knockoff plush toys that are nearly identical to Finite's hostile hawks. Finite seeks a temporary restraining order that would enjoin Stuffies from any further manufacturing or selling of the merchandise that infringes Finite's trademarks. Assuming that Finite has a viable claim and that it may suffer imminent harm, under which of the following circumstances will the court issue the TRO *ex parte*?

(A) Finite offers some evidentiary support for the notion that Stuffies' knockoffs may pose a public health risk, as they may not be in compliance with state and federal laws that regulate the material composition of products.

(B) The judge is aware that Stuffies is a repeat offender. In two recent actions brought by different video game manufacturers, Stuffies was found liable for copyright and trademark infringement under similar circumstances.

(C) Finite's counsel alleges that Stuffies might destroy or conceal their infringing goods and records relating to those goods if they are given notice of the relief requested.

(D) None of the above.

98. What are the four traditional legal requirements for the issuance of a preliminary injunction?
ANSWER:

99. Marjan Bistro entered into a contract with SVN Builders to remodel its restaurant for the sum of $100,000, of which approximately half the contract amount was for labor and the other half for materials. Marjan paid SVN $25,000 when the agreement was signed, and the remainder was due upon completion of the work. SVN purchased all of the building materials and stored them at the restaurant, which was then closed for the remodel. SVN had promised to complete the remodel within three weeks, but at the end of the third week, less than 20% of the work was done. Marjan ordered SVN to stop work on the project, intending to find another contractor. The next day, SVN began removing the purchased building materials from the premises. Marjan sued for breach of contract and sought a preliminary injunction enjoining SVN from removing, hiding, or destroying the building materials. Which one of the following facts would, if verified, provide the strongest support for Marjan's argument that he will suffer irreparable injury unless interlocutory relief is ordered?

(A) From the outset of their agreement, SVN had no intention of performing the contract.

(B) It is November 1, and the winter holiday season is the busiest for restaurants in this area.

(C) SVN has already used a small amount of the building materials on a different construction project.

(D) Marjan is struggling financially.

100. The City of Troxy heard testimony from residents who were frustrated by the delivery of unwanted "yellow pages" telephone directories to their doorsteps. Residents complained that these unwanted deliveries were wasteful and violated their right to privacy. Troxy City Council responded by passing an ordinance that curtailed the ability of companies to distribute phone books. The ordinance created a regime that required these companies to obtain a license, to pay 4 cents for each distributed book, and to establish and maintain an opt-out registry for residents. One of these publishing companies, Medallion Inc., has sued for violation of its First Amendment rights. This ordinance would effectively terminate Medallion's yellow pages directories business, which is one of its three principal sources of revenue. Accordingly, Medallion seeks a preliminary injunction to enjoin the City from enforcing the ordinance. Under these circumstances, the judge will likely grant the preliminary injunction provided:

(A) Medallion's First Amendment claim is "plausible" on the merits.

(B) Medallion's First Amendment claim raises "serious questions going to the merits."

(C) Medallion has a "likelihood of success on the merits."

(D) Medallion has a "strong likelihood of success on the merits."

101. Princess Ulla, a famous international figure, has been continually hounded by the media and paparazzi since her marriage to a Prince. One reporter in particular, Heinrik Kronel, has harassed her and continually invaded her privacy over the last ten years. In the past six months, Kronel has printed thirty stories about Ulla and her children. While no article or picture has appeared in the last few weeks, Ulla is interested in taking legal action to stop Kronel from violating her privacy, and files a lawsuit against him. If a court were to award injunctive relief at this stage of the litigation, which type(s) would it likely order?

(A) Temporary restraining order.

(B) Temporary restraining order and preliminary injunction.

(C) Preliminary injunction.

(D) Preliminary and permanent injunctions.

102. Bunnik owns a beautiful suburban house that was insured under a homeowner's policy issued by Venago Insurance Co., a prominent insurer. On January 2, Bunnik's house was damaged by vibration from construction that was taking place on an adjacent lot. City inspectors found Bunnik's house to be unsafe and ordered her to vacate. For approximately six weeks, Venago paid for Bunnik's family to live in temporary housing. On February 15, Venago disclaimed coverage and informed Bunnik that it would discontinue paying for temporary housing, effective March 1. The insurance policy provides coverage for up to 24 months of temporary housing, but has an "Earth Movement" exclusion that exempts the insurer for loss caused by "sinking, rising, shifting, expanding, or contracting of earth. This includes but is not limited to earthquake, landslide, mudflow, mudslide, sinkhole, erosion, or similar natural forces." Bunnik immediately filed a lawsuit, alleging that her insurance policy provided coverage, and sought a preliminary injunction directing Venago to continue to pay the temporary housing costs. Establishing which of the following is the biggest hurdle confronting Bunnik?

   (A) Likelihood of success on the merits

   (B) Irreparable injury

   (C) Balance of hardships

   (D) Public interest

103. Stephan sold snacks on a street corner at First and Main on the premises of a university campus. Stephan, who is unaffiliated with the university, parked his push-cart at this location for four years, before his business dwindled this year due to the construction of a new university library near his usual site. Stephan then moved his snack cart to a new location at Second and Elm directly in front of the library, and his business picked up. Coffee Mart, a company that is licensed by the university to sell coffee inside the library, complained to the University. The University, in turn, filed a complaint against Stephan for trespass and now seeks a preliminary injunction enjoining him from selling coffee anywhere on campus. Assuming satisfaction of the four prerequisites for preliminary relief, what is the most likely scope of the court's order?

   (A) Enjoin Stephan from selling snacks anywhere on campus.

   (B) Enjoin Stephan from selling snacks anywhere on campus other than at the corner of First and Main.

   (C) Enjoin Stephan from selling snacks within 300 (or *x*) feet of the library.

   (D) Enjoin Stephan from selling snacks at the corner of Second and Elm.

104. Two months ago, the State of East Dakota passed the Motor Vehicle Fuel Tax Act, which levies a new tax on sales of motor vehicle fuel within the state. Two Indian tribes in the state manufacture motor vehicle fuel on their reservations, and then sell the fuel to other local Indian tribes for retail sales. The two manufacturers immediately filed a federal lawsuit against the state seeking to clarify that the mandate does not apply to these manufacturer-to-retailer transactions; the state insists that the tax is due on all sales. The plaintiffs seek a preliminary injunction enjoining the state from collecting the tax on the manufacturer-to-retailer sales.

The disputed tax revenue is $200,000 per month, with $400,000 (and counting) now owed. Assuming that the four perquisites for preliminary relief are satisfied, will the plaintiffs also be required to post security (e.g., a bond) to get preliminary relief?

(A) Yes, and the amount must be $400,000 and should increase by $200,000 each month that this litigation continues.

(B) Yes, in an amount the judge considers proper.

(C) No, because the posting of a bond puts a price on equitable relief that some litigants (maybe even these plaintiffs) would be unable to pay.

(D) No, because government entities are not required to post bonds.

Topic 10

Contempt

105. Which of the following circumstances constitutes a basis for criminal contempt?

    (A) A mother accidentally pays $5,000 less than the amount of court-ordered child support.

    (B) A corporate defendant does not produce a document during discovery that is directly responsive to a document request (and the document is not privileged from disclosure).

    (C) A company implements a workplace policy regarding family leave that is a knowing and willful violation of existing laws.

    (D) A defendant in a civil matter who was ordered to deliver a dog to the plaintiff instead sold the dog on a classified advertisement website.

106. The contemnor described in the correct answer to the previous question could be subject to which of the following punishments?

    (A) A fine (but not a jail term).

    (B) A jail term (but not a fine).

    (C) A fine and/or a jail term.

    (D) Neither a fine nor a jail term because those would be excessive punishments; but some other, more modest punishment that is limited to what is sufficient to deter repetition of the conduct.

107. After the court denied Camden's motion in Aidan's suit against Camden, Camden's lawyer (Bunker) orally moved the court to reconsider its ruling. Bunker made no legal arguments but instead indulged in an unprofessional rant that impugned the integrity of the court—including a suggestion that Aidan may have prevailed on the motion because he is related to someone in town with considerable legal and political clout. The court held Bunker in contempt and fined her $100. What kind of contempt is this?

    (A) Summary/Direct (criminal) contempt.

    (B) Indirect (criminal) contempt.

    (C) Civil coercive contempt.

    (D) None of the above. Contempt is inappropriate here, because Bunker is not a party.

108. The government brings a (criminal) contempt motion against Microcorp for violating the terms of a consent decree that prohibited Microcorp from entering into licensing agreements that tied products to its operational software in violation of the antitrust laws. The government reluctantly concedes that Microcorp's behavior does not necessarily violate the terms of the consent decree, because the consent decree is vague on a key point. Microcorp reluctantly concedes that it entered into the subject agreement without reviewing the consent decree—that is, without relying on the vagueness of the key term. The court should:

(A) Deny the motion because contempt cannot be used to enforce consent decrees.

(B) Deny the motion because the order was vague.

(C) Grant the motion because Microcorp violated the spirit of the order.

(D) Grant the motion because Microcorp acted in bad faith.

109. Susan McDonagal refused to testify as a witness in the infamous Bluewater trial against President Clintex. The court ordered McDonagal jailed until she agreed to testify. McDonagal ultimately served two years for her refusal to testify, at which time the Bluewater case had ended. What kind of contempt remedy did the Court impose?

(A) Summary contempt.

(B) Criminal contempt.

(C) Civil coercive contempt.

(D) Civil compensatory contempt.

110. In a disability discrimination case, Sherman Industries is ordered by the trial judge to make five accommodations in its warehouse building. After extensive fact finding and hearing from both parties, the judge described the accommodations in great detail, and gave Sherman 90 days to complete the work. The judge states that Sherman will be fined $100,000 if it fails to comply, and she promises to tolerate "no excuses" from Sherman. Ninety-two days later, the plaintiff and his counsel returned to court with video footage showing the five projects in various stages of completion, but with none finished. The judge has no reason to doubt the authenticity of the video, and the video includes footage of the previous day's newspaper (to authenticate its date). The judge orders Sherman to pay a $100,000 fine. What result if Sherman appeals the sanction?

(A) The order should be affirmed because this is criminal contempt. This is a willful violation of the court's order which allowed for no excuses.

(B) The order should be affirmed because this is civil coercive contempt. The court properly crafted the remedy so that the defendant could purge the contempt remedy through compliance.

(C) The order should be reversed because the judge failed to conduct the necessary procedures prior to imposing criminal contempt.

(D) The order should be reversed because the judge failed to conduct the necessary procedures prior to imposing civil coercive contempt.

111. What are the legal strategies and defenses defendants can use to defend against motions for contempt?

ANSWER:

112. During a trial in an unfair competition (civil) case, the judge repeatedly instructs defendant, a taxicab driver, to be silent and to stop disrupting the proceedings. The judge warns defendant's counsel to control his client, and the lawyer replies: "I am doing the best I can with him, your Honor." After an adverse ruling, the defendant stands up and begins to storm out of the courtroom, muttering expletives as he goes. The judge:

(A) May order the defendant to be taken immediately into custody.

(B) May order the defendant to be taken into custody after a proper hearing.

(C) May order the defendant to be taken into custody after a proper hearing and an opportunity for the defendant to be heard.

(D) May not order the defendant into custody, and must refer the case to the criminal prosecutors' office for further review.

113. During a fight in a parking lot, Devlin shot and killed Vic, a known drug dealer. Devlin readily admitted to the slaying, but claimed he acted in self defense. Before his trial, Devlin contacted newspaper staff writer Liesl Moran and spoke with her on several occasions, providing Moran with details of the shooting and of his clash with Vic and other dealers. Based on this information, Moran authored several articles for the Patriot Ledger. State prosecutors found that certain portions of the newspaper pieces were inconsistent with statements Devlin made to authorities. With the murder trial already underway, prosecutors subpoenaed Moran's notes and other memorializations of her conversations with Devlin. When Moran refused, the court heard oral argument and ruled that Moran was obligated to produce them under state and federal law. Moran still refused to produce them. After another hearing, the court ordered that Moran would be fined $100 per minute of trial starting at 12:00 noon the following day until compliance or until the state rested its case. Moran still refused to produce her notes. The state rested a couple of days later. The judge held one more hearing and ordered Moran to pay a sanction of $40,000 for the 400 minutes of trial time covered by the contempt order. All of the hearings provided Moran with the protections of civil procedure, but not of criminal procedure. What result if Moran appeals the sanction?

(A) She might prevail by arguing that, even if the contempt sanction was proper (as a civil coercive remedy), the magnitude of the fine was an abuse of discretion.

(B) She might prevail by arguing that the contempt sanction was improper, because she was denied the protections of criminal procedure.

(C) Both (A) and (B).

(D) None of the above.

114. Jemma Nabors obtained a court order requiring her neighbor, Ryan Hislop, to comply with a restrictive covenant that prohibited a freestanding garage in their neighborhood. The trial judge's order required Hislop to attach his freestanding garage to his residence within six months. Hislop then constructed a pergola/breezeway between the residence and the garage. Nabors now argues that the pergola/breezeway did not connect the garage to the residence *with a common wall*, and therefore is still not "attached." The judge agrees with Nabors' interpretation of the meaning of "attached." The judge finds Hislop in contempt, orders Hislop to pay Nabors' $7,100 of counsel fees, and gives Hislop another three months to comply with the order. The hearing provided Hislop with the protections of civil procedure, but not of criminal procedure. What result if Hislop appeals the sanction?

(A) The appeals court will reverse this finding of criminal contempt because Hislop did not receive all of the protections of criminal procedure.

(B) The appeals court will reverse this finding of contempt because Hislop made a good faith effort to comply.

(C) The appeals court will affirm this finding of civil compensatory contempt (because of the collateral bar doctrine) even if the trial court's construction of the restrictive covenant was erroneous.

(D) The appeals court will affirm this finding of civil compensatory contempt unless the trial court's construction of the restrictive covenant was erroneous.

Topic 11　　　　　　　　　　　　　　　　　　　　　　　　　　Questions

Unjust Enrichment

115. Joe agreed to pay Builder $1 million to construct a new Bananas restaurant for him. Joe is a new franchise owner of the national Bananas chain that is known for its banana-shaped restaurants and delicious banana splits. Builder negligently constructs the restaurant by making it the shape of a hot dog, rather than a banana. Joe estimates it will cost $250,000 to make the necessary alterations to the building. Can Joe sue Builder for restitution?

   (A) No, because Builder has no unjust benefit to disgorge.

   (B) No, because Joe has suffered irreparable injury.

   (C) Yes, because Joe is entitled to punish Builder for the breach of contract.

   (D) Yes, because Joe is entitled to be compensated for his losses.

116. Tenant leased Landlord's building to manufacture its specialty toys. Tenant produces brain challenger puzzles for toddlers made out of wood. Tenant discovered a shrink wrap machine hidden in one of the closets of the building and began to use it to package its toys. The machine saved Tenant the $20/day cost of paying workers to wrap the toys by hand. One day, while visiting the plant, Landlord discovered that Tenant was using the machine. Landlord had not used the machine in over ten years, and offered to rent it to Tenant for $100 per month. Tenant refused the offer, and Landlord sued Tenant for restitution. What is the legal theory upon which restitution can be based?

   (A) Quantum meruit.

   (B) Constructive trust.

   (C) Quasi-contract.

   (D) Rescission.

117. Assume the same facts as in the previous question. What is the most appropriate measure of restitution in this case?

   (A) The rental value of the machine.

   (B) The market value of the machine.

   (C) The cost savings from the use of the machine.

   (D) The total profits from the sale of the toys.

118. The University solicits bids for artists to design the mural at its new student activity center. Artista submits a low bid of $5000 to design the plans for the mural. Artista's bid is accepted contingent upon funding from the National Arts Council. She shows her initial designs to the University board and it approves her work. However, six months into the project, the University's funding for the mural is lost. Artista has completed 90% of the design work when she is told that the project is cancelled pursuant to the terms of the contract. By this time, she has expended $9000 worth of work on the project. What action can Artista take against the University?

    (A) Sue in quasi-contract for $5000.

    (B) Sue in quasi-contract for $9000.

    (C) Sue in quantum meruit for $5000.

    (D) Sue in quantum meruit for $9000.

119. Lego Builders wanted to compete for a bid to build the new city hall in town. It then began receiving sub-contract bids. The lowest bid was made by Bionicle Builders for $180,000, which was $25,000 less than the next lowest bid. Based upon this low bid, Lego submitted its general bid to the City Council. Lego's general bid was $20,000 lower than the City Council originally anticipated, due to the low sub-bid from Bionicle. The City Council accepted Lego's bid. After the acceptance, Bionicle informed Lego that there had been a mistake in computing the sub-bid, and that the correct amount was $220,000. Lego was unaware of this mistake. In a suit for rescission of the contract with Lego, Bionicle should:

    (A) Not succeed because the mistake was made before the bid was accepted.

    (B) Not succeed unless Lego actually knew or should have known of the mistake.

    (C) Succeed because the mistake was bilateral.

    (D) Succeed because this was a unilateral mistake.

120. Accountant volunteers to help his elderly neighbor with her taxes. Unbeknownst to him, the neighbor has a confusing array of stocks and properties that makes the taxes quite complicated. Accountant ends up spending five times as long on the taxes as he expected, and loses a significant amount of time at the office from working on his neighbor's account. When the ungrateful neighbor refuses to even say thank you for the tax preparation, Accountant decides to sue in restitution. What result?

    (A) Accountant will receive restitution in the amount of the services rendered.

    (B) Accountant will receive restitution in the amount of the time lost at work.

    (C) Accountant will be denied restitution because he was a volunteer.

    (D) Accountant will be denied restitution because neighbor had no unjust benefit.

121. Distributor, a food service company, enters into oral negotiations with Almondia, a locally owned company that manufacturers gourmet foods for a trendy almond diet. Distributor wants to establish an exclusive arrangement for distributing the Almondia products in the southern states. During the initial negotiations, the parties agreed on the important terms of the agreement, but had not yet worked out all the details. Both parties were excited about the new deal, and Almondia assured Distributor, "Don't worry. We'll work the rest of the things out." Assuming that he had the deal sealed, Distributor hired additional workers, leased larger space, and purchased delivery equipment. Shortly thereafter, Almondia told Distributor that it had signed a deal with Florida Brothers to handle the distribution. Which of the following theories would help Distributor prevail in a lawsuit against Almondia?

(A) Implied-in-fact contract.

(B) Promissory estoppel.

(C) Unjust enrichment.

(D) Quasi-contract.

122. Pizza driver is involved in a three-car accident while racing to deliver pizzas on time. Driver suffers injuries to his leg and requires medical treatment. The medical expenses are paid by his insurance company. After investigation, it is established that Driver and the driver of a second car were both causes of the accident. Driver was speeding in order to follow his restaurant's new policy of promising customers a 29-minute delivery. The restaurant also promised their drivers that they would cover them for any legal problems regarding the policy. What restitution claims are likely to be raised in this case?

ANSWER:

123. Insurance Co. insured the chief executive officer of Big Corporation for $3 million. The CEO, a young man of 45, represented in his insurance application that he was in good health, had no preexisting medical conditions, and was a non-smoker. Less than one year after issuance of the policy, CEO died of a heart attack. Upon investigation, Insurance Co. discovered that CEO had in fact been a heavy smoker. What result if Insurance Co. sues for restitution?

(A) Rescission of the contract and retention of the $3 million.

(B) Enforcement of the contract and payment to Big Corporation of $3 million.

(C) Enforcement of the contract and payment to Insurance Co. of the additional cost of premiums for smokers.

(D) Rescission of the contract, retention of the $3 million, and return of the premiums paid.

124. Public Agency sues Computer Co. for failure to deliver 100 computer screens which it says it purchased for $200 each. Agency still wants the screens, and seeks their immediate delivery. At trial, there is no evidence proven of a written contract or any testimony about an offer and acceptance. The two parties who negotiated the alleged contract for each side no longer work for the organizations and cannot be located. Evidence is presented that Public Agency wrote a check to Computer Co. for $20,000 and that Computer Co. deposited that check in its bank account. Upon what basis would Public Agency be entitled to relief?

(A) Rescission.

(B) Express contract.

(C) Quasi-contract.

(D) Implied-in-fact contract.

Topic 12   Questions

Equitable Restitution

125. Which of the following is not an equitable restitution remedy?

    (A) Quasi-contract.

    (B) Constructive trust.

    (C) Equitable lien.

    (D) Accounting of profits.

126. In recent cases before the U.S. Supreme Court, the Court has distinguished equitable from legal restitution. What are the hallmark characteristics of equitable restitution?

    ANSWER:

127. Winifred and Harry are newlyweds. Harry's parents own farm land and agree to let Harry and Winifred build a home on the land worth $20,000. The couple uses $30,000 of their savings to secure a $140,000 mortgage for the house. Harry helps the contractor build the house in order to save money. Winifred helps paint the house and does small jobs on the construction, services valued at approximately $22,000. Ten years later, Winifred and Harry divorce, splitting everything equally. At the time of the divorce, the house and land are valued at $220,000 and the mortgage has been paid in full by Winifred and Harry. If Winifred successfully sues Harry's parents under a theory of constructive trust, what amount will the court award?

    (A) $22,000.

    (B) $85,000.

    (C) $100,000.

    (D) $107,000.

128. Assume the same facts as in Question 127, except that Winifred sues under a theory of equitable lien. What amount will the court award?

    (A) $22,000.

    (B) $85,000.

(C) $100,000.

(D) $107,000.

129. Bonnie Ray is the latest TV cooking sensation. Her new cookbook, "The Hot Mama's Guide to Baking" is number one on the bestsellers list. It turns out, however, that Bonnie stole all of the recipes from her mother-in-law. She had told her mother-in-law that she wanted to have all the family's secret recipes to continue the traditions in her own family. However, Bonnie really intended to publish the recipes in her new book. What equitable theory of restitution would assist Mother-in-law in disgorging all of Bonnie's unjust profits?

(A) Equitable lien.

(B) Quasi-contract.

(C) Constructive trust.

(D) Accounting of profits.

130. Bob and Gretta decide to move in together. Bob moves into Gretta's house that she owns and which is valued at $80,000. The couple decides to add a second floor to the house, and Bob contributes $55,000 of his own money from a savings account to pay for the cost of the construction work. Five years later, the remodeled house is valued at $150,000. However, after 6 years, the couple has grown apart and Bob moves out. When Gretta refuses to compensate Bob for his contribution to the house, he brings a lawsuit against her. What restitution remedy is available to Bob?

(A) Quantum meruit for the value of his services.

(B) Constructive trust for the appreciated value of the house.

(C) Equitable lien for the debt owed to Bob.

(D) Indemnification by Gretta for the cost of the construction work.

131. In modern times, civil justice advocates have petitioned the legal process to try and obtain redress for the injustice of slavery in the United States. The slavery reparations cases seek, among other things, monetary relief on behalf of the survivors of slaves for their forced labor. Restitution has been the primary legal avenue upon which these reparations claims have been based. How would you frame these arguments for slavery reparations as restitution claims?

ANSWER:

QUESTIONS · TOPIC 12: EQUITABLE RESTITUTION 57

132. Erb's Root Beer infringes on the trademark of Beerman's Brew. Erb's takes the design and color of Beerman's label as its own. Beerman's proves that this caused consumers to believe that Erb's product was affiliated with the popular best-selling Beerman's beer. At trial, the evidence shows that during the time of the infringement, Erb's earned $3 million in sales. No evidence is submitted as to whether or not Beerman in fact lost any sales from the infringement. Erb's documents show that it cost them $2 million to produce the root beer, and that Erb's engaged in a targeted advertising campaign during the time of infringement that generated $250,000 in new sales. What amount is Beerman likely to recover as a measure of restitution?

    (A) $3 million.

    (B) $1 million.

    (C) $750,000.

    (D) $0.

133. LeMar Ivory was the treasurer of the Great Lakes church when he embezzled $200,000 from church funds. He gave $100,000 of the monies to his girlfriend, Betty. She purchased a Mercedes Benz automobile for $50,000 and purchased stocks with the remaining $50,000. The stocks have now increased in value to $100,000 and the car has depreciated in value to $30,000. Ivory fled to Costa Rica and cannot be located. The church sues Betty for restitution of the stolen funds. What result?

    (A) The church is awarded $100,000.

    (B) The church is awarded $130,000.

    (C) The church is awarded $150,000.

    (D) The church is awarded $200,000.

134. Sally, Dick and Jane are neighbors on the Gulf Coast of Florida. During a particularly bad hurricane, Sally and Dick move into Jane's two-bedroom house to ride out the storm. The homes of Sally and Dick are destroyed in the storm, and Jane offers to let the neighbors stay. Sally and Dick begin to pay Jane a reasonable monthly rent. After three years, the roommates decide to build a third bedroom and second bathroom onto the house. Dick builds the addition himself and uses $10,000 of his savings to purchase construction supplies. This increases the value of Jane's home to $200,000, from the original price of $60,000, though part of this increase is due to market factors related to the lack of housing after the storm's destruction. One year later, Jane notifies her roommates that she is going to be married, and needs them to move out of the house. When Dick asks for compensation for his addition to the home, Jane refuses. If Dick sues Jane for restitution, what result?

    (A) Dick will be awarded an equitable lien for the value of his services.

    (B) Dick will be awarded an equitable lien in the amount of his savings and services.

    (C) Dick will be awarded a constructive trust for the return of his savings.

    (D) Dick will be awarded a constructive trust for the value of the appreciated house.

Topic 13   Questions

Declaratory Judgment

135. Prime Advertisers Co. paid Oliver Oldham $15 million for Oldham's billboard business. As part of the deal, Oldham was allowed to retain ownership of several billboards; but in the purchase and sale agreement, Oldham promised to use those billboards only for advertising businesses that he owned. A few months after the deal closed, Prime suspects that Oldham's wife, Devi, may be marketing the (retained) billboards for advertising by third parties. Legal research suggests that it is an open question whether certain restrictive covenants can also bind a party's family members to the covenants. Prime will file a declaratory judgment suit when the case is ripe. Which of the following facts is relevant to the ripeness inquiry?

    (A) Devi is an accomplished and successful businesswoman in her own right, but has never been in the outdoor advertising business.

    (B) Devi signed a promissory note agreeing to pay $2,000,000 to her husband for the retained billboards, toward which no payment has yet been made.

    (C) A longtime customer of Prime recently declined to renew its advertising contract with Prime, stating that lower prices were available from a new seller.

    (D) All of the above.

136. Consider the same facts as in the previous question. Should Prime file an action seeking a preliminary injunction *instead* of filing a declaratory judgment suit?

    ANSWER:

137. On successive weekends earlier this month, Apollo and Artemis were passing out anti-war leaflets in a shopping center in Rometown. Twice, the police warned them that they must stop leafleting or they will be arrested and prosecuted for criminal trespass. Last weekend, Apollo (alone) was passing out leaflets, and he was arrested and prosecuted by Rometown. Now, Artemis (alone) sues for declaratory relief, stating that the criminal trespass statute as applied violates her First Amendment rights. Is Artemis entitled to declaratory relief?

    (A) No, because only Apollo was passing out leaflets last weekend.

    (B) Yes, because Artemis wants the court to order the police to stop arresting protesters.

    (C) No, because there is no definite and concrete controversy between Artemis and Rometown.

    (D) Yes, because the controversy is ripe.

59

138. Sales owned three Burger Queen restaurants when she entered into an agreement with Perch. In their agreement (1) Perch purchased the personal property associated with the operation of the restaurants for a stated sum; (2) Perch agreed to lease the real property from Sales for scheduled amounts; and (3) Perch was given an option to purchase any of "the premise[s]" at fair market value (for an amount to be determined by an independent appraiser). Pursuant to a term in the agreement, Perch notifies Sales of his intent to exercise the option to purchase. But the parties differ as to the nature and extent of the property interests to be appraised as "the premises." Sales maintains that the contract requires the appraisal of the land together with all improvements, while Perch contends that only the land must be evaluated. Is Sales entitled to declaratory relief to clarify the scope of "the premises"?

(A) Yes.

(B) No, because the controversy is not ripe for judicial determination.

(C) No, because issues of contract interpretation present questions of law reserved to the courts.

(D) No, because declaratory relief would not definitively resolve the parties' dispute.

139. Jean Paul files a declaratory judgment action challenging Catalog Co.'s customer-satisfaction guarantee policy. Six months ago, Catalog Co. added two conditions to its lifetime guarantee: customers must produce proof of purchase (e.g., a receipt), and products must not be damaged beyond normal wear and tear. Paul purchased an expensive winter coat for $750 from the company three weeks before the policy changed. She is currently pleased with the coat. But because these new conditions on the lifetime guarantee purport to apply retroactively, Paul seeks declaratory relief on the grounds that this policy violates applicable consumer protection laws. Is a declaratory judgment likely?

(A) No, because the dispute is trivial.

(B) No, because the dispute is not ripe.

(C) Yes, because Paul has a strong likelihood of success on the merits of the consumer protection claim.

(D) Yes, because the case presents a pure legal issue that is well-suited for resolution by a declaratory judgment.

140. What is the reason that a litigant might choose a declaratory judgment remedy over other remedies?

(A) Declaratory relief, like preliminary relief, may be awarded before plaintiff suffers harm (or further harm). And unlike preliminary relief, there is no irreparable injury requirement.

(B) Cases seeking only declaratory relief may be expedited under some rules of civil practice and procedure.

(C) Declaration of the parties' rights and responsibilities might be all that is necessary for the parties to proceed in accordance therewith.

(D) All of the above.

141. Pat is an inpatient of Oldtown Psychiatric Hospital. The Hospital is administering involuntary medication treatments pursuant to State Law § 33-12, which prescribes a decision-making process for treatments and also ensures notice to the patient and the patient's appointed health advocate. Following the regulations, the Hospital provides notice of its intent to begin a more aggressive treatment regimen in 48 hours from the time that notice was received. Pat's advocate files, on his behalf, an action against the Hospital, seeking a declaration that § 33-12 violates his due process rights provided under the state and federal constitutions. If the court denies declaratory relief, what is the most likely reason?

(A) The case is not ripe.

(B) A declaratory judgment will not provide practical relief.

(C) The parties are not adverse.

(D) The disputed issue is not a question of law.

142. A shooter entered the Millenium nightclub and injured four people. One of the injured guests (Gerson) sues the nightclub in state court arguing that it failed to protect him from a foreseeable harm. The Millenium's insurer, A1 Insurance Co., files an action in federal court seeking a declaration that the policy's exclusion for claims related to assault and battery exempts it from any obligation to defend or indemnify Millenium in litigation filed by injured guests. The insurer and the insured dispute whether the shooter's violent attack constitutes "assault" and/or "battery." Is declaratory relief appropriate?

(A) No, because the insurer's liability must be litigated as part of the state court action.

(B) No, because a declaratory judgment would not settle the controversy.

(C) Yes, provided the federal action was filed after the state court action.

(D) Yes, provided Gerson's state court claim expressly alleges that the shooter committed "assault" and/or "battery."

143. A middle school teacher is arrested for sexually molesting one of his students. He is arraigned on charges of sexual molestation, assault, and a lesser misdemeanor. The teacher's insurance company sues for declaratory judgment seeking an order stating that there is no coverage for molestation. How should the court rule?

(A) Issue a declaratory judgment because there is an actual controversy.

(B) Issue a declaratory judgment because the case is ripe.

(C) Deny the declaratory judgment because the order will not terminate the uncertainty.

(D) Deny the declaratory judgment because the defendant seeks a tactical advantage.

144. Datsun Motor Co. is America's third largest automaker and is located in Detroit, Michigan. A separate unaffiliated company named Old Datsun Car Parts, a small company in South Carolina, began selling parts online. Attorneys for Datsun Motor Co. send a letter to Old Datsun Car Parts demanding that the latter quit using/copying the former's trademarks and threatening to sue. Old Datsun Car Parts promptly responds with a letter defending its use of the trademarks and immediately files for a declaratory judgment of non-infringement in the U.S. District Court for the District of South Carolina. How should the court rule?

(A) Issue a declaratory judgment because there is an actual controversy.

(B) Issue a declaratory judgment because the case is ripe.

(C) Deny the declaratory judgment because the order will not terminate the uncertainty.

(D) Deny the declaratory judgment because the defendant seeks a tactical advantage.

145. Gremlin Motor Co. is America's fourth largest automaker and is located in Detroit, Michigan. A separate unaffiliated company named Old Gremlin Car Parts, a small company in North Carolina, began selling parts online. Attorneys for Gremlin Motor Co. send a letter to Old Gremlin Car Parts demanding that the latter quit using/copying the former's trademarks and threatening to sue. Old Gremlin Car Parts promptly responds with a letter defending its use of the trademarks. For time period *x*, counsel for the two companies exchange emails carefully arguing their respective positions. If Old Gremlin Car Parts is inclined to file for a declaratory judgment of non-infringement in a federal district court in North Carolina, which of the following periods of time is the most advantageous value of *x*?

(A) Twenty-four hours; or even less if possible.

(B) One or two weeks.

(C) Six to twelve months.

(D) Two years; or even more if possible.

Topic 14   Questions

Remedial Defenses

146. Radia secured the domain name fashionplate.com in the late 1990s. She did little to develop the site and ultimately sold it three months ago to Casey for $20,000, payable in ten monthly installments of $2,000. Casey, a recent art school graduate, was not represented by counsel and did not consult a lawyer. Radia's lawyer prepared the contract, which included a provision that gave Radia a unilateral right to cancel the contract within six months. Radia triggers the cancellation right, and when Casey refuses to return the website, she sues for rescission and equitable relief. Which of the following defenses might be available to Casey?

    (A) Waiver.

    (B) Unconscionability.

    (C) Laches.

    (D) Unfairness.

147. What is the difference between the defenses of *in pari delicto* and unclean hands?

    (A) *In pari delicto* applies to statutory claims, and unclean hands applies to common law claims.

    (B) *In pari delicto* applies when plaintiff has engaged in illegal activity, and unclean hands when the plaintiff's activity is wrongful even if not illegal.

    (C) *In pari delicto* applies when the plaintiff's losses were substantially caused by its own forbidden actions; unclean hands applies when the plaintiff has engaged in fraud or misconduct that is related to its equitable claim.

    (D) They mean exactly the same thing; *in pari delicto* is the Latin term.

148. Landlord leases a commercial property to a private childcare center. To comply with child safety laws, the Center starts to build a chain-link fence around the playground. Landlord drives by the property and notices that the fence is being installed too close to the edge of the property line. This violation of zoning law could subject the landlord to penalties. Landlord talks with the Center's director, who explains the need for the fence before the business can open. Landlord says "I understand," and drives away. The Center finishes the fence and immediately begins operation. Four weeks later, the landlord sends the Center an eviction notice because the fence violates zoning regulations which, in turn, violates a term of the lease. What remedial defense should the Center pursue?

(A) Estoppel.

(B) Laches.

(C) Unclean hands.

(D) Unconscionability.

149. Medal Jeans, Inc., an apparel brand and owner of a trademark "MEDAL," files a trademark infringement claim against Medal Sport, Inc., a powerlifting brand, seeking preliminary and permanent equitable relief. Which of the following facts would be most relevant to an unclean hands defense?

(A) Medal Jeans, Inc., recently lost a substantially similar trademark infringement suit that it filed against Medal Racing Co., an organizer of running events.

(B) Medal Jeans, Inc., has provided varying accounts of how it acquired the trademark.

(C) Medal Sport, Inc.'s infringement of the mark was deliberate and willful.

(D) Medal Sport, Inc., previously made a false statement to the U.S. Patent and Trademark Office, which led that Office to cancel Medal Sport's registration of its "CLEAN/JERK" trademark.

150. Four years ago, Dugal Products Co. breached a supply contract with its vendee, Pangaea Restaurants Inc. Pangaea's many efforts to resolve the suit without litigation were unsuccessful. Pangea now files suit against Dugal, pursuing damages and injunctive relief. The statute of limitations on contract claims is three years. Are Pangaea's claims timely?

(A) The legal and equitable claims are barred by the statute of limitations.

(B) The legal claim is barred by the statute of limitations, and the equitable claim is subject to the doctrine of laches.

(C) The equitable claim is barred by the statute of limitations, and the legal claim is subject to the doctrine of laches.

(D) The legal and equitable claims are subject to the doctrine of laches.

151. Rufus brings a lawsuit to enjoin his neighbor, Natalie, from trespassing. Natalie has started building a swimming pool in her backyard that extends 18 inches onto Rufus's property. Natalie observes that, at another segment of their shared property line, the roof on the tool shed that Rufus built two years ago extends 18 inches onto her (Natalie's) property. What remedial defense might be available to Natalie?

(A) In pari delicto.

(B) Waiver.

(C) Unclean hands.

(D) Laches.

152. Eleven years ago, Gakh purchased a 2-acre lot in a subdivision. The lot sat vacant until one year ago, when Gakh installed a mobile home and moved in. Restrictive covenants prohibit mobile homes in the neighborhood. One week after moving in, Gakh's neighbors notified him of their intent to enforce the covenants and, if necessary, to file suit. Gakh responded immediately with a letter expressing his intent to remain and, if necessary, to litigate his right to remain. Every few weeks for the next six months, the neighbors made various gestures to Gakh of their discontent — letters from lawyers, petitions from neighbors, invitations to public meetings — which Gakh ignored. The neighbors recently filed an equitable action against Gakh seeking to enforce the restrictive covenant prohibiting mobile homes. Gakh raises the defense of laches. Approximately how long have the plaintiffs delayed in asserting their right?

(A) Eleven years.

(B) One year.

(C) Six months.

(D) No delay.

153. Consider the same facts as in the previous question. On the defense of laches, the court will also consider whether Gakh has suffered prejudice as a result of the neighbors' delay. Which of the following additional facts would be helpful to Gakh with this defense?

(A) Before installing the mobile home on the property, Gakh spent $50,000 outfitting the property with water/septic/electrical systems that are uniquely appropriate for mobile homes (and not suitable for any other home or use).

(B) Once installed on the premises, the mobile home could not be removed therefrom without substantially impairing the value of the mobile home. (In other words, this mobile home was designed to be moved only once.)

(C) Two months ago, Gakh's spouse and three children moved across country to join him and live in the mobile home.

(D) All of the above.

Topic 15   Questions

Attorney Fees

154. Baker and Simpson entered into an oral contract for the sale of 500 widgets. Simpson refused to deliver the widgets to Baker at the agreed upon date, because Simpson had found a buyer who paid a higher price for the widgets. In a breach of contract action by Baker against Simpson, which of the following is true?

   (A) Baker will be entitled to recover attorney fees from Simpson if Simpson breached the contract without legal excuse or justification.

   (B) Baker will be entitled to recover attorney fees from Simpson if Simpson willfully breached the contract.

   (C) Baker will not be entitled to recover attorney fees from Simpson because Simpson's breach was an "efficient breach."

   (D) Baker will not be entitled to recover attorney fees from Simpson regardless of Simpson's reasons for breaching the contract.

155. Polly Pilot sued Able Airlines on behalf of herself and all similarly situated pilots. In her suit, Pilot alleged that Able breached its collective bargaining agreement with its pilots by failing to reimburse pilots for certain professional licensing fees incurred by the pilots. Able agreed to pay the class an amount equal to the value of all the licensing fees paid by its pilots. If Pilot files a motion to recover attorney fees, which of the following is true?

   (A) The court can order Able to pay Pilot's attorney fees, because Pilot is a prevailing party in the litigation.

   (B) The court can order Pilot's attorney fees paid out of the settlement fund, because each of the class members benefited from the fund.

   (C) The court can order Pilot's attorney fees paid out of the settlement fund provided all class members attempt to collect a share of the fund.

   (D) The court cannot order Pilot's attorney fees paid out of the fund.

156. The state legislature of East Dakota passes a law creating the tort of educational malpractice. The law outlines the elements of the cause of action, outlines applicable affirmative defenses, and provides that a court "may award reasonable attorney fees to a prevailing party." Is a defendant who prevails at trial likely to receive an award of attorney fees?

   (A) Definitely not.

   (B) Probably not.

(C) Probably yes.

(D) Definitely yes.

157. Landers is a commercial landlord who rented a building to Tenneson. The 20-year lease included a fee-shifting provision that required either party to pay the other's reasonable attorney fees in the event of litigation arising from a breach of their agreement. Beginning in the third year of the lease and continuing for more than a year thereafter, the parties disputed the amount of rent that was due under various complex calculations required by the lease. Landers eventually files suit and, two years later, wins at trial. Is she entitled to an award of her reasonable attorney fees?

    (A) Yes, because the parties included a fee-shifting provision in their agreement.

    (B) Yes, provided Landers recovered legal (and not merely equitable) relief.

    (C) No, provided Tenneson litigated in good faith.

    (D) No, because the American Rule disfavors fee-shifting.

158. Dugal is a residential landlord who rented a flat to Lavoie. The one-year lease includes a fee-shifting provision that obliges the tenant to pay the landlord's attorney fees in the event landlord prevails in any litigation arising from the tenant's breach. Dugal breaches a term of the lease; Lavoie sues and recovers damages. Which of the following is true?

    (A) Lavoie may recover her attorney fees because this is a two-way fee-shifting provision that courts will enforce as an exception to the American Rule.

    (B) Lavoie may recover her attorney fees because this is a one-way fee-shifting provision that courts will enforce (as written) because of party autonomy.

    (C) Lavoie may recover her attorney fees because this is a one-way fee-shifting provision that courts may, for public policy reasons, interpret as a two-way

    (D) Lavoie will not recover her attorney fees because this is a two-way fee-shifting provision; these provisions are presumptively void because they are contrary to public policy.

159. The buyer of a bar examination preparation program brought suit against the seller for seven distinct breaches of covenants and warranties in their purchase and sale agreement. Plaintiff complained of millions of dollars in damages. A jury found for plaintiff on two of its claims and awarded plaintiff $125,000 in damages. The purchase and sale agreement included a provision that "Each party shall pay the other party's reasonable costs and fees incurred in successfully enforcing against the other party any covenant, term, or condition herein." Is Buyer entitled to an award of attorney fees?

    (A) Buyer is entitled to recover the full amount of the fee billed by Buyer's attorney.

    (B) Buyer is entitled to recover the lodestar amount — the number of hours reasonably expended on the case multiplied by a reasonable hourly rate.

(C) Buyer may be entitled to recover an amount of fees that is apportioned to reflect its relative success.

(D) Buyer is not entitled to recover any of its attorney fees, because its victory was trivial given the difference between the amount of damages it sought and the amount it recovered.

160. Which of the following facts is relevant when determining the reasonableness of an award of attorney fees?

(A) The novelty of the claim and the skill required to litigate it.

(B) Awards in similar cases.

(C) The nature and length of the attorney-client relationship.

(D) All of the above.

161. Parker sued Sheriff pursuant to 28 U.S.C. § 1983, alleging that Sheriff unlawfully detained Parker without probable cause in violation of Parker's constitutional rights. More than 10 days before trial, Sheriff served Parker with a written offer to accept judgment for $50,000 inclusive of costs and attorney fees. At the time of the offer, Parker had incurred $10,000 in attorney fees. Parker rejected the offer, and the case went to trial. At trial, a jury returned a verdict for Parker in the amount of $30,000. The court entered judgment on the verdict, and Parker filed a motion for attorney fees, seeking $25,000 in fees. Which of the following best describes how the court should rule on the motion?

(A) The court should award Parker $25,000 in attorney fees plus costs because Sheriff's offer of judgment improperly offered one lump sum for both the substantive claim and costs and attorney fees.

(B) The court should award Parker $25,000 in attorney fees because the $30,000 judgment for Parker recovered at trial combined with Parker's $25,000 in attorney fees exceed Sheriff's $50,000 offer of judgment.

(C) The court should award Parker $10,000 for Parker's pre-offer attorney fees but refuse to award any post-offer attorney fees.

(D) The court should deny Parker's motion because Parker's recovery at trial was less favorable than the offer of judgment.

Topic 16

Right to Jury Trial

162. Paula sues Deng for a state common-law breach of contract claim in a South Virginia state court. What authority determines Deng's constitutional right to a jury trial?

    (A) The state constitution.

    (B) The Seventh Amendment to the U.S. Constitution.

    (C) The state constitution *and* the Seventh Amendment to the U.S. Constitution.

    (D) None; Deng has no right to a jury trial, because the right to a civil jury trial belongs to the plaintiff, not the defendant.

163. The Seventh Amendment ensures a right to jury trial for which of the following suits in federal court?

    (A) A diversity action arising under state law, seeking $80,000 in damages for negligence arising out of an automobile accident.

    (B) An action filed by the State of Texas against an Indian Tribe under federal law seeking an injunction that would halt the Tribe's bingo operations on its Reservation.

    (C) A claim by a trademark holder seeking injunctive relief under federal law for infringement and unfair competition.

    (D) All of the above.

164. Adams sues Benkert in federal court on a state-law claim for breach of contract. Adams seeks $100,000 in damages for harm already suffered and a permanent injunction to prevent further loss. If Adams demands a jury trial on all claims so triable, what should the judge order?

    (A) Allow a jury to resolve Adams's legal and equitable claims.

    (B) Allow a jury to resolve Adams's claim for damages, and then decide the equitable claim in a manner that is consistent with the jury's determination.

    (C) Decide Adams's equitable claim, and then allow the jury to resolve the claim for damages.

    (D) Deny a jury trial, because the equitable clean-up doctrine allows the judge to resolve both the legal and equitable claims.

165. Congress passes a statute that creates a new cause of action to benefit certain essential workers whose employers failed to provide employees with adequate personal protective equipment during a recent pandemic. The text of the statute does not mention the availability *vel non* of a jury trial. Which of the following will help the court determine whether the Seventh Amendment confers a right to jury trial on such claims?

    (A) An historical inquiry into whether the most analogous claims from the Eighteenth Century were legal or equitable.

    (B) An examination of whether the remedies available under the statute are legal or equitable in nature.

    (C) Both (A) and (B).

    (D) Examination of the legislative history, since congressional intent is determinative.

166. Congress passes a statute that creates a new private right of action to protect consumers from data collection by certain internet companies. The text of the statute provides a right to a jury trial. Gardiner brings a claim against a social media company under the new statute. Is Gardiner entitled to a jury trial?

    (A) Yes.

    (B) Yes, provided the two-step analysis required by the Seventh Amendment is also satisfied — as it surely is here.

    (C) No, because the two-step analysis required by the Seventh Amendment must also be satisfied — and that is not established here.

    (D) No, because the Seventh Amendment of the U.S. Constitution supersedes a congressional mandate.

Practice Final Exam: Questions

Questions

Practice Final Exam

Instructions: This exam consists of 44 questions, some of which are multiple choice questions and some of which are short answer questions. Try to answer these questions in no more than 90 minutes.

167. Bradford entered into a contract to purchase Sally's used car for $1500. The bluebook value of the car was $2000. After Bradford and Sally entered into the contract, Tina offered to purchase Sally's car for $1800. Sally refused to deliver her car to Bradford. In an action for breach of contract by Bradford, what will be the measure of damages if Bradford does not cover?

   (A) $500

   (B) $1500

   (C) $2000

   (D) Bradford is not entitled to damages.

168. Your client is considering whether to file suit for an injunction or declaratory judgment. How would you advise your client as to the advantages of declaratory relief?

   ANSWER:

169. Plaintiff suffered damage to her cornea as a result of an infection caused by a defective contact lens. Plaintiff was treated by a physician and put on a medicine regimen that lasted ten days to cure the infection. Plaintiff also had to undergo a surgical procedure to repair the damage to her cornea. Plaintiff missed two months of work while recovering from the surgery. Medical experts agree that most people who contract this type of infection make a full recovery and have no lasting vision problems. However, a small number of people suffer recurring vision problems as a result of the corrective surgery. Plaintiff's vision has been completely restored and, thus far, she has shown no signs of recurring vision problems. In an action by Plaintiff against the manufacturer of the contact lens, which of the following will not be recoverable?

   (A) The reasonable value of the surgery because Plaintiff acted unreasonably in having a surgery that posed a risk of future complications.

   (B) The medical expenses related to the treatment of any vision problems Plaintiff might suffer in the future because such expenses are too speculative.

(C) Lost wages for the time that Plaintiff missed work because Plaintiff's employer continued to pay her salary during that period.

(D) Plaintiff will be entitled to recover all of the above.

170. Larry Litigator is up against Sammy Slime in yet another personal injury case. Given Slime's general reputation for dishonesty, Larry is concerned that Slime will refuse to play by the court's rules and will fail to provide the appropriate documents during discovery. At the initial conference in the case, Larry asks for a general order against Slime requiring him to produce all relevant documents in the case. What result?

(A) Injunction granted due to Slime's propensity towards dishonesty.

(B) Injunction granted because the order conforms to the regular discovery rule.

(C) Injunction denied because there is no irreparable injury.

(D) Injunction denied because there is no threat of imminent harm.

171. Baker and Simpson entered into a contract for the sale of land. Simpson refused to deliver title to the land. If Baker sues Simpson for breach of contract, which of the following are true?

(A) Baker will be entitled to a jury trial only if Baker seeks money damages.

(B) Baker will be entitled to a jury trial only if Baker seeks specific performance of the contract.

(C) Baker will be entitled to a jury trial if Baker seeks either money damages or specific performance.

(D) Baker will not be entitled to a jury trial

172. Betty Crocker Hershey, the owner of Sweets-R-Us, has soured on the candy business. She decides to turn her business over to her son, Mr. Clean. Betty agrees to employ Mr. Clean as corporate president, and they enter into a written contract for twenty years at an annual salary of $350,000. Mr. Clean loves being president and is thankful for the once-in-a-lifetime opportunity to run a family business. However, after three years of retirement, Betty is tired of eating bon-bons all day. She fires her son and resumes the presidency of Sweets-R-Us. Mr. Clean sues to enforce the terms of the contract. What result?

(A) Specific performance is granted because of Clean's detrimental reliance.

(B) Specific performance is granted because of the uniqueness of the contract.

(C) Specific performance is denied because Clean can find another job.

(D) Specific performance is denied because it is difficult to enforce.

173. A class of women prisoners in the state of Gilead bring suit alleging violations of the Eighth Amendment's prohibition of cruel and unusual punishment for their conditions of confinement. The inside of the prison is unsanitary and kept at a temperature of 50 degrees. Women who are pregnant are denied adequate medical care. It is also established at trial that guards routinely sexually harass and assault the women. As the attorney for the successful plaintiffs, what injunctive relief will you request from the court?

ANSWER:

174. Porter was seriously injured when an industrial press that Porter was operating malfunctioned. Porter sued the manufacturer of the press for personal injuries. Porter sought damages for pain and suffering as well as for medical expenses and diminished earning capacity. At trial, Porter's counsel made the following closing argument to the jury:

> Let's talk about one element of damages. We have talked about pain and suffering. What would be fair compensation for pain and suffering? Ladies and gentlemen of the jury, it is entirely up to you. But let me make a suggestion. If you think about what it is like for Porter to go through one day with the pain that Porter has, what do you think would be fair? Would it be $100 to go through that in a day? Would it be $75? I want to be scrupulously fair in my request to you. So I am going to suggest that you award Porter $50 a day for the pain and suffering. Now consider that there are 365 days in a year and 30 years of pain and suffering that Porter should be compensated for. So that's $547,500 for 30 years of pain and suffering.

What objections, if any, might defense counsel raise to this closing argument?

ANSWER:

175. Homeowner bought a house for $250,000 from a man anxious to sell, and secured the purchase with a $240,000 mortgage. After moving into the house, Homeowner noticed seepage from the sewage disposal and called in a repair person to fix the problem. It was discovered after further investigation that the land was not an approved home site because of the lack of sufficient topsoil. Homeowner now wants to cancel the contract and be paid for the costs of moving and hiring an expert to assess the problem. What restitution remedy can Homeowner seek?

(A) Implied-in-fact contract.

(B) Quasi-contract.

(C) Quantum meruit.

(D) Rescission.

176. Approximately 300 minority Big City police officers claim that a test administered to determine promotions to sergeant is racially biased. They seek a preliminary injunction to prohibit the City from making sergeant promotions pending the outcome of their lawsuit. The district court finds that under the law, it is a close question as to whether the officers have a meritorious claim. It also finds that any temporary denial of a promotion could later be addressed by monetary damages. Based on these findings, how should the court rule on the request for preliminary injunction?

    (A) Grant the injunction because of the likelihood of success on the merits.

    (B) Grant the injunction because of the harm to the plaintiffs.

    (C) Deny the injunction because of the undue hardship to the City.

    (D) Deny the injunction because of the lack of irreparable injury.

177. The court held a hearing in an admiralty case as to why contempt sanctions should not issue for an attorney's failure to appear at trial. The case had been continued three times to accommodate the attorney's schedule. The attorney told two federal judges that he was appearing before the other on the same date, when in fact he was appearing before neither. What action can the judge take?

    (A) Jail the attorney for 10 days.

    (B) Order the attorney to pay $2500.

    (C) Order the attorney to pay the costs of the defendants' attorney fees.

    (D) Order Rule 11 sanctions for frivolous conduct.

178. Which of the following cases would *not* support an award of punitive damages?

    (A) A jubilant casino patron hugs his dealer after winning a large sum of money, causing serious physical injury to the dealer.

    (B) A frustrated law student punches her professor after receiving a disappointing grade, causing serious physical injury to the professor.

    (C) A repair person knowingly misrepresents the length of time needed to complete the repairs in negotiating a service contract with a customer.

    (D) An award of punitive damages would be appropriate in all of the above.

179. Father wants Daughter to move back home to Small Town from the dangers and high prices of New York City. He promises to give his successful daughter her own interior design business. Father lets Daughter use a piece of business property he owns, and Daughter secures a loan in the amount of $25,000 to purchase office equipment and inventory for her business. Daughter runs a successful business and voluntarily gives her Father a 10% share of the busi-

ness profits. Ten years later, Father informs Daughter that he is selling the property in order to obtain funds to retire to Florida. Daughter is incensed and sues her Father in restitution for his promise to give her the business. What result?

(A) Constructive trust to Daughter for the value of the property.

(B) Equitable lien to Daughter in the amount of the improvements to the property.

(C) Constructive trust denied because of absence of fraud or breach of trust.

(D) Equitable lien denied because of the lack of property to secure.

Questions 180 and 181 are based on the following fact pattern.

Victor suffered a severe head injury during a bar fight with Dan. Victor never regained consciousness after suffering the head injury. He spent several weeks in a coma, and ultimately died as a result of the head injury.

180. In an action by Victor's Representative against Dan, which of the following most accurately describes the Estate's recovery?

(A) Victor's Estate will be entitled to recover damages for the medical expenses Victor incurred before death, pain and suffering, and the wages Victor would have earned over the course of his natural worklife span.

(B) Victor's Estate will be entitled to recover damages for the medical expenses Victor incurred before death and Victor's pain and suffering.

(C) Victor's Estate will be entitled to recover damages for the medical expenses Victor incurred before death and the wages Victor would have earned over the course of his natural worklife span.

(D) Victor's Estate will be entitled to recover damages for the medical expenses Victor incurred before death.

181. In a wrongful death action against Dan brought on behalf of Victor's next of kin, which of the following most accurately describes the probable recovery?

(A) Victor's Beneficiaries will be entitled to recover damages for the loss of Victor's financial support and for the loss of his companionship.

(B) Victor's Beneficiaries will be entitled to recover damages for the loss of Victor's financial support only.

(C) Victor's Beneficiaries will be entitled to recover damages for the loss of Victor's companionship only.

(D) Victor's Beneficiaries will not have a wrongful death claim against Dan.

182. Sampson agreed to sell 15 used delivery trucks to Bivens at a price of $7500 per truck. The fair market value of the trucks was $7000 per truck. Bivens refused to accept delivery of the trucks. Sampson resold the trucks to Thompson at a private sale for $3000 per truck. In an action for breach of contract by Sampson, what will be the measure of Sampson's damages?

(A) $7500 per truck.

(B) $4500 per truck.

(C) $500 per truck.

(D) Sampson is not entitled to damages.

183. The People Against Coffee are planning a protest next week against Coffee Incorporated at its national headquarters. The police would like to avoid any harm to people and property from the protest, and thus seek a temporary injunction to prohibit the protest. The police file a complaint and motion for temporary relief, and deliver a copy of the papers to the protest leader. The court conducts an *ex parte* hearing. Will the temporary injunction be granted?

(A) No, because there was inadequate notice to the defendant.

(B) No, because there is no legal harm threatened.

(C) No, because the threatened harm is not imminent.

(D) No, because *ex parte* hearings are unconstitutional.

184. Paula Smith sued President Clintex for alleged sexual harassment. The court issued an order carefully defining "sexual relations" for purposes of questioning in the case. During deposition, President Clintex testified that he did not have sexual relations with Mona Monica. Subsequently, on national television, Clintex admitted that he had "inappropriate relations" with Monica. Upon the plaintiffs' motion for contempt, the judge awards the plaintiff $90,000 for its attorney fees in bringing the contempt motion and the costs of the deposition in which Clintex lied, and says she will conduct a hearing if Clintex so requests. What result on appeal?

(A) The criminal contempt remedy is invalidated for improper procedures.

(B) The civil compensatory remedy is upheld as valid.

(C) The civil compensatory remedy is invalidated for improper procedures.

(D) The criminal contempt remedy is upheld as valid.

185. While driving too fast for conditions, Davis lost control of the car that Davis was driving and collided with Patterson. Patterson was uninjured, but Patterson's car suffered substantial damage. In an action by Patterson against Davis for damage to the car, what is the likely measure of Patterson's recovery?

(A) Patterson is entitled to recover the cost to repair the car as long as the car can be restored to its pre-accident condition.

(B) Patterson is entitled to recover the cost to repair the car if the car can be restored to its pre-accident condition and the cost to repair the car does not exceed the pre-accident value of the car.

(C) Patterson is entitled to recover the cost to repair the car if the car can be restored to its pre-accident condition and Patterson has a personal reason for repairing the car.

(D) Patterson is not entitled to recover the cost to repair the car under any circumstances.

186. A test preparation company, Get U Ready, has been accused of sending representatives to take secure standardized tests in order to obtain confidential questions. Secure questions are kept secret by the creators of the tests and reserved for possible use on future tests. A lawsuit is filed against Get U Ready and trial is set for a date eight months later. In the interim, the testing company would like to obtain a court order barring Get U Ready from using copies of its test questions. What relief is available to the standardized testing company at this stage of the litigation?

(A) Temporary injunction.

(B) Preliminary injunction.

(C) Temporary, preliminary, and permanent injunctions.

(D) Temporary and preliminary injunctions.

187. Beasley Middle School ordered 200 t-shirts at a cost of $4.00 per t-shirt from Super Tees. The t-shirts contained a specially designed logo commemorating graduation which incorporated the class year and the date of graduation. Super Tees purchased 200 blank t-shirts at a cost of $1.00 per shirt. Super Tees also purchased ink for the shirts at a cost of $0.30 per shirt. Super Tees estimated its overhead expenses to be $0.20 per shirt. After Super Tees completed 100 t-shirts, Beasley repudiated the contract. Super Tees sold the remaining 100 blank t-shirts for $0.50 per shirt and paid $0.10 per shirt to ship the 100 blank shirts to the purchaser. In an action for breach of contract, what will be the measure of Super Tees damages?

(A) $800

(B) $760

(C) $650

(D) $500

188. Davidson, a restaurant server, intentionally spilled hot coffee on Peters, a customer, after Peters failed to leave Davidson an adequate tip. Peters suffered serious burns. Peters sued Davidson for personal injuries. If Peters' personal injury action is tried to a jury, which of the following is true?

(A) A jury must impose punitive damages on Davidson if it concludes that Davidson acted intentionally.

(B) A jury may impose punitive damages on Davidson if it concludes that Davidson acted intentionally.

(C) Only the judge can impose punitive damages on Davidson even if the jury finds that Davidson acted intentionally.

(D) Punitive damages are not appropriate in this case.

189. Billy agrees to sell his baseball card collection to Bobby for $150. Billy knows that there are no valuable cards in his collection, but he tells Bobby that there are two cards worth over one hundred dollars each. Bobby's roommate, who works at a baseball trading card store, overhears the conversation and interrupts to tell Bobby that there are no valuable cards in the collection. Bobby still goes through with the purchase. When he later discovers that the card collection is worth only $20, he sues for breach of contract. What defenses are available to Billy in the action?

(A) Waiver.

(B) Estoppel.

(C) Estoppel and Waiver.

(D) Unconscionability.

190. In a bench trial for personal injury damages, Plaintiff offered expert testimony to establish her future lost wages. Plaintiff's expert included an upward adjustment in Plaintiff's future wages to account for future increases in wages due to increases in the cost of living. Judge Grumpy, the presiding judge, excluded this testimony, prohibiting Plaintiff from offering any estimates of future wage increases based on increases in the cost of living. Judge Grumpy ruled that such evidence was too speculative. In awarding Plaintiff damages for future lost wages, Judge Grumpy discounted Plaintiff's damages to present value based on a the current market yield for certain bonds issued by the federal government. What basis, if any, does Plaintiff have to challenge Judge Grumpy's award of damages for future lost wages?

ANSWER:

191. Big, Bad and Boom fireworks opens up a new manufacturing site in Tylersville, where it employs 10 workers. The fireworks factory spews toxic chemicals into the air that have a putrid odor. Mrs. Small, who lives 3 blocks from the factory, develops lung problems. Upset and worried that she is seriously ill, Mrs. Small consults her doctor who believes the serious medical problem is caused by the fireworks plant. Can Mrs. Small seek an injunction to stop the hazardous pollution?

(A) No, because of the economic waste to Big, Bad and Boom.

(B) Yes, because of the serious physical and emotional harm to Mrs. Small.

(C) No, because of the public policy in favor of commercial manufacturing.

(D) Yes, because of Mrs. Small's preference for injunctive relief.

192. STOIL Co. brings suit seeking a declaratory judgment that a state excise tax levied on it for the storage of gasoline is invalid under the Commerce Clause and the Fourteenth Amendment of the Federal Constitution. The court should:

(A) Deny the declaratory judgment because there is no case or controversy.

(B) Grant the declaration because there is an actual controversy.

(C) Deny the declaratory relief because the claimant seeks an advisory opinion.

(D) Grant the declaration because it presents a hypothetical question.

193. Big Films Industry makes a movie using a story it received in the mail from an eighteen-year-old novice writer from Indiana. Without contacting the writer, Big Films proceeds to make the movie. It gets the biggest star in Hollywood, Betty Devine, to play the lead in the film. Devine alone can generate $30 million in movie profits. The film is a box office smash and generates $65 million in revenues for the low-budget film that cost only $5 million to make. Writer sues Big Films for copyright infringement. If she is successful, what is the likely amount of recovery in restitution?

(A) $10,000, the typical cost of a royalty payment to a new author.

(B) $65 million, the total profits to Big Film.

(C) $60 million, the total profits offset by costs to produce the film.

(D) $30 million, the total profits offset by production costs and profits from Devine.

Questions 194 and 195 are based on the following fact pattern.

Farmer Brown owns a small farm. The property has been used by the Brown family as a farm for over 100 years. The property is divided into four fields. Shortly after planting one of the fields, Farmer Brown discovered that chemicals from a nearby manufacturing plant were leaching into the soil on that field. Experts agree that while the chemicals themselves are not harmful to humans, the chemicals have stripped the soil of vital nutrients, rendering the soil unfit for agriculture. Experts also agree that the chemicals can be removed from the soil, but that the soil cannot be restored to productive agricultural use. Farmer Brown brought suit against the owner of the manufacturing plant.

194. What is the likely measure of recovery for damage to the land?

   (A) Farmer Brown will be entitled to recover the cost to remove the chemicals from the soil unless the cost exceeds the pre-contamination value of the land.

   (B) Farmer Brown will be entitled to recover the cost to remove the chemicals from the soil unless the cost exceeds the diminution in the value of the land.

   (C) Farmer Brown will be entitled to recover the pre-contamination value of the land because the land is destroyed.

   (D) Farmer Brown will be entitled to recover the diminution in value to the land because the damage to the land is permanent.

195. What is the likely measure of recovery for the lost crops?

   (A) Farmer Brown will be able to recover the lost profits that Brown would have earned on the crops.

   (B) Farmer Brown will be entitled to recover the fair market value of the crops.

   (C) Farmer Brown will not be entitled to recover damages for the lost crops because they will be duplicative of damages for the injury to the land.

   (D) Farmer Brown will not be entitled to recover damages for the lost crops because they are too speculative.

196. The Urban City Transit Workers Union went on strike in reaction to the City's failure to provide adequate funding for the Union's health insurance costs. The district court found that the strike by public safety workers violated the federal labor laws and ordered the workers to return to work. When the workers had not returned to work five days later, the judge gave notice to the Union and conducted a hearing to address the workers' past violations of her order. The judge then ordered the Union to pay $10,000 per day until its workers returned to work. This fine is:

   (A) Valid civil coercive contempt.

   (B) Invalid civil coercive contempt.

   (C) Valid criminal contempt.

   (D) Invalid criminal contempt.

197. Plimpton worked for Big Brother Credit Card Company. Plimpton also held a Big Brother credit card for personal use. After Plimpton called in sick for several days in a row, Plimpton's supervisor at Big Brother accessed Plimpton's personal credit card records without authorization. Plimpton's supervisor was attempting to determine whether Plimpton was abusing her sick leave. When Plimpton discovered the unauthorized intrusion, Plimpton sued Big Brother for invasion of privacy. The evidence at trial revealed that several other employees had complained to Big Brother management that the same supervisor had accessed their

personal credit card records. A jury awarded Plimpton $100,000 in compensatory damages for emotional distress and $1 million in punitive damages. If Big Brother challenges the award as unconstitutionally excessive, what arguments can be advanced to set aside the award? What arguments can be advanced to sustain the award?

ANSWER:

198. Explain the difference between the remedial defenses of laches and statute of limitations.

ANSWER:

Questions 199 and 200 are based on the following fact pattern.

Software Co. entered into a three-year contract with Fashion Mavens (FM) to develop software for FM's use in delivering fashion consultations over the Internet. FM initially paid Software $60,000 to secure the contract, and agreed to pay Software royalties from future profits. One year into the contract, FM stopped paying royalties to Software in violation of the terms of the contract. After adversarial negotiations produced no agreement, Software sued FM to rescind the contract and seek payment of all profits FM generated from the use of its software products.

199. What is the legal basis for Software's claim for rescission?

(A) The inadequacy of damages.

(B) The mistaken payment of royalties.

(C) The substantial breach of contract.

(D) The implied-at-law contract.

200. Assume that the court grants Software's request for rescission. What is the proper measure of relief?

(A) The amount of profits made by FM using the software.

(B) The amount of profits made by FM attributable to the software and not attributed to FM's own contributions.

(C) The amount of profits made by FM attributable to the software and not attributed to FM's own contributions, offset by a return to FM of the $60,000.

(D) The amount of Software's loss under the contract.

201. Iggy Insured entered into a contract for professional liability insurance with Massive Mutual. A client sued Insured for malpractice, and Insured tendered the claim to Massive Mutual for defense in accordance with the terms of the insurance contract. Massive Mutual refused to defend the claim. As a result, Insured had to retain an attorney at his own expense to defend against the client's claim. Insured ultimately prevailed in client's suit and sued Massive Mutual for breach of insurance contract and bad faith refusal to defend the claim. If Insured prevails on his breach of contract claim against Massive Mutual *only*, which of the following best describes what Insured's recovery will be?

    (A) Insured will be entitled to recover the attorney fees he incurred in defending client's claims and the attorney fees he incurred in prosecuting his breach of contract claim against Massive Mutual.

    (B) Insured will be entitled to recover the attorney fees he incurred in defending client's claims.

    (C) Insured will be entitled to recover the attorney fees he incurred in prosecuting his claims against Massive Mutual.

    (D) Insured will not be entitled to recover any of his attorney fees.

202. Landlord rents an old racquetball building to New Church for a term of six years with an option to buy. New Church renovates the building to make it suitable for services. It adds many improvements to the building, adding a sanctuary, improving the grounds, and installing a kitchen. After six years, New Church is not able to purchase the building due to a lack of funds. Landlord is quickly able to rent the church building to another developing church group at double the monthly rent he was receiving from New Church. New Church requests that the Landlord reimburse it for the improvements it made to the building, but Landlord refuses, saying it was a risk the church took as a tenant. If New Church sues Landlord on an equitable restitution theory, what is the likely result?

    (A) Constructive trust awarded to New Church for the appreciation of the building.

    (B) Accounting of profits awarded to New Church in the amount of the increased rent.

    (C) Quantum meruit for the value of the church's construction services.

    (D) Equitable lien in the amount of the church's services and financial investments.

203. Parker retained Anderson as counsel to represent Parker in a personal injury action. The retainer agreement between Parker and Anderson provided that Parker would pay Anderson 33% of any judgment or settlement that Parker ultimately obtained. Parker discharged Anderson and retained a new attorney, Baker. Baker ultimately settled Parker's claim for $500,000. Anderson sued Parker to recover attorney fees. What amount, if any, should Anderson be entitled to recover?

    ANSWER:

204. Contractor is denied a building permit by the town of Hudson. The administrative regulations provide that Contractor may appeal the denial within twenty days of the order. Sixty-two days later, Contractor files an action for declaratory judgment against the town. The declaration is inappropriate because:

(A) The declaration will not terminate the uncertainty.

(B) The controversy is not ripe.

(C) The controversy is not definite and concrete.

(D) The declaration is used for tactical advantage.

205. The Big Fig sued Newton Co. for trademark infringement because Newton Co. was selling a product with the same name as its product called "California Fig Syrup." The testimony at trial revealed that neither company's syrup is made from figs. How should the case be resolved?

(A) Case dismissed because of plaintiff's unclean hands.

(B) Judgment for Big Fig because of defendant's fraud.

(C) Judgment for Big Fig because of defendant's unclean hands.

(D) Case dismissed because of *in pari delicto*.

206. Dudley Do-Right sued the National Regulatory Commission ("NRC"), the State of Utopia and KMG Corp., seeking an injunction preventing the NRC and Utopia from granting KMG a permit to mine uranium. Do-Right contended that certain federal environmental laws prevented the NRC and Utopia from granting a permit until the permit applicant filed an environmental impact statement and that KMG had failed to file an environmental impact statement. Do-Right ultimately prevailed in his lawsuit, and the court issued an order enjoining the NRC and Utopia from granting the permit. If Do-Right files a motion to recover attorney fees, which of the following is true?

(A) Do-Right will be entitled to recover his attorney fees because his lawsuit involves an important public policy issue.

(B) Do-Right will be entitled to recover his attorney fees because his lawsuit will affect how the NRC and Utopia handle future permit applications.

(C) Do-Right will not be entitled to recover his attorney fees because KMG will be able to obtain a permit once it files the environmental impact statement.

(D) Do-Right will not be entitled to recover attorney fees because his lawsuit did not generate a determinative fund to which an identifiable class of third parties has a claim.

207. Specialty Products, Inc. agreed to manufacture a specially designed press for Manufacturer's assembly line. At the time of contracting, Manufacturer explained to Specialty Products that Manufacturer was in the business of manufacturing and selling widgets. Manufacturer explained that it needed the press to complete the manufacture of its widgets. Specialty Products delivered a press that did not fit into Manufacturer's assembly line. Manufacturer promptly sought repair of the press. In a breach of contract action by Manufacturer, what will be the measure of Manufacturer's damages?

   (A) Manufacturer will be entitled to recover the difference between the value of the press as delivered and value of the press as contracted for.

   (B) Manufacturer will be entitled to recover its lost profits on the sale of widgets that it was unable to manufacture and sell while the press was being repaired.

   (C) Manufacturer will be entitled to recover both the difference between the value of the press as delivered and value of the press as contracted for and Manufacturer's lost profits.

   (D) Manufacturer will not be entitled to recover damages.

208. Surfer Dude enters into a contract with Best-O-Wax for 100 cans of surf board wax at a price of $5.00 per can. Best-O-Wax fails to deliver the wax due to a manufacturing error that leaves it with no inventory to sell. Dude is able to find 50 cans of OK-Wax for sale at $6.00 per can, but prefers the Best-O-Wax. Surfer Dude sues Best-O-Wax for specific performance of the contract. What result?

   (A) Specific performance granted because the goods are unique.

   (B) Specific performance granted because the replacement goods cost more.

   (C) Specific performance denied because of the burden of enforcement.

   (D) Specific performance denied because damages are adequate.

209. Princess Virginia obtains a cease and desist order against Photo Joe for his invasion of her privacy through the taking and printing of personal pictures. Joe fails to abide by the order, and continues to climb the trees near her castle in order to get exclusive photos with the use of his high-powered camera. Virginia files a motion to modify the injunction. What result?

   (A) Denied because of the lack of changed circumstances.

   (B) Denied because of Photo Joe's substantial and good faith compliance.

   (C) Granted, and modified to require Joe to stay 25 feet away from Virginia's castle.

   (D) Granted, and modified to prohibit Joe from printing any stories or pictures of Princess.

210. Tyson stole a painting from Potter's collection, mistakenly believing that the painting was a previously undiscovered Vermeer. In fact, the painting was an imitation by a lesser-known artist. At the time that Tyson stole the painting, the painting had a fair market value of $5000. Tyson sold the painting to an unsuspecting buyer for $1 million. What potential claims can Potter assert against Tyson? Which theory would be most advantageous to Potter?

ANSWER:

Practice Essay Question One

(Answer this question in approximately 75 minutes.)

Four years ago, Sherman Keefe started and has since managed a chain of tax preparation service stores in the State of Watopia called SK Tax Services Inc. ("SK Tax" or "the company"). All fifteen of the SK Tax stores are located in low-income areas, and all of the company's marketing targets people who may qualify for the earned income tax credit ("EITC"). The EITC is a federal tax benefit for working people with low incomes. Since its formation, SK Tax has prepared and filed approximately 10,000 tax returns—all of which are federal Form 1040 tax returns. Keefe hired and trained all of the company's tax return preparers, and he has personally prepared about 10% of all of the tax returns that were filed by the company.

Last week, the United States government ("the Government") filed a civil complaint against Keefe and SK Tax in the U.S. District Court. The complaint offers a short and plain statement of a cause of action under a section of the (federal) Internal Revenue Code that provides:

> If, in any action filed by the United States, the court finds that a tax return preparer systematically has
>
> (a) recklessly or intentionally disregarded Internal Revenue Service ("IRS") rules or regulations; or
>
> (b) engaged in other fraudulent or deceptive conduct that interferes with the proper administration of the IRS
>
> the court may enjoin such person from further engaging in such conduct when such injunctive relief is appropriate and necessary to prevent the recurrence of such conduct. Equitable relief is in addition to and not exclusive of any and all other remedies.

26 U.S.C. § 26000. The Government's complaint includes a number of allegations that SK Tax manipulated many of their customers' returns so that each filer's income would fall within the income levels necessary to qualify for the EITC. The complaint seeks preliminary and permanent relief enjoining

> Keefe and SK Tax from acting as a federal tax return preparer or requesting, advising, assisting, or directing the preparation or filing of federal tax returns, amended returns, or other related documents or forms for any person or entity other than himself.

Complaint and Prayer for Relief ¶ 42.

Coincident with the filing of its complaint, the Government filed a motion for a preliminary injunction. In support of its motion for preliminary relief, the Government included affidavits from three IRS officers and twelve taxpayers. The affidavits from the IRS officers describe the tax returns of twelve taxpayers and the informal audits that the IRS conducted over the past four years of those taxpayers' returns. All twelve of these taxpayers' returns were prepared by SK Tax. The IRS officers testify that, in all twelve instances, the tax returns claimed fictitious dependents, fabricated business expenses, and/or reported bogus education credits. In the twelve affidavits signed by the taxpayers, the taxpayers testify that the submitted tax returns included information that the taxpayers knew to be false, and that such information was included at the suggestion and direction of the SK Tax preparers. Ten of the twelve audited returns were prepared personally by Keefe.

The IRS officers further testify that the Government does not have the resources to review, much less audit all of the tax returns that have already been filed — or that will in the future be filed — by SK Tax. The Government estimates that SK Tax has prepared approximately 10,000 returns over the past four years. In the Government's sample of the twelve aforementioned returns, all twelve contained false statements. Accordingly, the Government argues, it is reasonable to draw the inference that all, most, or at least many of the other 10,000 returns likewise contain false statements, as will the returns that Keefe and SK Tax file in the future. The Government also claims that pursuing individual remedies against former and future customers of SK Tax would be "unproductive" and would consume "an impossibly disproportionate share of the Government's limited resources."

The Government also produced evidence that the practice at SK Tax was not to charge its customers upfront fees for the preparation of tax returns, but rather to extract the fees from the customers' tax refunds. That practice is not itself unlawful. But the Government argued that SK Tax charged its customers excessively high return preparation fees. One of the taxpayers who submitted an affidavit was charged $1,150 for preparing and filing a simple return. According to the Government, the national average fee for preparing and filing a Form 1040 is $150. The Government thus claims that Keefe and his employees engage in pervasive tax fraud by making (and/or directing or encouraging others to make) false claims on their customers' tax returns and by engaging in other fraudulent activities aimed at maximizing their customers' refunds and, in turn, their fees. The Government requests that the district court preliminarily enjoin Keefe from employing his tax return preparation business in order "to prevent Keefe's continued and repeated fraud" during the pending trial proceedings. According to the court's Tentative Scheduling Order that is issued automatically by the clerk's office upon the filing of a case, trial in this case is unlikely to occur within twelve months.

Keefe admits that those twelve taxpayers' returns contain errors. But adds that it is difficult to know whether all of those errors are the fault of lying tax filers or careless tax preparers: "We tell our customers what the EITC can do for them. Once they understand that more dependents, more business expenses, or more education expenses will help their bottom line, it's sort of out of our hands." Keefe described himself as more of a businessperson than a tax expert. Twenty years ago, he completed a 70-hour tax preparation certification program offered by H&R Block, an established tax preparation company. Other than that training, he is self-taught and has no formal degrees. He and all fifteen of his SK Tax employees (one for each store) are formally certified as Tax Preparers by the Internal Revenue Service.

The court has scheduled a hearing on the Government's motion for a *preliminary* injunction. How likely is the court to grant the requested relief?

ANSWER:

Practice Essay Question Two

(Answer this question in approximately 60 minutes.)

DG Electronics, Inc. (DG) is a large manufacturer of electronic devices. DG opened a new manufacturing plant in the State of Watopia. DG hired Pocket Technologies Co. (Pocket) to develop software that DG could use in its manufacturing process to diagnose problems and to control the quality of its products. Pocket is a small but experienced technology company that develops tailored software to a manufacturer's specification for industrial processes. Pocket is paid an up-front charge for the software development; it then licenses its software for use by the manufacturer—typically for many years thereafter.

A few months after getting this job, Pocket delivered software to DG that met DG's specifications. DG promptly paid Pocket $250,000 for developing the software. Shortly thereafter, DG installed the software on 100 computers in its plant. Going forward, DG was obligated to pay a license fee of $60 per machine per month (i.e., annualized rate of approximately $72,000) for as long as it used the software. DG made the contractually required payments for six months.

After six months, DG told Pocket that DG was no longer using its software, and therefore would not be paying any further license fees. When Pocket sought additional information, DG claimed that it was not using Pocket's software but was instead using a product developed by Contrafite Software, Inc. (Contrafite).

After six months of negotiations, Pocket filed a lawsuit against DG. After 18 more months of litigation, Pocket prevailed on its claims that DG (i) infringed Pocket's copyright on its database-scripts source code and (ii) unlawfully used Pocket's software to aid Contrafite's development of a new testing program. A jury awarded compensatory damages of $144,000, which was based upon the license fees that DG avoided paying during the 24 months from the date that DG quit paying through the date of the trial. Further, the court entered a permanent injunction enjoining DG from using either the Pocket software or the Contrafite software (which was derivative of Pocket's intellectual property). DG wrote Pocket a check for $144,000.

The judge then stayed (postponed) enforcement of the injunction for six months to give DG sufficient time to develop replacement non-infringing software. DG was also ordered to pay Pocket a $100 per machine per month (i.e., annualized rate of $120,000) until a replacement non-infringing software program was installed, fully operational, and certified by a special master named by the judge. This amount was invoiced and paid monthly.

DG hired a company to develop new software, but their work was not completed on time. Immediately before the injunction was set to go into effect, the parties appeared before the judge for a status conference. DG's lawyer complained that a global disruption in supply chains had delayed progress, but things were back on track and the new software would be installed and operational in three months at the latest. The judge ordered DG to pay a fine of $50,000 to the court, and outlined an escalating penalty structure for further delays beyond DG's new expected completion date: in the first month after the new expected completion date, DG would be fined $25,000 and each month thereafter that fine would double. (E.g., $50,000 in the second month; then $100,000 in third month; then $200,000 in the fourth; and so on.) These fines were to be imposed unless and until the replacement non-infringing software was certified as installed.

DG finally had the new replacement non-infringing software certified five months after the expected completion date. At this point DG had paid Pocket, in addition to the compensatory damages awarded by the jury, $130,000 pursuant to the fines imposed by the initial order staying effect of the judgment ($100 per month × 13 months × 100 computers). DG has yet to pay either the $50,000 fine that was imposed at the status conference or the $775,000 in escalating fines that accrued during the five months from the amended anticipated completion date until final certification ($25k + $50k + $100k + $200k + $400k).

You are an associate at the law firm that represents DG. The senior partner wants you to analyze the propriety of the $130,000, $50,000, and $775,000 awards, and evaluate the prospects for appealing any of the trial judge's errors. What is your response?

ANSWER:

Answers

Topic 1 — Answers

Introduction to Remedies

1. **Answer (A) is the correct answer.** Although a specific remedy, replevin was a remedy traditionally available in the courts of law to a plaintiff in a case of conversion of goods or chattels.

   Answer (B) is incorrect. Specific performance is an equitable remedy available in a breach of contract case only if money damages and other forms of legal relief are inadequate.

   Answer (C) is incorrect. Constructive trust is an equitable remedy.

   Answer (D) is incorrect. Even though backpay involves the award of money to the plaintiff, courts have consistently characterized backpay as an equitable remedy.

2. A specific remedy grants the plaintiff the very object or benefit the plaintiff would have received had the defendant not committed the wrong. A substitutional remedy grants the plaintiff a benefit that is of equal value to the object or benefit lost as a result of the defendant's wrong.

3. **Answer (B) is the correct answer.** Even though both involve the award of money to the plaintiff, courts have consistently characterized backpay and frontpay as equitable remedies to which no right to a jury trial attaches.

   Answer (A) is incorrect. Plaintiff's amended complaint seeks only equitable relief. Thus, no right to a jury trial attaches. If Plaintiff's claims had raised mixed claims of law and equity, Plaintiff may have been entitled to a jury trial. In many jurisdictions, including the federal courts, Plaintiff would have a right to a jury trial on Plaintiff's legal claims if Plaintiff's case raised mixed claims of law and equity. However, in jurisdictions employing the "equitable clean-up" doctrine, Plaintiff may not have a right to a jury trial on legal claims if the court determines that the legal claims are ancillary to the equitable claims.

   Answer (C) is incorrect. The right to a jury trial attaches only to claims that arise at law. Even though Plaintiff seeks only monetary relief, courts have consistently characterized backpay and frontpay as equitable remedies to which no right to a jury trial attaches.

   Answer (D) is incorrect. Plaintiff's amended complaint seeks equitable relief only. If Plaintiff's claims had raised mixed claims of law and equity, Plaintiff may have been entitled to a jury trial. In many jurisdictions, including the federal courts, Plaintiff would have a right to a jury trial on Plaintiff's legal claims if Plaintiff's case raised mixed claims of law and equity. However, in jurisdictions employing the equitable clean-up doctrine, Plaintiff may not have a right to a jury trial on legal claims if the court determines that the legal claims are ancillary to the equitable claims.

4. **Answer (C) is correct.** Plaintiff's complaint seeks both equitable relief in the form of reinstatement and backpay, and legal relief in the form of compensatory damages. If the court concludes that the legal claims significantly overlap with the equitable claims, the case will be deemed essentially equitable and no right to a jury trial will attach. When a plaintiff's case raises mixed claims of law and equity such as Plaintiff's case in this problem, the equitable clean-up doctrine requires the court to determine whether the case is "essentially equitable." If the court determines that the claims are essentially equitable, the right to a jury trial will not attach. Instead, the court will "draw the legal claims into equity" and resolve them as ancillary to the equitable claims. A case will be considered essentially equitable when the core questions presented in the legal claims overlap significantly with those presented in the equitable claims.

   Answer (A) is incorrect. Under the equitable clean-up doctrine, the right to a jury trial does not attach to all cases raising mixed legal and equitable claims. Instead, when a case raises mixed legal and equitable claims, the right to a jury trial will attach only if the legal claims are sufficiently distinct and severable from equitable legal claims.

   Answer (B) is incorrect. Under the equitable clean-up doctrine, the presence of equitable claims does not preclude a right to a jury trial. Instead, the parties will have a right to a jury trial in cases raising mixed legal and equitable claims if the legal claims are sufficiently distinct and severable from the equitable claims.

   Answer (D) is incorrect. Under the equitable clean-up doctrine, if the legal claims significantly overlap with the equitable claims, the court will deem the case as essentially equitable. As such, no right to a jury trial will attach, and the court should grant the motion to strike the jury demand.

5. Potter can argue that the court should order Potter's reinstatement with backpay to effectuate the purposes of the Act. The Act is intended to prevent an employer from making employment decisions based on an employee's credit history. However, $500 in statutory damages is too minor a sanction to effectively deter an employer from violating the Act. Additionally, $500 and attorney fees is inadequate to compensate Potter for the harm suffered from the violation because Potter has lost his or her primary source of income. Conversely, Darko can argue that the statute provides express remedies and that the statutory language does not envision remedies in addition to those provided in the statute. Additionally, Darko can argue that the right created by the statute was unknown at common law, and as such, the statute should be strictly construed to preclude additional remedies.

6. **Answer (C) is correct.** Generally, a plaintiff cannot recover twice for the same loss. However, an order of specific performance by its terms can only compel future performance. As such, an order of specific performance in this case would only protect Publisher from future losses. Thus, if compensatory damages are limited to what is necessary to compensate Publisher for past losses, Publisher will not be receiving a double recovery.

Answer (A) is incorrect. While a plaintiff cannot recover twice for the same loss, a court may award both equitable relief and compensatory damages as long as they are complementary rather than duplicative. Where compensatory damages are limited to compensation for past losses, they will be complementary to rather than duplicative of equitable relief.

Answer (B) is incorrect. An award of specific performance can only compel future performance and, hence, may only protect the plaintiff from future losses. Thus, a court may consistently conclude that money damages would be inadequate and award specific performance to protect against future losses while also recognizing the plaintiff is entitled to compensatory damages to compensate it for past losses.

Answer (D) is incorrect. A plaintiff is precluded from recovering twice for the same loss regardless of the defendant's culpability. Thus, a defendant's good or bad faith is irrelevant, and the court should only award specific performance and compensatory damages if they are complementary rather than duplicative.

Topic 2   Answers

Compensatory Damages

7. **Answer (C) is the correct answer.** Under the Restatement (Second) of Contracts, the non-breaching party to a contract can recover the cost to remedy defects or complete performance if that cost is not clearly disproportionate to the loss in value to the non-breaching party. A court is most likely to award the cost to remedy a defect in performance even though it exceeds the loss in value to the owner where the defect frustrates the purpose of the contract. Here, the defect frustrates the purpose of the contract because the defect prevents Owner from using the prevailing winds to cool the building.

    Answer (A) is incorrect. Because the building has to be torn down and rebuilt, a substantial part of the cost to remedy the defect will consist of the cost to undo the defective performance. Where a large part of the cost to remedy the defect consists of the cost to undo the defective performance, courts generally will not award the cost to remedy. *See Jacob & Youngs v. Kent*, 230 N.Y. 239 (1921); Restatement (Second) Contracts § 348, cmt. c.

    Answer (B) is incorrect. Because this is an office building that Owner presumably holds for commercial rather than personal reasons, the aesthetic appearance of the office building is not likely central to the purpose of the contract. Therefore, the court would be unlikely to award the cost to remedy if it exceeds the diminished market value of the property.

    Answer (D) is incorrect. As discussed above, the court is likely to award the cost to remedy the defect under the circumstances described in **Answer (C)**.

8. **Answer (B) is the correct answer.** Generally, the non-breaching party is entitled to recover its expectancy interest under the contract. Here, Benson's expectancy interest would be the profits Benson would have earned from operating the franchise. However, if a party cannot prove its expectancy with reasonable certainty, the party can recover as damages any expenses the non-breaching party incurred in reliance on or in furtherance of performance of the contract. Here, Benson likely cannot prove lost profits with reasonable certainty, because Benson has no previous restaurant experience on which to base an estimate of lost profits. Thus, Benson will be entitled to recover any expenses Benson incurred in performing the contract. Here, Benson incurred the advertising expenses in furtherance of performance under the franchise agreement because the agreement required Benson to use best efforts to promote the franchise. Thus, Benson will be entitled to recover the advertising expenses.

Answer (A) is incorrect. To recover lost profits, Benson would have to prove past success in a sufficiently similar enterprise. Benson's success as an attorney is not sufficiently similar to be predictive of Benson's likely success as a restaurant owner.

Answer (C) is incorrect. Reliance damages are an alternative to expectancy damages and can be recovered only if the non-breaching party cannot establish its expectancy. Thus, Benson is entitled to recover either lost profits or the advertising fees but not both.

Answer (D) is incorrect. Even if Benson cannot prove the lost profits from the franchise with reasonable certainty, Benson will be able to establish the amount that Benson expended on advertising in reliance on the franchise agreement. Thus, Benson will be able to recover the advertising expenses as reliance damages.

9. **Answer (B) is the correct answer.** Benson did not incur the advertising expenses in performance of obligations under the contract with Contractor. Benson's only likely obligation under the agreement with Contractor was to pay Contractor the purchase price. Thus, the advertising expenses were incidental to or collateral to Benson's obligations under the agreement with Contractor. The non-breaching party may recover incidental expenses only if the breaching party could have foreseen those expenditures at the time of contracting.

   Answer (A) is incorrect. Essential reliance expenses include only those expenses which the non-breaching party necessarily incurs in performance of its obligations under the contract. Here, Benson was not obligated to advertise in order to perform Benson's obligations under the contract with Contractor. Rather, Benson's only likely obligation under the agreement with Contractor was to pay the purchase price. Thus, the expenses incurred for advertising are not incurred in essential reliance.

   Answer (C) is incorrect. Although the breaching party is required to prove its reliance damages with reasonable certainty, Benson likely will not have trouble establishing the cost of advertising expenses with reasonable certainty.

   Answer (D) is incorrect. This answer places the burden of proof on the wrong party. The non-breaching party cannot recover reliance damages in excess of its anticipated expectancy. Thus, here, if Benson's advertising costs exceed the anticipated profits, Benson's recovery will be limited to the value of the lost profits. However, the breaching party bears the burden of proving the loss. Thus, in this case, Contractor would be required to prove the value of the anticipated profit with reasonable certainty. In the absence of such proof, Benson will be entitled to recover the full value of the advertising costs.

10. **Answer (D) is the correct answer.** Special damages are those damages which do not flow necessarily and inherently from the breach but instead are caused by the particular needs of the non-breaching party. Generally, special damages are those that arise from the use of the object of the action rather than the injury or loss of the object itself. Under the Restatement (Second) of Torts, damages like the medical expenses in **Answer (A)** are considered special damages. Damages for loss of use of an automobile in **Answer (B)** are special damages. They are not damages to compensate for the actual damage to the vehicle. Instead,

they are damages that arise from the owner's particular use of the automobile. Lost earnings in the defamation action in **Answer (C)** are also special damages. An injured party's specific lost earnings will depend on the particular individual's circumstances. Thus, all of the circumstances described in the problem are examples of special damages. **That result is found in Answer (D), making Answer (D) the correct answer and Answers (A), (B) and (C) incorrect.**

11. **Answer (B) is the correct answer.** In order to recover lost profits, the non-breaching party must make reasonable efforts to avoid lost profits and can only recover those portions of the lost profits which could not be avoided through reasonable efforts. The non-breaching party need not make extraordinary efforts to avoid the loss but need only take reasonable steps to avoid the loss. The reasonableness of the non-breaching party's efforts is determined by the individual circumstances of the non-beaching party. Here, because the sole proprietor is an individual, she may lack the means to locate a replacement truck in a different state or transport the replacement truck to the sole proprietor's home state. If so, she will be entitled to recover lost profits even though she did not purchase a replacement truck.

    Answer (A) is incorrect. The buyer failed to take reasonable efforts to avoid lost profits because the buyer could have purchased substitute component parts at a cheaper price than producing the components itself and, thereby avoided some of its lost profits.

    Answer (C) is incorrect. The farmer could have avoided lost profits by searching for a replacement tractor during the three months between the time of breach and the start of the planting system.

    Answer (D) is incorrect. As discussed above, the sole proprietor in **Answer (B)** likely will be able to recover lost profits.

12. Generally, comparative or contributory negligence applies to the plaintiff's actions or omissions before an accident occurs and which contribute to the injury. A failure to mitigate arises when the plaintiff fails to act after the accident in a manner that would have minimized or eliminated the plaintiff's injuries. One exception to this general rule is the failure to wear a seatbelt. Even though this failure occurs before an accident, some courts have considered the failure to wear a seatbelt to be a failure to mitigate damages.

13. **Answer (D) is the correct answer.** An injured party is entitled to recover any costs it incurs attempting to mitigate or avoid a loss as long as the injured party's efforts were reasonable at the time they were undertaken. The fact that the efforts at mitigation ultimately prove unsuccessful does not render them unreasonable. This is a corollary to the injured party's duty to take reasonable steps to avoid or mitigate a loss. Because the injured party must take reasonable efforts to avoid or mitigate any potential losses after a breach, the injured party should be able to recover the costs of those reasonable efforts. To hold otherwise would require the injured party to risk bearing the cost of a loss if it fails to act or to risk bearing the cost of mitigation if its efforts proved unsuccessful.

Answer (A) is incorrect. An injured party can recover the costs of even unsuccessful mitigation efforts as long as the efforts were reasonable at the time they were undertaken.

Answer (B) is incorrect. An injured party need not notify a breaching party of its intent to mitigate, and, indeed, notifying the breaching party of its intent to mitigate after the breach will be insufficient to permit recovery. In order to recover mitigation costs, the loss that the non-breaching party seeks to avoid through mitigation must have been foreseeable to the breaching party at the time of contracting.

Answer (C) is incorrect. The breaching party's good faith or lack thereof does not affect the non-breaching party's entitlement to recover mitigation costs.

14. **Answer (A) is the correct answer.** Executive will be entitled to the remaining salary under the employment agreement with Corporation. A non-breaching employee has a duty to use reasonable efforts to seek comparable substitute employment. Having searched for a new job, the only offer Executive received was not comparable to Executive's position with Corporation. Thus, Executive is entitled to the full value of Executive's expectancy under the employment agreement.

Answer (B) is incorrect. Executive is required only to use reasonable efforts to seek comparable substitute employment. Here the offer from the smaller corporation does not appear to be substantially similar. The position is an inferior position in that Executive would be one of six executive vice presidents rather than the sole Chief Executive. Because the offer was not for comparable employment, Executive reasonably declined the offer and Executive's recovery will not be limited.

Answer (C) is incorrect. As stated above, Executive reasonably declined the job offer from the smaller corporation because it was not comparable to Executive's position at Corporation. Had the offer from the smaller corporation been comparable, Executive's damages would be limited to the difference in earnings under the two contracts.

Answer (D) is incorrect. As stated above, Executive reasonably declined the job offer from the smaller corporation because it was not comparable to Executive's position at Corporation. Had the offer from the smaller corporation been comparable, Executive would not be precluded from recovery. Instead, Executive's damages would be limited to the difference in earnings under the two contracts.

15. **Answer (C) is the correct answer.** A prevailing plaintiff is entitled to pre-judgment interest if the plaintiff's claim is liquidated or ascertainable. A claim is liquidated when damages will be computed by reference to an objective source or formula such as the fair market value of the automobile.

Answer (A) is incorrect. Tort claims can be liquidated claims as long as damages are readily ascertainable, such as when damages will be based on an objective source or formula.

Answer (B) is incorrect. A dispute over liability will not render a claim unliquidated.

Answer (D) is incorrect. Parker will be entitled to pre-judgment interest only if Parker's fraud claim is a liquidated claim.

16. **Answer (D) is the correct answer.** Post-judgment interest as distinguished from pre-judgment interest is interest that accrues from the date of judgment until the defendant satisfies the judgment. In most jurisdictions, it is awarded automatically by statute regardless of the nature of the claim.

    Answer (A) is incorrect. Post-judgment interest is awarded regardless of the legal theory under which the plaintiff sues.

    Answer (B) is incorrect. Post-judgment interest, unlike pre-judgment interest, is available even if a claim is unliquidated. Thus, post-judgment interest is available even if the amount of damages is committed to the discretion of the jury.

    Answer (C) is incorrect. Both pre-judgment and post-judgment interest are available if the defendant disputes liability.

Topic 3 Answers

Contract Damages

17. **Answer (B) is the correct answer.** When a seller has wrongfully failed to deliver goods, Uniform Commercial Code (UCC) §2-712 allows a buyer to "cover" by purchasing substitute goods and recover from the seller as damages the difference between the cost of cover and the contract price. However, the buyer's failure to cover does not preclude the buyer from recovering damages. Instead, under UCC §2-713(a), a buyer is entitled to recover as damages the difference between the market price at the time for tender and the contract price. Here, Seller wrongfully failed to deliver 2000 widgets. Buyer has failed to cover. However, Buyer is entitled to recover damages under §2-713(a). Buyer's damages will be measured as the difference between the market price at the time for tender which equals $8000 ($4.00 per widget × 2000 widgets) and the contract price of $2000 ($1.00 per widget × 2000 widgets). Thus, Buyer will be entitled to recover $6000. This result is found in **Answer (B), making Answer (B) the correct answer** and **Answers (A), (C), and (D) incorrect answers.**

18. **Answer (A) is the correct answer.** When a buyer lawfully rejects non-conforming goods, UCC §2-712 allows a buyer to "cover" by purchasing substitute goods and recover from the seller as damages the difference between the cost of cover and the contract price. Here, Bombay lawfully rejected non-conforming sprockets and purchased commercially reasonable substitute sprockets. Therefore, Bombay is entitled to recover damages under §2-712. Bombay's damages will be measured as the difference between the cover price of $30,000 ($3.00 per sprocket wheel × 10,000 wheels) and the contract price of $10,000 ($1.00 per sprocket wheel × 10,000 wheels) or $20,000.

    Answer (B) is incorrect. Bombay is entitled to recover the difference between the cost of cover and the contract price. Bombay is not entitled to recover the entire cost of cover.

    Answer (C) is incorrect. Cover goods need only be reasonable substitutes. The fact that the cover goods cost more than the original goods by itself does not make the cover goods unreasonable substitutes. Indeed, by allowing the buyer to recover the difference between the cost of cover and the contract price, the UCC implicitly recognizes that commercially reasonable substitute goods may cost more than the original goods.

    Answer (D) is incorrect. Bombay will not be entitled to recover *consequential* damages resulting from Bombay's intended use of the sprockets such as lost profits because Bombay did not inform Super Sprockets of its intended use of the sprockets at the time of contracting. However, Bombay may recover its *general* damages. General damages are those damages that compensate Bombay for the loss of the actual object of the contract—here, the sprockets—rather than its use of that object. The law presumes that such losses are foreseeable to the seller. Here, the loss of the sprockets themselves will be measured as the difference between the cost of the cover sprockets and the contract price.

19. **Answer (A) is correct.** When a seller such as Super Sprockets breaches, UCC § 2-715 allows a buyer such as Bombay to recover the expenses reasonably incurred in effecting cover as incidental damages.

    Answer (B) is incorrect. The UCC does not limit recovery of incidental damages to merchants.

    Answer (C) is incorrect. Incidental damages need not be foreseeable at the time of contracting. They need only be reasonable.

    Answer (D) is incorrect. When a buyer lawfully rejects non-conforming goods, UCC § 2-712 allows a buyer to "cover" by purchasing substitute goods. A buyer is then entitled to recover the reasonable costs incurred in effecting cover under UCC § 2-715.

20. **Answer (C) is correct.** When a seller tenders non-conforming goods, the buyer generally is entitled to recover the difference between the market price as warranted and the market price as delivered. However, under certain circumstances, a court may allow a buyer to offer evidence of the cost to repair as evidence of the difference in value. This is particularly true when the repairs are necessary to ensure that the goods function for their intended purpose. In this case, damage to the oxygen sensor would seem to prevent the tractor from functioning in its intended manner.

    Answer (A) is incorrect. As stated above, repairing the oxygen sensor appears to have been necessary to ensure that the tractor functioned as intended. Thus, the repairs would be reasonable mitigation efforts.

    Answer (B) is incorrect. The usual measure of damages when a seller delivers non-conforming goods is the difference in value as warranted and as delivered, not the difference between the market price and the contract price.

    Answer (D) is incorrect. The UCC allows the buyer to recover for damages for any "non-conformity." A buyer need not show a breach of an express warranty to recover.

21. **Answer (B) is the correct answer.** Under UCC § 2-715, a buyer can recover consequential damages such as lost profits if those losses were foreseeable and unavoidable. Under the UCC, consequential damages must be foreseeable to the seller at the time of contracting. Consequential damages are foreseeable when the seller has reason to know of the particular needs of the buyer that cause the consequential loss. The UCC also requires the buyer to take reasonable steps through cover or otherwise to prevent the loss. If the loss occurs despite the buyer's reasonable efforts, the buyer can recover damages for the loss. Here, Betty's lost profits are consequential damages because they arise from Betty's intended use of the van. Betty has taken reasonable steps to avoid her lost profits by searching for a comparable van. Because no comparable van was available, her lost profits are unavoidable. However, Betty failed to communicate her intended use of the van to Stan until the time and place for delivery of the van. Thus, Stan had no reason to know of her intended use at the time of contracting and could

not foresee her lost profits at the time of contracting. Accordingly, even though her lost profits are unavoidable, they were not foreseeable at the time of contracting, and hence, Betty is not entitled to recover damages for the lost profits. This result is found in **Answer (B)**, **making Answer (B) the correct answer** and Answers (A), (C), and (D) incorrect answers.

22. **Answer (C) is the correct answer.** Here, the contract is a mixed contract for goods and services. The contract obligated Electric Company to both deliver a good—the transformer—and perform a service—the installation of the transformer. While Electric Company performed its obligations by delivering a conforming transformer, Electric Company breached the contract by improperly installing the transformer. Metals Company is entitled to general damages for Electric Company's breach of the contract. These damages will be measured as the difference in the value of the installation as promised and the value of the installation as performed.

    Answer (A) is incorrect. Under UCC § 2-714, the measure of damages when the buyer accepts non-conforming goods is the difference between the value of the goods as accepted and the value of the goods had the goods been delivered in the condition warranted by the seller. The cost to repair nonconforming goods may be an appropriate measure of difference in value in some cases. However, Metals Company is precluded from recovering damages for harm to the transformer in this case. Here, the transformer was delivered in the condition in which it was warranted. Thus, Metals Company received conforming goods. The harm to the transformer occurred as a result of Electric Company's negligent installation of the transformer. Thus, the harm to the transformer is a form of consequential damages. Ordinarily, the buyer would be entitled to recover consequential damages for the harm to the transformer. However, here, the parties have expressly limited such damages in the contract. Thus, Metals Company is not entitled to recover damages for the harm to the transformer.

    Answer (B) is incorrect. Here, the transformer was delivered in the condition in which it was warranted. Thus, Metals Company received conforming goods. The harm to the transformer occurred as a result of Electric Company's negligent installation of the transformer. Thus, the harm to the transformer is a form of consequential damages. Ordinarily, the buyer would be entitled to recover consequential damages for the harm to the transformer. The lesser of the cost to repair or the diminution in value would be an appropriate measure. However, here, the parties have expressly limited such damages in the contract. Thus, Metals Company is not entitled to recover damages for the harm to the transformer.

    Answer (D) is incorrect. While Metals Company is entitled to general damages measured by the difference in value from the improper installation of the transformer, Metals Company is not entitled to consequential damages for the harm to the transformer because the contract expressly precludes such damages.

23. **Answer (D) is the correct answer.** The economic loss rule precludes a plaintiff who is in a contractual relationship with the defendant from recovering economic loss in a tort action absent personal injury or damage to property other than the property that is the subject of the contract. Instead, such a plaintiff is limited to whatever recovery is available in a breach of contract claim. Economic losses include purely pecuniary damages such as the lost profits at

issue in this problem. Here, the only property damage that Metals Company suffered was the physical damage to the transformer. Because the transformer was the subject of the contract between the Metals Company and the Electric Company, the economic loss rule precludes Metals Company from recovering its lost profits in tort. Further, Metals Company is precluded from recovering lost profits in a breach of contract action because the contract precludes consequential damages.

Answer (A) is incorrect. While the lost profits may have been foreseeable to Electric Company at the time of contracting, they are a form of consequential damages under the contract. Here, the contract precludes recovery of consequential damages.

Answer (B) is incorrect. Under the economic loss rule, a plaintiff in a contractual relationship with the defendant may recover damages in tort for economic loss if the defendant's conduct caused personal injury or damage to property other than the property that is the subject of the contract. While Electric Company's conduct caused harm to the transformer in this case, the transformer is the subject of the contract. Thus, Metals Company is precluded from recovering in tort.

Answer (C) is incorrect. The non-breaching party to a contract has a duty to mitigate its lost profits by seeking substitute goods or through other reasonable means. Its recovery is limited to only that portion of its profits which could not have been avoided through cover or other reasonable means. In this case, purchasing a substitute transformer may have been appropriate means to avoid the lost profits if a substitute transformer was available at a reasonable cost. However, even if Metals Company had attempted to purchase a substitute transformer, Metals Company would have been precluded from recovering any unavoidable lost profits because the contract precludes recovery of consequential damages.

24. Simon is entitled to recover $0.02 per brick for the 200,000 bricks that Barbara rejected, or $4000. When a buyer refuses to accept conforming goods and the seller does not resell those goods, UCC § 2-708 provides that the seller is entitled to recover the difference between the contract price and the market price at the time and place for tender.

25. **Answer (B) is the correct answer.** Under UCC § 2-706, a seller is entitled to resell goods in a commercially reasonable manner and collect the difference between the resale price and the contract price. Here, because the greetings cards had a time-sensitive theme, Stone acted reasonably in attempting to sell the cards until Valentine's Day then waiting until the next Valentine's Day season to attempt a second resale.

Answer (A) is incorrect. A seller such as Stone is entitled to recover price only if the goods are identified to the contract and cannot be resold through reasonable efforts. Here, the greeting cards were resold through reasonable albeit not immediate efforts.

Answer (C) is incorrect. Given the seasonal nature of the greeting cards, Stone could reasonably wait until the appropriate season to attempt to resell the goods.

Answer (D) is incorrect. Under UCC § 2-706, a seller such as Stone is entitled to resell goods at a private sale as long as the seller provides the buyer with reasonable notice of the resale.

26. **Answer (A) is the correct answer.** Under UCC § 2-706, a seller such as Stone is entitled to recover any incidental damages incurred as a result of the breach. Under UCC § 2-710, incidental damages include commercially reasonable expenses incurred in the care and custody of goods after the breach as well as expenses incurred in reselling the goods. Here, Stone incurred the rental fee in connection with the care and custody of the greeting cards after Brown's breach and so that Stone could resell the goods at an appropriate time. Further, Stone acted reasonably in storing the greeting cards until the appropriate season.

    Answer (B) is incorrect. A seller need not be successful in its resale efforts to recover expenses incurred in connection with the resale. The seller need only be reasonable in its efforts. Here, Stone acted reasonably in attempting to resell the greeting cards during the appropriate season, so Stone would be entitled to recover the rental fees even if Stone had not been able to resell the greeting cards.

    Answer (C) is incorrect. While a seller such as Stone generally is precluded from recovering consequential losses, the rental fee is incidental to the contract between Stone and Brown rather than consequential because Stone incurred the rental fee in attempting to mitigate Stone's loss under the contract with Brown.

    Answer (D) is incorrect. Stone need not inform Brown of the rental fees. Expenses incurred in attempting to mitigate the loss under the contract are presumed to be foreseeable to the breaching buyer.

27. **Answer (C) is the correct answer.** A lost volume seller is entitled to recover its profit under § 2-708(2).

    Answer (A) is incorrect. A seller may elect to recover the difference between the market value and the contract price. However, if that measure of damages would be inadequate, a seller may elect to recover its lost profits under UCC § 2-708(2). Here, if the standard retail price is less than the market value of the laptop computers, Super Computers may elect to recover the difference between the market value and the standard retail price. However, if the standard retail price is equal to or greater than the market value of the computers, this measure of recovery would be inadequate as it would yield no damages. Super Computers would not be precluded from recovering. Instead, it could recover its lost profits under UCC § 2-708(2).

    Answer (B) is incorrect. UCC § 2-708(2) allows a seller to recover its lost profits when market or resale damages would be inadequate. One of the circumstances under which § 2-708(2) applies is when the seller is a "lost volume seller." A lost volume seller is a seller who would have made a sale to a third party even if the original buyer had not breached. In other words, the seller would have made a sale to both the breaching party and the third party if the buyer had not breached. Under these circumstances, the seller has lost one sale and the profit on that one sale, even though the seller has resold the breaching buyer's goods.

    Answer (D) is incorrect. A lost volume seller is entitled to recover only its profits on the lost sale. The lost volume seller is not entitled to recover the entire contract price.

28. **Answer (D) is the correct answer.** Under UCC § 2-709, a seller is entitled to recover the price of the contracted-for goods under three circumstances: (1) if the buyer has accepted the goods; (2) if conforming goods are lost or damaged after the risk of loss has passed to the buyer; or (3) if the buyer rejects conforming goods and the seller is unable to sell those goods after reasonable efforts. Thus, if Seller is not able to resell the molding machine, here, because it is designed for Buyer's specific uses, Seller will be entitled to recover the price of the molding machine. Likewise, if Buyer accepts delivery of the molding machine but refuses to pay for the molding machine, Seller will be entitled to recover price. Finally, because the contract requires Seller to ship the molding machine via common carrier but provides no express term allocating risk of loss while the goods are in the possession of the railroad, it is a shipment contract under the UCC. Under a shipment contract, the risk of loss passes to the buyer once the seller delivers the goods to the carrier and makes a contract for their shipment. Here, Seller delivered the molding machine to the railroad and made a contract for its shipment before the molding machine was stolen. Thus, the risk of loss passed to Buyer before the molding machine was stolen. Hence, Seller is entitled to recover the price. As such, Seller is entitled to recover price under all three circumstances. This result is found in **Answer (D), making Answer (D) the correct answer** and **Answers (A), (B), and (C) incorrect answers.**

29. Super Salty will be entitled to recover $1900. Super Salty will be entitled to recover the price of $500 ($5.00 per pound × 100 pounds) for the 100 pounds of processed nuts it completed. Under UCC § 2-709, a seller is entitled to recover price for goods identified to the contract that the seller is unable to resell through reasonable efforts. Here, Super Salty completed 100 pounds of processed nuts which are identified to the contract with Benny's Best. Super Salty was unable to resell the nuts because they were processed pursuant to Benny's Best's unique recipe. Super Salty also will be entitled to recover its lost profits for the remaining 400 pounds of nuts. UCC § 2-704 allows a seller that has not completed manufacturer of the contract goods prior to the breach to cease manufacturing if to do so would be commercially reasonable. Here, Super Salty acted reasonably in ceasing production because no market appears to exist for the processed nuts. When a seller ceases production, market and resale differential damages will be inadequate. The measures envision that the seller will be able to resell finished goods. Thus, such a "components seller" is entitled to lost profits under § 2-708(2). Here, because Super Salty ceased production of the remaining 400 pounds of processed nuts, it has no finished goods. Accordingly, it is entitled to lost profits. Under UCC § 2-708(2), lost profits are measured as the seller's profits including reasonable overhead plus due allowance for costs reasonably incurred and less any payments or proceeds on resale. Profit is measured as the contract price less the seller's production costs. Here, Super Salty's anticipated profit was $2.00 per pound or $800 (($5.00 contract price − $2.00 cost of nuts − $0.50 cost of ingredients − $.050 cost of equipment and rent) × 400 pounds). The depreciation on its equipment and the rent on its plant would be considered overhead. Thus, assuming Super Salty's estimate of $0.50 per pound was reasonable, Super Salty will be entitled to recover $200 ($0.50 × 400 pounds) as well. Super Salty also is entitled to recover costs it has reasonably incurred. Here, Super Salty already has paid $800 for the 400 pounds of unprocessed nuts ($2.00 per pound × 400 pounds). Assuming Super Salty acted reasonably in purchasing the unprocessed nuts, it will be entitled to recover this cost as well. Finally, Super Salty's recovery will be reduced by any

proceeds it received on resale of the components. Here, Super Salty was able to sell the unprocessed nuts for $400 ($1.00 per pounds × 400 pounds). Thus, Super Salty's recovery will be $1900 ($500 (price for completed nuts) + $800 (profit on unprocessed nuts) + $200 (overhead attributable to unfinished nuts) + $800 (costs incurred for unprocessed nuts) – $400 (profit earned on resale of unprocessed nuts)).

30. **Answer (C) is the correct answer.** Under the Restatement (Second) of Contracts, a court will uphold a liquidated damages provision if: (1) the damages resulting from a breach would be difficult to determine at the time the parties entered into the contract; and (2) the stipulated amount bears a reasonable relationship to either the anticipated or actual harm resulting from the breach. Here, if Contractor does not complete construction by the start of the school year, School District will be harmed in that it will have to find a new location to hold classes or re-configure existing facilities. This, in turn, could harm the educational experience of students who may be forced to attend classes in overcrowded facilities or move from one location to another during the course of the semester. The injury to the students' educational experience would be difficult to quantify. Moreover, the clause bears a reasonable relationship to the harm, because the rental value of comparable space is the most quantifiable measure of the harm.

    Answer (A) is incorrect. The liquidated damages clause allows the shipper to recover the full contract price for goods that it does not have to ship and, hence, does not have to incur the costs of shipping. Thus, the clause provides for a greater recovery than either the actual or anticipated harm.

    Answer (B) is incorrect. The harm to Landlord in the event of a breach likely will not be the loss of the entire rent. Rather, because Landlord can re-let the property, the harm is the difference between the rent due under the lease with Tenant and the fair rental value of the property. Here, the clause does not account for Landlord's ability to re-let the property. Thus, in the absence of evidence that Landlord would encounter difficulty in re-letting the property, the clause does not bear a reasonable relationship to the anticipated or actual harm.

    Answer (D) is incorrect. Courts generally do not give controlling weight to the parties' characterization of the clause.

31. **Answer (C) is the correct answer.** Courts generally consider earnest money or down payment forfeiture clauses to be liquidated damages provisions that are presumptively valid. Courts will uphold such clauses unless the breaching party can show that the amount forfeited does not bear a reasonable relationship to the anticipated or actual harm to the seller. The actual harm to Smith would be the difference between the contract price and the market value or resale price of the condominium plus any consequential damages. If Brown can show that Smith could have resold the condominium for an amount significantly greater than $15,000 over the contract price, Brown likely can show that the forfeiture clause does not bear a reasonable relationship to Smith's actual or anticipated harm.

    Answer (A) is incorrect. Most courts have abandoned the rule against allowing a breaching party to maintain an action for restitution.

Answer (B) is incorrect. Down payment or earnest money forfeiture clauses generally are considered liquidated damages clauses. The enforceability of such clauses does not turn on the willfulness of the breaching party.

Answer (D) is incorrect. Courts generally analyze forfeiture clauses as liquidated damages clauses and consider clauses that liquidate damages at 10 percent of the purchase price to be presumptively valid.

32. **Answer (A) is the correct answer.** Most courts adhere to the American rule. Under the American rule, a buyer such as Baker is entitled to recover full benefit of the bargain damages when a vendor such as Stone fails to deliver marketable title regardless of the reasons for the vendor's default. However, some jurisdictions adhere to the English rule. Under the English rule, when the vendor is unable to deliver marketable title through no fault of her own, a buyer's recovery is limited to the return of any purchase price paid and any expenses incurred in connection with the transaction. Here, if Stone was unaware of the easement, Stone will be without fault in the breach. Thus, Baker's recovery will be limited to the return of any purchase price paid in a jurisdiction that adheres to the English rule.

    Answer (B) is incorrect. While Baker's recovery will not be limited to restitution of purchase price in a jurisdiction that adheres to the American rule, Baker's recovery will be so limited in a jurisdiction that adheres to the English Rule. Thus, **Answer (A)** is preferable.

    Answer (C) is incorrect. Even under the more restrictive English rule, Baker will not be limited to restitution of purchase price and, instead, will be entitled to recover benefit of the bargain damages if Stone acted in bad faith.

    Answer (D) is incorrect. A buyer's compensatory damages are measured by the benefit that the buyer would have gained from the transaction, rather than the benefit that the seller would have gained from the transaction. This usually will be measured as the difference between the contract price and the fair market value of the property.

33. **Answer (D) is the correct answer.** Biggs was able to purchase a comparable home at a cheaper price and, hence, needed to borrow less money. However, Biggs still suffered harm, because Biggs had to take out a loan at a higher interest rate. As a result of the higher interest rate, Biggs ultimately will end up paying more for the second house than Biggs would have paid under the contract with Stanton. Under these circumstances, Biggs is entitled to recover the interest rate differential between the two loans. This would be measured by the difference between the total amount of interest and principal due under the $280,000 loan at 6% and the total amount of interest and principal due under the $270,000 loan at 7.5%. This result is found in **Answer (D)**, making **Answer (D) the correct answer** and Answers (A), (B), and (C) incorrect answers.

Topic 4 Answers

Damages for Bodily Injury and Death

34. **Answer (B) is the correct answer.** Penny is entitled to recover the reasonable value of any necessary medical services or treatments.

    Answer (A) is incorrect. Penny is entitled to recover the reasonable value of any necessary medical services regardless of whether she has paid for the services at the time of trial. The amount paid for the treatment may be offered as evidence to show the reasonable value of services. Likewise, the fact that Penny has paid for the treatment may be offered to show that the treatment was medically necessary.

    Answer (C) is incorrect. Penny can recover the reasonable value of necessary services even if the treating physician is unlicensed.

    Answer (D) is incorrect. Penny will be entitled to recover damages for her medical expenses regardless of whether her personal health insurance covers the loss. Indeed, under the collateral source rule, Dan will not be able to introduce into evidence the fact that Penny has insurance coverage for the losses. However, if Penny's insurance carrier has paid for her treatment, her insurance carrier may be entitled to recover from Penny any damages she receives from Dan.

35. **Answer (D) is the correct answer.** None of the circumstances provided will preclude an injured plaintiff from recovering damages for lost earning capacity.

    Answer (A) is incorrect. While damages for lost wages are awarded to compensate a plaintiff for wages lost from a specific job while the plaintiff was injured, lost earning capacity compensates a plaintiff for a decrease in her ability to work. Thus, lost earning capacity as distinguished from lost wages does not require a record of past earnings. As such, a child who has not yet entered the workforce can recover for lost earning capacity if she can demonstrate that she would have been able to earn more money over her worklife had she not been injured.

    Answer (B) is incorrect. A plaintiff who returns to her previous employment may recover for lost earning capacity if she can demonstrate that her opportunities for advancement, promotion or change of careers have been limited because of her injuries.

    Answer (C) is incorrect. A full-time care provider can recover for lost earning capacity if he can demonstrate that he would have been able to re-enter the workforce but is unable to do so or can do so only at a decreased salary because of his injuries. Alternatively, the full-time care provider may recover the replacement value of his child care services if he is unable to provide child care services as a result of his injuries.

36. A jury can consider numerous factors including the plaintiff's age, past employment history, education, training, opportunities for employment or promotion, and stated career intentions in determining the plaintiff's lost earning capacity.

37. **Answer (C) is the correct answer.** Awards that compensate for future pecuniary expenses that will recur periodically must be reduced to present value. Here, expenses for Peterman's daily nursing care will recur periodically after trial.

    Answer (A) is incorrect. Most courts agree that damages for pain and suffering need not be reduced to present value.

    Answer (B) is incorrect. Only damages for future pecuniary losses must be reduced to present value. Future losses are those that the plaintiff will incur after trial. While damages that compensate Peterman for the wages he lost before trial are damages for pecuniary losses, they compensate Peterman for past losses rather than future losses. Therefore, these damages do not need to be reduced to present value.

    Answer (D) is incorrect. While damages for Peterman's future daily nursing care must be reduced to present value, damages for lost wages need not be.

38. **Answer (C) is correct.** Damages for lost wages and damages for diminished earning capacity compensate an injured plaintiff for two different types of lost economic opportunities. Damages for lost wages compensate the plaintiff for wages she loses when she is unable to work at a specific job which she held at the time of the accident. Damages for diminished earning capacity, meanwhile, compensate an injured plaintiff for a narrowing in the range of economic opportunities available to her and need not be tied to the loss of a specific job. Here, Penny appears to have suffered both. At the time of the accident, she was employed as a short-haul truck driver. She was unable to work in this job for a period of time while she underwent medical treatment for her injuries. Thus, she should be able to recover the wages she lost during this period. If she can establish that, but for the accident, she would have become a long-haul truck driver, she can also show that her range of economic opportunities has been narrowed. As such, she will be able to recover damages for future diminished earning capacity as measured by the difference in what she could have earned as a long-haul driver and what she can now earn as a short-haul driver over the course of her worklife.

    Answer (A) is incorrect. Even though she eventually returned to work, Penny was unable to work for some period of time. Thus, she is entitled to recover the wages she lost during that period of time in which her injuries precluded her from working. Furthermore, even if a plaintiff returns to the job she held prior to the accident, she will be entitled to recover damages if she can show that her economic opportunities have been narrowed as a result of her injuries. Thus, if she can return to her job as a short-haul driver but can show that her injuries will prevent her from advancing in her career to the position of long-haul driver, she will be entitled to recover damages for diminished earning capacity.

    Answer (B) is incorrect. Even if a plaintiff returns to the job she held prior to the accident, she will be entitled to recover damages if she can show that her economic opportunities have been narrowed as a result of her injuries. Thus, if Penny can return to her job as a short-haul driver but can show that her injuries will prevent her from advancing in her career to the position of long-haul driver, she will be entitled to recover damages for diminished earning capacity.

Answer (D) is incorrect. Damages for lost wages and damages for diminished earning capacity compensate an injured plaintiff for two different types of lost economic opportunities. Damages for lost wages compensate the plaintiff for wages she loses when she is unable to work at a specific job which she held at the time of the accident. Damages for diminished earning capacity, meanwhile, compensate an injured plaintiff for a narrowing in the range of economic opportunities available to her and need not be tied to the loss of a specific job. Thus, if Penny can establish both types of losses, she is entitled to recover damages for both types of losses.

39. **Answer (D) is the correct answer.** In *Jones & Laughlin Steel Corp. v. Pfeifer*, 462 U.S. 523 (1983), the Supreme Court recognized that the discount rate should be based on the interest rate earned on "the best and safest" investment. The Court also recognized that inflation affects both the estimate of lost earnings and the discount rate and held that the discount rate should be chosen on the basis of the factors that are used to estimate the lost earnings. Essentially, inflation should be treated consistently on both sides of the equation. If inflation is excluded from estimates of lost wages, inflation should also be excluded from the discount rate. Here, the method of discounting treats inflation consistently by including cost of living increases in the estimate of lost wages while using a market interest rate that reflects, in part, anticipated inflation. The discount rate also reflects the interest rate earned on reasonably safe investments because triple-A rated corporate bonds are reasonably safe investments.

Answer (A) is incorrect. Here, the discount rate is based on the yield on junk bonds. Junk bonds are not reasonably safe investments. Additionally, inflation has been excluded from the estimate of lost wages because the estimate excludes increases due to the cost of living. However, inflation has been factored into the discount rate because the discount rate uses a market interest rate.

Answer (B) is incorrect. The yield on triple-A rated corporate bonds reflects an interest rate earned on reasonably safe investments. However, the method treats inflation inconsistently between the estimate of lost earnings and the discount rate. The estimate of lost earnings excludes any increase in earnings due to inflation because it excludes cost-of-living increases. However, the discount rate includes an estimate of inflation. The current market yield on triple A rated corporate bonds reflects, in part, a predicted inflation rate. The yield is increased to account for anticipated price inflation before the bond's maturity. Thus, this method of discounting runs the risk of undercompensating Peterson.

Answer (C) is incorrect. This method of discounting treats inflation consistently by including cost of living increases in the estimate of lost wages while using a market interest rate that reflects, in part, anticipated inflation. However, a junk bond is not a reasonably safe investment.

40. A plaintiff can recover damages for any noneconomic harms resulting from the defendant's misconduct, including pain and suffering, loss of enjoyment of life, mental and physical an-

guish and disfigurement. Some jurisdictions treat each of these claims as a separate item of recovery, while other jurisdiction treat these all as components of pain and suffering.

41. **Answer (A) is the correct answer.** Patty received medical services, so she will be entitled to recover the reasonable value of those services, provided that they were medically necessary. While Patty also received the benefit of her Aunt's gratuitous services, she received that benefit from her Aunt who has no relationship to the defendant. Thus, under the collateral source rule, the defendant will not be entitled to offset the harm and the benefit.

    Answer (B) is incorrect. The plaintiff is entitled to recover the entire reasonable value of medical services provided.

    Answer (C) is incorrect. Generally, the defendant's state of mind does not affect the plaintiff's entitlement to compensatory damages. The defendant's state of mind, however, will affect the plaintiff's ability to recover punitive damages.

    Answer (D) is incorrect. Patty received a benefit when her Aunt provided the medical services gratuitously. However, that benefit was collateral to the defendant's misconduct. Thus, under the collateral source rule, the defendant will not be entitled to offset the harm and the benefit.

42. **Answer (B) is the correct answer.** The majority of jurisdictions today allow an injured plaintiff to recover the reasonable value of any medical services the injured plaintiff receives. Many of these jurisdictions allow defendants such as Dixon to offer evidence of the amount a health care provider actually accepted to satisfy a claim as evidence of the reasonable value of services. *See, e.g. Robinson v. Bates*, 857 N.E.2d 1195 (Ohio 2006); *but see Dedmon v. Steelman*, 535 S.W.3d 431 (Tenn. 2017) (holding that the collateral source rule precludes defendants from offering evidence of insurance write offs).

    Answer (A) is incorrect. At common law, the collateral source rule precluded a court from reducing a plaintiff's recovery by any amount that a third-party such as an insurance company had paid to satisfy a plaintiff's expenses. Thus, the collateral source rule would preclude a court from reducing Patton's recovery by the $10,000 Patton's insurance company paid to cover the medical expenses.

    Answer (C) is incorrect. Patton will be entitled to recover the reasonable value of the medical services regardless of how much Patton actually paid.

    Answer (D) is incorrect. A defendant's culpability does not affect how the court measures the reasonable value of medical services.

43. **Answer (C) is the correct answer.** An injured party must undergo reasonable treatment that is within her means. An injured party need not endure undue hardships, including financial hardships, to avoid a loss. If Pierson lacks the financial means to pay for the surgery, she will be entitled to recover damages for her pain and suffering.

Answer (A) is incorrect. While a defendant must take the plaintiff as the defendant finds her, the plaintiff has a duty to use reasonable and proper efforts to minimize harm and restore herself. The defendant is not required to compensate the plaintiff for harm that could be avoided through reasonable means. Here, surgery could alleviate Pierson's pain and suffering. Thus, Pierson will have a duty to undertake the surgery if a reasonable person would undergo the surgery, and Davidson will not have to pay damages for the pain and suffering that could be alleviated by the surgery if Pierson refuses to undergo the surgery.

Answer (B) is incorrect. Pierson must undertake all reasonable steps to avoid her pain and suffering. A reasonable person might undertake the surgery if it involved only a slight risk of failure.

Answer (D) is incorrect. Pierson need only undergo those treatments to which a reasonable person would submit. If a reasonable person would not undergo the corrective surgery, Pierson will be entitled to recover her full pain and suffering damages.

44. **Answer (B) is the correct answer.** A spouse such as Wilma is entitled to maintain an action for loss of consortium. However, a spouse's consortium recovery cannot be duplicative of the injured party's recovery. Wilma will be entitled to recover damages for her loss of consortium. Her damages for her noneconomic losses such as her loss of companionship will not be duplicative of Harrison's recovery, because she suffers a separate and distinct loss.

Answer (A) is incorrect. Here, if Harrison recovers damages for his lost wages, Wilma cannot recover damages for her loss of financial support from Harrison because these damages would be duplicative of the damages for lost wages.

Answer (C) is incorrect. Recovery for loss of financial support would be duplicative of Harrison's recovery for lost wages.

Answer (D) is incorrect. Wilma will be entitled to maintain an action for loss of consortium and recover any damages that are not duplicative of Harrison's damages.

45. **Answer (B) is the correct answer.** A spouse's claim for loss of consortium is derivative of the injured party's claim. As such, a claim for loss of consortium is barred or reduced in the same manner as the injured spouse's recovery. Here, Harrison's recovery will be reduced proportionally to his fault, so Wilma's recovery will be likewise reduced.

Answer (A) is incorrect. Wilma's recovery will be reduced in the same manner as Harrison's recovery. In a comparative fault jurisdiction, Harrison's recovery will be reduced by the percentage at which he is at fault rather than barred. Thus, Wilma's recovery will be reduced proportionally rather than precluded.

Answer (C) is incorrect. Loss of consortium protects the marital relationship from acts of third parties only. It does not give the non-injured spouse a right to recovery from the injured spouse.

Answer (D) is incorrect. Because Wilma's loss of consortium claim is derivative of Harrison's personal injury claim her recovery will be reduced in the same manner as Harrison's recovery.

46. **Answer (B) is the correct answer.** Traditionally, a plaintiff must maintain a single action for all past, present and future losses arising from a single transaction or occurrence. A plaintiff may recover damages for future losses only if the plaintiff demonstrates that those future losses are reasonably certain to occur. Here, Poppins must maintain a single action to recover damages for her injuries both from the burns and the potential cancer in a single action because they arise from a single occurrence. She can recover damages relating to future treatment for cancer if she proves with reasonable certainty that she is likely to develop cancer.

    Answer (A) is incorrect. Generally, courts have permitted plaintiffs to recover damages for an increased fear of future harms such as cancer if the plaintiffs are unable to prove to a reasonable certainty that they will incur the likely harm. However, the increased fear of future harm is a present harm rather than a future harm. The plaintiff suffers from a fear of future harm as soon as the exposure occurs. Thus, the plaintiff need not prove to a reasonable certainty that some future harm will occur. Instead, the plaintiff must show that her current fear is reasonable.

    Answer (C) is incorrect. Generally, res judicata precludes a plaintiff from splitting her cause of action. Instead, she must file a single cause of action to recover damages for all of her injuries arising from a single transaction or occurrence. Here, if Poppins files an action to recover damages for injuries relating to the burns, she will be precluded from filing a second action to recover damages for her treatment for cancer because both injuries arise from the same occurrence.

    Answer (D) is incorrect. A stated above, a plaintiff can recover for future losses as long as she proves those losses to a reasonable certainty.

47. **Answer (D) is correct.** A plaintiff who suffers physical bodily injury is entitled to recover noneconomic damages for all pain and suffering the plaintiff endures, including any emotional distress caused by the underlying tortious conduct. Thus, Passenger is entitled to recover damages for any pain and suffering the injuries cause and any emotional distress resulting from the accident.

    Answer (A) is incorrect. A plaintiff who suffers physical bodily injury is entitled to recover noneconomic damages for all pain and suffering the plaintiff endures regardless of the severity of the plaintiff's injuries.

    Answer (B) is incorrect. A plaintiff who suffers physical bodily injury is entitled to recover noneconomic damages for all pain and suffering the plaintiff endures regardless of the severity of the plaintiff's injuries or whether the plaintiff recovers.

    Answer (C) is incorrect. A plaintiff who suffers physical bodily injury is entitled to recover noneconomic damages for all pain and suffering the plaintiff endures, including any emotional distress caused by the underlying tortious conduct. This is true despite a lack of a causal connection between the emotional distress and the physical injuries. The distress need only be caused by the same tortious conduct.

48. **Answer (A) is the correct answer.** Most states now provide by statute that causes of action survive the victim's death. Under these survival statutes, an estate, like Watson's Estate, can maintain an action against a tortfeasor and collect any damages to which the victim would have been entitled had the victim survived.

    Answer (B) is incorrect. Most states now have created by statute a claim for wrongful death. The wrongful death claim allows specified beneficiaries to recover damages they suffer as a result of the victim's death. However, here, Watson's Beneficiaries would not have a wrongful death claim against Davis because Davis did not cause Watson's death.

    Answer (C) is incorrect. Watson's beneficiaries do not have a wrongful death claim against Davis because Davis did not cause Watson's death.

    Answer (D) is incorrect. States generally allow the victim's tort claim to survive her death and also allow specified beneficiaries to pursue a claim for wrongful death.

49. **Answer (C) is the correct answer.** Generally, an estate can recover damages only for wages lost between the time of injury and the time of death and cannot recover damages for lost future wages or future lost earning capacity. However, the beneficiaries of the decedent can recover damages for the loss of the financial support that the decedent would have provided had the decedent survived.

    Answer (A) is incorrect. Generally, the estate can recover damages only for past lost wages measured as the wages the decedent lost from the time of injury until death.

    Answer (B) is incorrect. Allowing Parker's Estate to recover for lost future wages and Parker's beneficiaries to recover for lost financial support would result in an impermissible duplicative recovery. Had Parker survived, the financial support to Parker's beneficiaries would have come from these future wages.

    Answer (D) is incorrect. Generally, the estate can recover damages for wages lost between injury and death.

50. **Answer (B) is the correct answer.** Most courts now recognize a claim for wrongful pregnancy. The trend is to limit recovery to damages for the pregnancy itself, including medical expenses, lost wages and pain and suffering from labor and delivery. However, courts have allowed claims for child-rearing expenses when the child is born with a disability.

    Answer (A) is incorrect. The Pattersons do have a claim for wrongful pregnancy rather than wrongful birth. However, the trend is to reject claims for child-rearing expenses unless the baby is born with a disability. Thus, the Pattersons are not likely to recover their child-rearing expenses unless the baby was born with a disability.

Answer (C) is incorrect. Courts generally have allowed claims for child-rearing expenses when a child is born with a disability.

Answer (D) is incorrect. The avoidable consequences rule only requires the injured party to take reasonable steps to avoid her loss. Requiring a parent to place a child up for adoption would impose an unreasonable burden on the parent. *See Smith v. Gore*, 728 S.W.2d 738, 751–52 (Tenn. 1987).

51. **Answer (A) is the correct answer.** The statute caps damages at the greater of $250,000 or three times economic damages. However, it also further caps damages at a maximum of $350,000 per plaintiff and $500,000 per occurrence. Here, Wendy was awarded $750,000 in economic damages ($250,000 in lost wages + $500,000 in medical expenses). Wendy was awarded $1 million in noneconomic damages (pain and suffering). Harold was awarded $500,000 in noneconomic damages because all of his loss of consortium damages were awarded to compensate for noneconomic losses. Thus, Wendy and Harold were awarded a combined total of $1.5 million in noneconomic damages. Neither Wendy's nor Harold's noneconomic damages exceed three times Wendy's economic damages or $2.25 million. However, both awards exceed the $350,000 limit for each plaintiff. Further, reducing both awards to $350,000 would exceed the $500,000 per occurrence cap. Both awards stem from a single occurrence because both arise from Wendy's use of the defective product. Thus, their combined total even if reduced to $350,000 per plaintiff would exceed the occurrence limit. As such, Wendy and Harold are entitled to a combined award of $500,00 for noneconomic damages, and the jury verdict must be reduced by $1 million to $1.25 million. **This result is found in Answer (A), making Answer (A) the correct answer and Answers (B), (C) and (D) incorrect.**

Topic 5   Answers

Property Damages

52. Hewlett is likely to recover either the $560 pre-tort value of the jalopy or the $60 diminution in value as damages. Hewlett is not likely to recover the cost to repair the jalopy. Generally, courts allow an injured plaintiff to recover the cost to repair damaged property if repairs are both physically and economically feasible. Courts differ as to at what point repairs become economically infeasible. For some courts, repairs become economically infeasible when the cost to repair exceeds the diminution in value to the property. For others, the repairs become economically infeasible when the cost to repair exceeds the pre-tort value. Here, the cost to repair the jalopy exceeds both the $60 diminution in value and the $560 pre-tort value of the jalopy. Thus, Hewlett will not recover the cost to repair under either standard and will recover either $560 or $60 in damages depending on which standard the court applies.

53. **Answer (A) is the correct answer.** Most jurisdictions permit a plaintiff to recover both for the physical damage to property and for the economic loss of the use of the property when property is destroyed. When property is destroyed, the pre-tort market value of the property compensates the plaintiff for the physical injury to the property only. The plaintiff is also entitled to damages for loss of use. However, the plaintiff's damages for loss of use are limited by the duty to mitigate. Thus, the plaintiff can recover damages for loss of use only for that period of time reasonably necessary to replace the destroyed property.

    Answer (B) is incorrect. A plaintiff is entitled to recover damages for loss of use regardless of whether the plaintiff's use of the property was commercial or personal.

    Answer (C) is incorrect. Historically, courts prohibited plaintiffs from recovering loss of use damages for destroyed goods under the theory that the market value of the goods encompassed the right to use the goods. However, most courts now recognize that damages paid to allow the plaintiff to purchase a replacement good, such as the pre-tort market value of the good, do not compensate the plaintiff for the economic loss resulting from the loss of the use of the good while the plaintiff seeks a replacement.

    Answer (D) is incorrect. The plaintiff's total recovery is not capped at the pre-tort value of the good.

54. **Answer (C) is the correct answer.** When a plaintiff has lost goods that fluctuate in value, most jurisdictions follow the "New York rule." The New York rule allows the plaintiff to recover the highest value of the property between the time the plaintiff learns of conversion and the expiration of a reasonable time after the person learns of the conversion. A reasonable time

after the conversion is measured by the time in which it would take a reasonable person with adequate funds to replace the converted goods. Here, Client learned of the conversion on June 1, so Client would be entitled to the highest market value of the stock between June 1 and a reasonable time in which to replace the stock. Because stock can be traded relatively easily and quickly, a reasonable investor likely would have replaced the stock by July 1. The highest price between June 1 and July 1 appears to be $110 per share.

Answer (A) is incorrect. When goods fluctuate in value, most jurisdictions would not limit the plaintiff's recovery to the market price at the time of conversion.

Answer (B) is incorrect. Under the New York rule, the court disregards the market value of the goods between the time of conversion and the time the plaintiff learns of the breach under the theory that if the plaintiff had intended to sell the goods during this period of time, the plaintiff would have learned of the breach sooner.

Answer (D) is incorrect. While the plaintiff has no obligation to replace the converted goods, the plaintiff's recovery is limited to those losses that the plaintiff could not reasonably avoid through cover. Thus, under the New York rule, the plaintiff's recovery is limited to the highest value of the goods between the time the plaintiff learns of the conversion and the reasonable period in which to purchase replacement goods.

55. **Answer (D) is the correct answer.** When clothing and other household items are lost or destroyed, the owner is entitled to recover the actual value of the goods to the owner. In determining the actual value, the trier of fact is to consider the original purchase price, the replacement cost and the age, wear and condition of the goods at the time they were destroyed or lost.

Answer (A) is incorrect. The owner is awarded the actual value to the owner rather than the market value for two reasons. First, the market value of goods such as used clothing is difficult to ascertain. Second, the market value for used clothing does not adequately compensate the owner because the owner is unlikely to replace the lost goods with used or second hand goods.

Answer (B) is incorrect. While the cost to replace the clothing is a factor for the trier of fact to consider, it is not dispositive. Instead, the owner is entitled to the actual value of goods to the owner. Actual value is measured by several factors in addition to the cost to replace.

Answer (C) is incorrect. As with the cost to replace the clothing, the original purchase price is one of the factors for the trier of fact to consider in determining the actual value of the goods to the owner. However, it is not dispositive.

56. **Answer (A) is the correct answer.** An owner is permitted to offer personal testimony as to the value even though not an expert. However, the owner must provide some basis for the opinion other than mere speculation.

Answer (B) is incorrect. Palmer may explain through testimony how he arrived at his opinion as to value. He need not provide supporting documentation.

ANSWERS • TOPIC 5: PROPERTY DAMAGES 125

Answer (C) is incorrect. Even if Palmer is not otherwise an expert in clothing, he is entitled to offer opinion testimony about the value of his own belongings.

Answer (D) is incorrect. A plaintiff need not offer expert testimony as to value. Instead, Palmer may offer his own testimony as to value as long as he also explains his basis for arriving at that value.

57. **Answer (B) is the correct answer.** When property that derives its primary value from sentiment is destroyed, most courts allow the owner to recover the actual value to the owner. However, most courts exclude any consideration of sentimental or emotional value from the measure of actual value. Instead, actual value includes factors such as the cost to replace and the original purchase price. Here, the photograph holds primarily sentimental value for Palmer. Thus, Palmer will be entitled to recover the actual value. However, the jury will be prohibited from considering Palmer's sentimental attachment to the photograph and, instead, will be limited to considering the cost to purchase the film and develop the photograph. The market value of comparable goods may be relevant. However, to be relevant, the market value must be the market value of truly comparable goods. Here, the informal snapshot taken by Palmer's friend is not comparable to professional photographs of the rock star sold to magazines and newspapers. Thus, evidence of their market value likely is not relevant. As such, only the cost of purchasing and developing the film are likely to be considered by the jury. **This result is found in Answer (B), making Answer (B) the correct answer and Answers (A), (C) and (D) incorrect.**

58. If LaSalle Realty does not recover the cost to repair its building, it will not be put in the position it enjoyed prior to Outdoor Advertising's improper conduct. Before Outdoor Advertising installed the sign, LaSalle Realty held real property worth $2 million. If awarded the diminution in value rather than the cost to repair as damages, after Outdoor Advertising's misconduct, LaSalle Realty would hold $2 million in assets. However, LaSalle Realty would hold real property worth only $1.8 million. If LaSalle Realty wished to hold $2 million in real property or wished to hold this particular piece of real property, LaSalle Realty would have to pay the cost to repair the building out of its own pocket or LaSalle Realty would have to sell the building and combine the proceeds from the sale with the damage award to purchase a new $2 million building. This would be particularly inadequate given that real property is considered unique. On the other hand, if LaSalle Realty recovers repair costs in excess of the diminution in value, it may be overcompensated. If LaSalle Realty were to sell the building without making the repairs, the repair costs combined with the sale proceeds would exceed the original fair market value of the building. Thus, LaSalle Realty would reap a windfall. This may be particularly true where a landowner such as LaSalle Realty holds the property for commercial purposes only.

59. **Answer (D) is the correct answer.** Under the Restatement (Second) of Torts § 929 and the accompanying commentary, a landowner is entitled to recover the cost to repair an injury to her land unless that repair cost is disproportionate to the diminution in value. Even when the repair cost is disproportionate to the diminution in value, the owner can recover reasonable

repair costs if the owner has a reason personal to the owner for repairing the land. Courts and commentators have interpreted this to mean that the owner must have a particular reason for restoring the land and that reason must be objectively reasonable. Here, the landowner in Answer (A) is entitled to the cost to repair the sand dune because it does not exceed the diminution in value to the land. Both the homeowner in Answer (B) and the church in Answer (C) are entitled to recover the cost to repair, even though the repair costs exceed the diminution in value because both have objectively reasonable particular reasons for restoring the land. Thus, all three cases support the award of repair costs. **This result is found in Answer (D), making Answer (D) the correct answer and Answers (A), (B) and (C) incorrect.**

60. **Answer (D) is the correct answer.** At common law, when a tree was wrongfully destroyed or removed from a landowner's property, the landowner was entitled to only the market value at the time of removal even if the tree had not yet reached its commercial maturity. Because this measure might undercompensate the landowner who would have otherwise raised the tree to commercial maturity and harvested it at that time, many states have enacted timber trespass statutes that allow a landowner to recover treble damages from a defendant who maliciously, intentionally or willfully removes or destroys a tree.

    Answer (A) is incorrect. Generally, when a tree is wrongfully destroyed or removed from a landowner's property, the landowner's recovery is limited to the market value at the time of removal even if the tree has not yet reached its commercial maturity. Any other measure might overcompensate the landowner and would be speculative.

    Answer (B) is incorrect. Awarding the current market value for mature trees might overcompensate the injured landowner and is speculative. Loud has saved the expense of growing the walnut trees to maturity. Further, Loud may begin re-generating the land sooner than he would have been able to had he grown the walnut trees to maturity. Finally, even if Bunyan had not removed the walnut trees, the trees could have died before they reached maturity or the market price could have dropped before the trees reached maturity.

    Answer (C) is incorrect. Generally, when a tree with commercial value is removed from the landowner's property, the landowner is entitled to the market value at the time of removal rather than the cost to replace the tree.

61. **Answer (A) is the correct answer.** Generally, when shrubs or trees without market value are removed or destroyed, the landowner is entitled to recover only the diminution in value to the land as a result of their destruction because the cost to replace the trees likely exceeds the diminution in value.

    Answer (B) is incorrect. The landowner likely cannot recover the cost to replace the trees because the cost to replace the trees generally exceeds the diminution in value and because awarding the cost to replace when it exceeds the diminution in value would result in economic waste or a windfall to the landowner.

ANSWERS · TOPIC 5: PROPERTY DAMAGES

Answer (C) is incorrect. The original purchase price is not an accurate measure of the harm caused by the later destruction of the property.

Answer (D) is incorrect. A landowner is entitled to recover damages for the destruction of property even if the property has no marketable use.

62. **Answer (C) is correct.** Regardless of the use the landowner intended to make of mineral rights such as those at issue in this problem, the landowner is entitled to damages for the commercial value of minerals that are wrongfully removed from the landowner's land. How a court measures the commercial value of the minerals will vary depending on the landowner's capacity to exploit the minerals for commercial use. Where, as in this case, the landowner lacks the capacity to extract the minerals and bring them to market herself, the plaintiff will be entitled to recover the royalty payments she would have received from licensing the rights to a third party because that is the commercial use the landowner could have made of the minerals but for the tort.

    Answer (A) is incorrect. Regardless of the use the landowner intended to make of mineral rights such as those at issue in this problem, the landowner is entitled to damages for the commercial value of minerals that are wrongfully removed from the landowner's land.

    Answer (B) is incorrect. The cost to remove the well and restore the land would be measures of damages for the injury to the land itself. Parker may be entitled to recover such damages. However, the removal of the minerals constitutes a separate loss. Parker is also entitled to be compensated for the loss of the minerals that have been wrongfully removed.

    Answer (D) is incorrect. A landowner may be entitled to recover the profits that the landowner may have made from the sale of the minerals if the landowner possesses the capacity to have extracted the minerals and brought them to market herself. However, Parker lacks the capacity to do so. As such, she would be limited to the royalty value of the mineral rights.

63. **Answer (D) is correct.** The economic loss rule precludes a plaintiff from recovering for purely economic loss in tort. Here, Homeowner's lost profits are purely economic loss. Homeowner has suffered no property damage or personal injury. Thus, the economic loss rule precludes Homeowner's claims.

    Answer (A) is incorrect. The economic loss rule applies to "stranger" claims even though the plaintiff and defendant are not in privity of contract.

    Answer (B) is incorrect. While a plaintiff can recover in tort for property damage, lost profits are a form of economic loss rather than property damage.

    Answer (C) is incorrect. Courts do recognize an exception to the economic loss rule when the defendant owes a special duty to the plaintiff. However, no such special duty exists in this case.

Topic 6 Answers

Punitive Damages

64. **Answer (B) is the correct answer.** Punitive damages are imposed on a defendant who has engaged in serious misconduct with a bad state of mind. Generally, a defendant must act maliciously, oppressively, wantonly or at least recklessly. Here, the fact that Dirk drove his car into Peterson's house for revenge suggests that Dirk acted intentionally to cause harm to Peterson's house. This, in turn, suggests that Dirk acted maliciously.

    Answer (A) is incorrect. Punitive damages are imposed to punish a defendant for a limited type of misconduct — serious misconduct undertaken with a bad state of mind. A defendant generally must intend to cause harm to the plaintiff or at least act recklessly in the sense that defendant consciously disregard the risk of harm to the plaintiff. Here, while Dirk acted wrongfully in driving while his license was suspended, the act of driving with a suspended license does not demonstrate that Dirk intended to harm Peterson's house or even that Dirk acted recklessly in consciously disregarding a risk of harm to Peterson's house.

    Answer (C) is incorrect. As discussed above, **Answer (A)** would not support the imposition of punitive damages.

    Answer (D) is incorrect. An invasion of only economic rights can rise to the requisite level of misconduct as long as the invasion is sufficiently serious and the defendant acts with the requisite state of mind.

65. Punitive damages are imposed primarily to punish a defendant and to deter the defendant and others from engaging in similar misconduct. Some courts and commentators have recognized some additional non-compensatory functions such as financing the cost of litigation.

66. **Answer (B) is the correct answer.** Although punitive damages are not available in breach of contract cases, punitive damages may be awarded if the conduct constituting a breach of contract also constitutes an independent tort. Bad faith denial of insurance coverage constitutes an independent tort. Therefore, Palmer may be entitled to punitive damages if Palmer succeeds on the bad faith claim.

    Answer (A) is incorrect. Punitive damages are not available for breach of contract claims.

    Answer (C) is incorrect. Punitive damages are not available for breach of contract claims.

    Answer (D) is incorrect. Punitive damages are available in claims involving a contractual relationship if the facts constituting breach of contract also constitute an independent tort.

130   ANSWERS · TOPIC 6: PUNITIVE DAMAGES

67. **Answer (C) is the correct answer.** In most states, a principal such as Big-Mart can be held vicariously liable for punitive damages based on the acts of its agent under two circumstances: (1) if the principal authorized, participated in or ratified the agent's conduct; or (2) if the agent was employed in a managerial capacity. A few states allow a principal to be held vicariously liable for punitive damages based on the acts of its agent so long as the agent acted within the scope of her authority. Under either test, Big-Mart can be held liable either if the employee at issue acted in a managerial capacity or if Big-Mart managers were aware of the practice and failed to stop it. This would demonstrate that the managers condoned or ratified the practice.

Answer (A) is incorrect because it is underinclusive. While Big-Mart may be held vicariously liable if its managers were aware of the discriminatory practice, it also may be held liable if the employee at issue was a manager.

Answer (B) is incorrect because it is underinclusive. While Big-Mart may be held vicariously liable if the employee at issue was a manager, it also may be held liable if its managers were aware of the discriminatory practice and failed to stop it.

Answer (D) is incorrect. As discussed above, employers may be held vicariously liable for punitive damages based on the acts of their employees.

68. **Answer (B) is the correct answer.** Most jurisdictions allow punitive damages for "reckless indifference" or "gross negligence." Under either formulation, jurisdictions allow punitive damages in a products liability action if the defendant had actual knowledge of a defect and acted in bad faith by marketing the product without correcting the known defect or failing to warn consumers of the defect. Here, Neptune had actual knowledge of the defect through its internal testing data and acted in bad faith by marketing the car without taking steps to correct the defect.

Answer (A) is incorrect. While Neptune may be liable for punitive damages if it has engaged in intentional misconduct, intentional misconduct is not necessary. As discussed above, Neptune may be liable for punitive damages if it has acted with reckless indifference or gross negligence.

Answer (C) is incorrect. To be liable for punitive damages, a defendant must engage in something more than simple negligence. In the products liability context, this requires that the defendant have actual knowledge of the defect. Failure to detect a defect is insufficient.

Answer (D) is incorrect. A plaintiff is not prevented from seeking punitive damages in products liability. Even though proof of reckless indifference, gross negligence, or intentional misconduct is not required to prove liability for design defect, a plaintiff is entitled to offer proof of such misconduct. If the plaintiff can prove such misconduct, the plaintiff is entitled to recover punitive damages.

69. **Answer (D) is the correct answer.** Most states permit a jury to consider a defendant's net wealth or financial condition under the theory that a sanction must be greater to punish a wealthy defendant than a poor defendant. The use of financial condition or net wealth has been subject to much criticism recently, including by the Supreme Court. However, the Supreme Court has not prohibited the use of net wealth as a factor, and most courts continue to permit juries to consider net wealth. Indeed, one state, California, has mandated that juries must consider net wealth in determining the size of a punitive damage award. Perhaps more

controversial is the consideration of the plaintiff's litigation costs. Punitive damages are imposed to punish the defendant and deter the defendant and others from engaging in similar misconduct. The plaintiff's litigation costs would seem to have no relationship to these two goals. However, some commentators have recognized financing litigation as an ancillary goal of punitive damages. Additionally, some commentators have justified consideration of litigation costs on deterrence grounds. Awarding litigation costs increases the likelihood that a plaintiff will bring suit. Increasing the likelihood that a plaintiff will bring suit, in turn, deters a defendant from engaging in misconduct. Finally, most states permit a jury to consider the extent of the plaintiff's harm on the ground that the extent of the plaintiff's harm is one indicator of the gravity of the defendant's misconduct. Thus, all of the listed factors are appropriate for a jury to consider in determining an award of punitive damages. Indeed, each factor has been utilized in at least one state. **This result is found in Answer (D), making Answer (D) the correct Answer and Answers (A), (B) and (C) incorrect.**

70. The Court identified three guideposts that indicated that the award in *BMW v. Gore* was grossly excessive: (1) the degree of reprehensibility; (2) the ratio of punitive damages to the amount of harm inflicted on the plaintiff; and (3) the comparison between the punitive damage award and civil and criminal sanctions for comparable misconduct.

71. **Answer (C) is the correct answer.** In *State Farm v. Campbell*, 538 U.S. 408 (2003), the Supreme Court created a presumption against the constitutionality of a punitive damage award that exceeds a single-digit ratio of punitive to compensatory damages. However, the Court also recognized that awards in which the ratio is greater than 9-to-1 may comport with due process if the defendant engages in particularly egregious conduct that results in only slight economic harm. Here, Hospitality Inn has engaged in egregious conduct by knowingly letting guest rooms infested with bedbugs. However, its conduct has produced only slight economic harm. A greater award can be justified here on the grounds that such an award is necessary to prevent the defendant from profiting from its conduct and to encourage victims to bring suit and, hence, deter the defendant from engaging in the misconduct. *See Mathias v. Accor Economy Lodging*, 347 F.3d 672 (7th Cir. 2003).

Answer (A) is incorrect. While the *State Farm* Court recognized that awards exceeding a single-digit ratio rarely comport with due process, the Court did not set up an irrebuttable presumption. Instead, the Court recognized that awards in which the ratio is greater than 9-to-1 may comport with due process if the defendant engages in particularly egregious conduct that results in only slight economic harm.

Answer (B) is incorrect. While Pittman suffered only slight economic injuries, other guests appear to have suffered greater economic injuries as a result of their severe physical injuries. Because they have suffered greater economic injuries, they presumably have greater incentive to sue and are more likely to recover significant compensatory damages, thereby providing an effective deterrent to the defendant's misconduct.

Answer (D) is incorrect. In *State Farm*, the Court recognized that a punitive damage award in a case based on unrelated or dissimilar misconduct could not provide the basis for an increased punitive award.

72. In most jurisdictions, Peters will be entitled to punitive damages because Officer acted with the requisite state of mind by acting knowingly and intentionally and because Peters suffered actual damage as evidenced by the award of nominal damages. A minority of jurisdictions require an injured party to show not only actual harm but also compensatory harm to be entitled to punitive damages. In those jurisdictions, Peters would not be entitled to punitive damages because the jury found that Peters had suffered no compensable harm and, hence, failed to award any compensatory damages.

Topic 7   Answers

Qualifying for Injunctions

73. The court will not grant an injunction. Instead, Poitier can hire someone to fix his lawn; he should save his receipts; and can then sue Dunn Stables for damages. This is because the default remedy in our judicial system is damages, not injunctive relief. More specifically, the irreparable injury rule requires that a plaintiff establish that her legal injury cannot adequately be remedied by damages. Irreparable injury is established where damages are difficult to measure, where the subject of a contract is unique, or where intangible or personal harm is threatened. The rule establishes the doctrinal line between remedies at law and equity, which historically were awarded by different courts with separate jurisdiction.

74. **Answer (D) is the correct answer.** Because damages are the default remedy, the expectation is that someone like Poitier will cure the problem and then sue for damages. To access equitable relief, then, the plaintiff needs facts that make it difficult (or impossible) for them to cure the problem themselves. Accordingly, if there isn't some business that Poitier can hire to remove this statue (because it's heavy or because removal poses some unique danger), then his legal remedies are inadequate and equitable relief may be appropriate.

    Answer (A) is incorrect because clarity about Lewis's motives does not change whether Poitier is entitled to equitable relief. The issue, rather, is whether Poitier's legal remedies are adequate.

    Answer (B) is incorrect because Lewis's culpability does not change whether Poitier is entitled to equitable relief. Again, the issue here is whether Poitier's legal remedies are adequate.

    Answer (C) is incorrect because Lewis's future intentions with respect to others do not change whether Poitier is entitled to equitable relief. Equitable relief is not supposed to be punitive. So here (and with Answers (A) and (B), too), the plaintiff will not get the equitable relief that he seeks by arguing that the defendant should be punished. In fact, such an argument would likely backfire if made expressly.

75. **Answer (B) is the correct answer.** Specific performance of a contract is available where the subject of the contract is unique and cannot easily be replaced on the market. Here, the uniqueness and rarity of the soccer team itself makes it difficult to replace the team on the market. Also, the damage to the civic pride and reputation of the city as a result of the loss of the team would be difficult to measure.

    Answer (A) is incorrect. Specific performance is not always available for breach of contract. Only where the subject of the contract is unique, difficult to replace on the market, or where damages are difficult to measure will the equitable remedy be awarded. Where such uniqueness or difficultly is missing, the contractual party is limited to the remedy of damages.

Answer (C) is incorrect because the burden of supervision on the court is not any more difficult than a routine injunction, as the court will just monitor whether the Aquas play their home games in Municipal Stadium.

Answer (D) is incorrect. The public policy or public interest against the issuance of an injunction is relevant, but must be significant to outweigh the plaintiff's request for a particular injunction. Here, while law and economics scholars favor efficient breaches of contract, the law permits specific performance to enforce contractual promises where damages are inadequate or the subject of the contract is unique.

76. Poseidon's best argument against the issuance of the injunction is that the balance of the hardships weighs against the plaintiff's request for an injunction. First, Poseidon can argue that the City's loss of the team can easily be replaced by monetary damages measured by the amount remaining to be paid on the lease plus any incidental losses to the City. Second, Poseidon will argue that the livelihood and continued existence of the team depend upon his ability to make a profit. Forcing a business to close or go out of business would impose an undue hardship upon a defendant sufficient to outweigh the plaintiff's irreparable injury. Finally, Poseidon might argue that public policy in favor of free market competition favors the denial of the injunction so that the team might breach an inefficient contract and maximize profits through the citizens of Treasure Island.

77. **Answer (A) is the correct answer.** Avoiding a multiplicity of suits is one traditional justification for equitable relief. Dugal should not have to sue Torre every few months for the previous months of interference. Because it appears that Torre has no intention of stopping this behavior (notice what Torre says in the fact pattern), Dugal is entitled to injunctive relief.

    Answer (B) is incorrect because the extent of the damage/injury is irrelevant. The trespass is unlawful whether or not Torre causes substantial or lasting damage.

    Answer (C) is incorrect. To be sure, Dugal's legal remedies may be adequate for the past three months of interference; for that period of time, Dugal's damages are quantifiable, and paying them may, in fact, make Dugal whole. Yet Dugal's legal remedies are inadequate, because it shouldn't have to sue *again* when Torre *again* interferes. This likely prospect of multiple suits makes Dugal's legal remedies inadequate.

    Answer (D) is incorrect because the harm is imminent. Torre has a pattern of conduct, and that pattern is likely to continue.

78. **Answer (A) is the correct answer.** The undue hardship on Kelvin Cline outweighs the harm to plaintiffs. Closing down the factory causes tremendous economic waste by shuttering a factory that produces an economic good, includes significant capital investment, and employs hundreds of people. In addition, plaintiffs' harm is mere annoyance rather than harm to physical health. Where such economic waste outweighs plaintiffs' harm, an injunction will not be granted, and plaintiffs will instead be awarded compensatory damages.

ANSWERS · TOPIC 7: QUALIFYING FOR INJUNCTIONS

Answer (B) is incorrect because there is no undue burden on the court from shutting down the plant, as the order would be a simple, negative injunction that would require no ongoing monitoring or necessary oversight.

Answer (C) is incorrect. To be sure, the interference with the plaintiff's enjoyment of their property is a big deal. (Property rights are rather sacrosanct!) However, given the enormous economic waste that is loaded into the fact pattern, the balance of the hardships surely tips in favor of the defendant, not plaintiffs. To this end, notice also how the plaintiffs are suffering only a perfume smell — not a more odious smell, and also not some physical interference (like acid rain, confetti, dust, etc.).

Answer (D) is incorrect because, although the sequence of events strengthens the neighbors' claim, an order ceasing operation of the plant would impose too severe a hardship, as discussed in Answer (A). These plaintiffs will be expected to accept monetary relief.

79. **Answer (B) is the correct answer.** A prerequisite for issuing injunctions is a real threat of imminent harm. There is no mention of expert (or otherwise compelling) testimony here suggesting that an actionable nuisance is imminent. The Odens' subjective fears are speculative, and thus do not establish a real threat.

    Answer (A) is incorrect because there is insufficient evidence that nuisance (or some other actionable wrong) will occur. Accordingly, there is no legal harm for the court to prevent.

    Answer (C) is incorrect. To be sure, once the building is built, a court is not likely to order that it be torn down (because of the hardship to the defendant) even if it is an actionable nuisance. But that is not a legal reason for qualifying for an injunction.

    Answer (D) is incorrect. The zoning code permits the land use of an apartment building, but it does not authorize nuisances or other interferences with the enjoyment of the neighbors' properties. Therefore the zoning code is not an absolute barrier to an injunction. Rather, to get an injunction, the plaintiffs must first show some violation of the law, which is made more difficult by the authorization of the specific land use.

80. **Answer (B) is the correct answer.** Courts consider public policy or public interest when weighing the factors in favor of an injunction. The policy against forcing an employee to work for an employer, embodied in the Thirteenth Amendment, is a strong legal policy that weighs strongly against the issuance of the injunction in this case. The Nightclub might instead pursue a negative injunction (merely) prohibiting Woo from working for the other club. A court is more likely to grant a negative injunction, because the policy against forced employment is more muted: if enjoined, she might DJ for Nightclub because she can't DJ anywhere else, but she wouldn't be obligated to do so.

    Answer (A) is incorrect. Woo may be famous, but not necessarily unique, as there are other famous DJs. But even assuming that Woo is unique, the public policy against personal servitude outweighs the plaintiff's preference for an injunction in this case.

Answer (C) is incorrect because damages probably won't make Omnium whole. It could be difficult for Omnium to prove with reasonable certainty the full value of an "inventive" DJ to their business operations. Damage to the club's reputation; damage to their related businesses; arguments that the club's profits would have crescendoed over the remaining months of the contract — these will seem highly speculative and thus, perhaps, unrecoverable.

Answer (D) is incorrect. The law does enforce written promises, but usually by the remedy of compensatory damages rather than injunction. The general moral policy of enforcing promises alone is insufficient to qualify for an injunction.

81. Yes, Byun could expect both damages and an injunction. Damages would compensate him for the money he has already lost, and an injunction would prevent further loss. As described here, damages and injunctive relief would not be a double recovery, because the former is retrospective, and the latter is prospective; thus, they do not overlap.

82. **Answer (D) is the correct answer.** A court will issue a preventive injunction to protect the plaintiff against a real threat of imminent harm. Here, the existence of a dangerous animal in a residential neighborhood poses a real threat of imminent harm and assault.

    Answer (A) is incorrect because even though the tigers are the neighbor's property, the neighbor may not lawfully use her property to threaten harm to others.

    Answer (B) is incorrect. Although the tigers have not yet caused harm to anyone, the court need not wait until harm occurs before acting. The serious and imminent danger posed by adult tigers in a residential neighborhood is presumed obvious. All that is required for an injunction is a real threat, not an actual completed event. Courts prefer to avoid personal injury rather than wait for the physical harm to occur. While damages could be awarded to the plaintiff, courts sometimes prefer as a matter of public policy to protect individuals from physical harm — that is, to prevent the damages from occurring in the first instance.

    Answer (C) is incorrect. The rule of strict liability regarding inherently dangerous objects is irrelevant to the question of whether an injunction should issue. While it might help establish the basis for tort liability, the dangerous nature alone does not justify the issuance of an injunction.

83. **Answer (D) is the correct answer.** If equitable relief is required by statute, then a plaintiff is entitled to receive it. A judge would still have considerable discretion, however, in crafting the order. Even when statutes require equitable relief, they seldom specify what — exactly — the court must order.

    Answer (A) is incorrect because the statute has displaced the traditional test. The inadequacy of the legal remedy is the traditional test.

    Answer (B) is incorrect. The supervisory burden is not a disqualifying factor if the statute prescribes it. That said, the supervisory burden will likely influence what — exactly — the court includes in that order.

    Answer (C) is incorrect. The availability of equitable relief is an issue for the judge, not the jury.

Topic 8 — Answers

Injunctions

84. **Answer (B) is the correct answer.** A preventive injunction seeks to prevent future harm by stopping the current illegality. This preventive measure requires Macrocorp to stop the current illegality, thereby preventing the same legal harm in the future.

    Answer (A) is incorrect. This is a prophylactic provision designed to impose an additional, precautionary measure on Macrocorp of requiring a revised, standardized contract for future transactions. A judge might order this, but we wouldn't call it a preventive injunction.

    Answer (C) is incorrect because it is a structural injunctive measure designed to address the illegality inherent in the structure of the company itself, which is too big and too powerful to act competitively in the market. Again, a judge might order this; but the question asks about a preventive injunction.

    Answer (D) is incorrect because it is a reparative measure that seeks to reverse or repair the past illegality by ordering corrective measures to the existing licensing. This is not a preventive injunction.

85. **Answer (B) is the correct answer.** Prophylactic injunctions, like prophylactic medicine, require the defendant to take extra steps or safeguards to ensure against the repetition of future harm. An employer who has engaged in pervasive employment discrimination, for example, might be ordered to install an ombudsperson or to post certain data on its corporate website. *But for* the (prophylactic) injunction, the absence of an ombudsperson or the failure to report certain data on the website would not be unlawful.

    Answer (A) is incorrect because it defines preventive injunctions.

    Answer (C) is incorrect because it defines reparative injunctions.

    Answer (D) is incorrect. Prophylactic injunctions are valid types of injunctions that can be issued by the courts—often in combination with other injunctions.

86. **Answer (C) correct.** The portion of the court order that keeps the protestors off the Lab's premises is a preventive measure that is designed to stop the ongoing harm in the future—that is, to prevent a trespass (which would harm plaintiff). The portion of the order that establishes a buffer zone (of 35 feet) is a prophylactic measure that establishes additional safeguards. The buffer between the protestors and the lab employees will help prevent trespass and assaults. But it's prophylactic in the sense that, *but for* the injunction, it would not be unlawful for a protestor to stand 5 feet from the lab's property.

Answer (A) is incorrect because it is not repairing prior harm done.

Answer (B) is incorrect because this injunction lacks the ambition and magnitude of a structural injunction; nor is it repairing prior harm done

Answer (D) is incorrect because it lacks the ambition and magnitude of a structural injunction. To be sure, there is no clear demarcation between an ordinary injunction and a structural injunction. But structural injunctions are those that challenge the limits of the judicial function. Structural injunctions typically present constitutional dilemmas, involve public (or other critical) institutions, and require extensive and ongoing judicial supervision.

87. First, preventive measures seek to stop the harm. On these facts, an example would be an order requiring Grant to cease the sexual harassment. Next, reparative measures seek to undo or reverse the continuing consequences of the harm: the court could order the firm to remove the adverse notation from her personnel file. Finally, the firm could also be ordered to comply with prophylactic measures that would provide additional safeguards to address the facilitators of the harm. For example, the firm could be ordered to draft a sexual harassment policy, establish a confidential employee grievance procedure, or train managers how to properly handle complaints of harassment.

88. **Answer (D) is the correct answer.** The illegality is the exclusion of men from Clarion, and thus, the appropriate injunctive measure that will stop that continued exclusion and restore the individual male plaintiffs to their rightful position is to allow them to apply. This was the relief ordered by the U.S. Supreme Court in a similar case involving Virginia Military Institute (VMI). *United States v. Virginia*, 518 U.S. 515 (1996) (*VMI*).

    Answer (A) is incorrect because a parallel-but-separate educational opportunity does not rectify the precise harm found by the court of unconstitutional exclusion. However, this was the relief originally ordered by the court of appeals in the *VMI* case, and the relief that one Supreme Court Justice found to be appropriate.

    Answer (B) is incorrect because eliminating the entire school is overbroad. It reaches beyond the harm of excluding male students.

    Answer (C) is incorrect because it, like Answer (B), is overbroad. This remedy reaches beyond the exclusionary harm of the gender discrimination in the admissions policy. Again, in the real *VMI* case, this was the option sought to be achieved voluntarily by the school alumni, because a *private* college would not be a state actor and thus would not be subject to the Equal Protection Clause.

89. The term "structural" injunction was first used in the 1970s to describe injunctions issued by courts in public law cases involving prisons, schools, and mental institutions. These injunctions seemed to differ from common forms of injunctive relief in their scope and in the detail by which they governed many aspects of the day to day functioning of the defendant public institutions. There are three main (overlapping) arguments against structural injunctions. First, it is asserted that judges are engaging in policymaking by inserting their own subjective

views of how public institutions should be run. For example, when a judge orders a school to be desegregated, she might decide that the school needs to fund a tennis team (but not necessarily a debate team), put computers in 70% of the classrooms (but not necessarily 75%), bus kids who live 2.5 miles from some landmark (but not if they live 2.6 miles away). The second argument against structural injunctions is that they violate principles of federalism, because it is usually federal courts dictating to state agencies how to manage their institutions. Finally, the third argument against structural injunctions is that, in issuing this relief, courts invade the separation of powers with executive and legislative branches by overreaching their realm of control by dictating the daily management of governmental functions.

90. **Answer (C) is the correct answer.** The structural injunction here is invalid because it is too broad in scope: it reaches myriad aspects of the prison law library that are unrelated to and disconnected from the legal harm of one illiterate inmate being denied access to the court. *See Lewis v. Casey*, 518 U.S. 343 (1996) (holding of a unanimous Court).

    Answer (A) is incorrect. This is a correct statement of the legal rule that the scope of injunctive relief must match the scope of the harm. However, the application of the rule to the facts shows that the injunction here is too broad in scope because it orders relief unconnected to the proven harm.

    Answer (B) is incorrect. As prospective relief, all injunctions must be necessary to prevent future harm. Put differently, the proposed measure suffers from "mission creep" in that the remedy ventures beyond the substantive violation that was litigated. (The propriety of the lighting, the hours, and the noise presumably were not litigated.) Even prophylactic measures must address the underlying substantive harm.

    Answer (D) is incorrect. Terms of injunctive relief do not need to be constitutionally required where they are prophylactic relief designed to remedy or prevent harm that is constitutionally protected. Prophylactic injunctions provide additional safeguards to address the facilitators of harm, where the prophylactic terms are causally connected to the underlying harm. Here, it is not the content of the injunctive terms that makes the relief invalid, but rather their lack of a nexus to the underlying harm.

91. **Answer (D) is the correct answer.** Specific performance, or an injunction ordering the seller to perform the contract, is available here because Spice's flavorings are unique. The UCC provides that specific performance is available as a remedy for the breach of a contract for the sale of goods where the goods are unique. The uniqueness of the goods is established here by the buyer's inability to find similar flavorings on the market and the distinctiveness of the combination of flavorings.

    Answer (A) is incorrect because it denies the injunction and awards incidental damages in the amount of reliance. While incidental damages caused by the defendant's breach are available under the UCC for breaches of contracts for the sale of goods, specific performance would be available here due to the uniqueness of the flavorings, which cannot be replaced on the market.

Answer (B) is incorrect because specific performance is available to Read Bull, and future lost profits as a measure of consequential damages flowing from the breach of contract are likely speculative and unforeseeable and thus not recoverable.

Answer (C) is incorrect because it awards duplicative remedies for Read Bull's future losses. A plaintiff cannot receive double remedies for the same loss. Here, the answer awards an injunction to avoid future loss but then also awards money in the amount of future lost profits.

92. **Answer (A) is the correct answer.** A defendant may seek modification of an injunction, when there are significant changed circumstances of fact or law. Here, the changed factual circumstances arguably provide a basis for him to seek modification.

    Answer (B) is incorrect because the standard for terminating an injunction is not changed circumstances, but rather requires a good faith compliance with a substantial portion of the injunction.

    Answer (C) is incorrect because it mixes the standard for termination (substantial, good faith performance) with the process of modification.

    Answer (D) is incorrect. While the answer states the correct standard for termination of an injunction, Masterman has only partially removed the levee: "Masterman retains more water than he would have if the levee were fully removed."

93. **Answer (C) is the correct answer.** Rocky may seek an injunction against the court to prevent it from requiring the counseling treatment. Mandamus is a more specific type of injunctive relief, defined as an injunction issued against a judicial or public official directing the official to perform some act which the law obligates the official to perform. Thus, Rocky may also seek the more specific common-law injunctive remedy of mandamus against the court. Declaratory relief also would be appropriate if Rocky wanted to obtain a judicial declaration that the counseling treatment was unconstitutional. The strategic advantage of the declaratory judgment would be that it would not order the sentencing judge to engage in specific conduct, as would an injunction, and thus might avoid any perceived animosity from the judge.

    Answer (A) is incorrect because it is incomplete. Rocky may seek an injunction, but he may also request mandamus and/or declaratory relief. Thus, (C) is the better, more complete answer.

    Answers (B) and (D) are incorrect because they include contempt as a possible option for Rocky. Contempt is not available here, because it is an ancillary remedy used to enforce a pre-existing order with which the defendant has failed to comply. Here, there is no prior injunction against the court which the sentencing judge has failed to follow. While Rocky himself might be held in contempt for failing to complete the counseling program as ordered, he cannot obtain the remedy against the judge in the absence of a previous order directing the judge's behavior.

Topic 9 Answers

Temporary and Preliminary Injunctions

94. **Answer (C) is the correct answer.** A temporary restraining order (or temporary injunction) is a bridge to a preliminary junction. A temporary restraining order will (in federal court) last for up to 14 (or 28) days. During this time, Shoe Co. will want to seek a preliminary injunction.

    Answer (A) is incorrect because, even with the lack of specificity, irreparable injury is still imminent.

    Answer (B) is incorrect because there may not be enough time to complete a preliminary injunction hearing before Kix releases the offending shoes into the marketplace. Shoe Co. could—and should—request a temporary restraining order *and* a preliminary injunction in the prayer for relief in its complaint. The temporary restraining order would then protect Shoe Co. until the preliminary injunction hearing occurs and the relief ordered.

    Answer (D) is incorrect because the plaintiff is not *automatically* entitled to equitable relief. Plaintiffs typically must demonstrate a threat of imminent irreparable injury.

95. **Answer (B) is the correct answer.** According to Federal Rule 65(b)(4), the defendant may move to dissolve the temporary restraining order. When ruling on that motion, the court will likely either (1) convert the temporary restraining order into a preliminary injunction or (2) dissolve the temporary restraining order because no form of equitable relief is necessary. Typically, a defendant is motivated to seek dissolution of the order because compliance is a hardship. Here, for example, the school is compelled to accommodate a dangerous student. Moreover, plaintiffs, too, typically are motivated to get a preliminary injunction before the TRO expires.

    Answer (A) is incorrect because a temporary restraining order would typically last for only 14 (or 28) days. *See* Fed. R. Civ. P. 65(b)(2). If equitable relief is moot 50 days hence, it would be the terminus of a preliminary injunction, not a temporary restraining order.

    Answer (C) is incorrect because a temporary restraining order would typically last for only 14 (or 28) days. *See* Fed. R. Civ. P. 65(b)(2). Only a preliminary injunction (not a temporary restraining order) could last until there is a trial on the merits and a final judgment.

    Answer (D) is incorrect. To be sure, the length of a temporary restraining order is "not to exceed 14 days." *See* Fed. R. Civ. P. 65(b)(2). Yet Answer (D) is not the best answer. For the reasons expressed in the explanation to Answer (B), above, plaintiffs and defendants will rarely sit idle for 14 days. Plaintiff runs the risk of the TRO expiring. And defendants want to communicate the hardship they are suffering. Another reason that this isn't the best answer is that the 14-day period can be doubled; judges who grant a 14-day TRO may be inclined to extend the order for an additional 14 days.

96. **Answer (B) is the correct answer.** Federal Rule of Civil Procedure 65, as interpreted by the Supreme Court, requires that a party requesting temporary relief make efforts to notify the adverse party of the request for temporary relief. When such efforts are unsuccessful, the rule does allow the court to issue a TRO *ex parte* if the reasons for the lack of notice are explained.

    Answer (A) is incorrect. The protestors do pose an immediate threat of harm given their past violent behavior towards people and property and their scheduled continuation of the protest.

    Answer (C) is incorrect. While actual notice to the defendant is not absolutely required for a temporary injunction, efforts to notify the defendant must be made. If that notice is ineffective, then the moving party must explain to the court why the temporary injunction can issue despite the lack of notice.

    Answer (D) is incorrect. It is true that *ex parte* injunctions (where only one party appears before the judge) are authorized by law. However, a moving party must qualify for such relief by making efforts to notify the defendant and by demonstrating immediate and irreparable harm. The failure to attempt notice here disqualifies the police from seeking temporary relief.

97. **Answer (D) is the correct answer.** An "*ex parte*" or one-sided order is issued by the court in the presence of only one party. Generally, a party may obtain a temporary restraining order *ex parte* only if it has attempted to provide notice to the adverse party. There are narrow exceptions to that general rule, but none of the scenarios offered in Answers (A), (B), and (C) would justify granting Finite's motion *ex parte*.

    Answer (A) is incorrect because the gravity of the harm is not a substitute for the due process requirement of notice. Even if the plush animals present a serious public health risk, Finite's lawyer could give notice to Stuffies' lawyer on her way to the courthouse to request the temporary restraining order. Stuffies may be unable to prepare fully for the hearing, Stuffies' participation in the hearing might be virtual, and/or the hearing might be abbreviated. But it is a non sequitur to deny Stuffies of notice merely because of the public health risk.

    Answer (B) is incorrect because Stuffies' culpability (in this or in other matters) is not a substitute for the due process requirement of notice.

    Answer (C) is incorrect. To be sure, proceeding *ex parte* is appropriate in a narrow class of cases where notice would lead the enjoined party to hide or destroy evidence. This exception is usually stated as something like: notice to the defendant would render fruitless the further prosecution of the action. (The other common exception to the notice requirement is impossibility — that is, when the identity of the defendant is unknown or cannot be located.) However, in Answer (C), we are told only that Finite "alleges" that Stuffies might destroy or conceal their infringing goods and records relating to those goods if they are given notice of the relief requested. An allegation alone will not suffice, however; the petitioner must offer evidence. If conclusory allegations by counsel were sufficient, then *ex parte* orders would be the norm, and this practice would undercut the notice requirements of Rule 65 (and the Due Process Clause).

98. The court will issue a preliminary injunction when: (1) the plaintiff is likely to succeed on the merits favors plaintiff; (2) the plaintiff shows irreparable injury during the pendency of trial; (3) the balance of the hardships between the parties weighs in favor of the plaintiff; and (4) the granting of the injunction advances the public interest.

99. **Answer (D) is the correct answer.** Without the means to buy replacement materials and hire a new contractor, Marjan cannot complete the remodeling of the restaurant unless the injunction is granted. This loss of business due to SVN's unlawful actions can be an irreparable injury. Put differently, Marjan is not seeking an injunction to compensate it for financial loss due to SVN's breach, but rather to prevent further injury to the business.

    Answer (A) is incorrect. SVN's bad faith may affect its liability, but not the adequacy of Marjan's legal remedy. The call of the question asks for facts that bolster the argument that Marjan will suffer an irreparable injury.

    Answer (B) is incorrect. The onset of the busy season affects the quantum of Marjan's damages, but not their irreparability. If Marjan had the means to pay for new materials and a substitute contractor, he would be denied injunctive relief; he would be expected to purchase new materials, hire a replacement contractor, save his receipts, and then recover all of his provable damages.

    Answer (C) is incorrect. The proffered fact would help establish the *imminence* of Marjan's injury, but not its irreparability. Again, if Marjan had the means to pay for new materials and a substitute contractor, he would be expected to use them and would be denied interlocutory relief.

100. **Answer (C) is the correct answer.** One of the prerequisites for a preliminary injunction is a likelihood (or a "reasonable likelihood") of success on the merits.

    Answer (A) is incorrect because *plausibility* is not the standard. Plausibility is instead a term that describes the pleading standard under Federal Rules of Civil Procedure 8(a)(2) and 12(b)(6).

    Answer (B) is incorrect. To be sure, some courts have used "serious question" as the threshold showing in circumstances where the plaintiff is exposed to an especially grave and irreparable harm. These courts apply what is referred to as a "sliding scale": the prerequisites of irreparable injury and likelihood of success on the merits are viewed in tandem, and an excess of either one can compensate for a deficiency in the other. But the U.S. Supreme Court's decision in *Winter v. Natural Resources Defense Council, Inc.*, 555 U.S. 7 (2008), cast doubt on the sliding-scale approach, and most (but not all) courts have shied away from it. If you were litigating the instant case in a jurisdiction that has stubbornly clung to the sliding scale, "serious questions going to the merits" would be enough if, but only if, Medallion's irreparable injury is especially pronounced. While the ordinance would be fatal to Medallion's yellow pages directories business, this is only one of the company's three main sources of revenue. Will the company collapse? Is the yellow pages business a profit center? Can the business do something different with these resources? How many people would be laid off? Without details like this in the fact pattern, it is difficult to make the case for especially grave and irreparable harm.

Answer (D) is incorrect because Medallion doesn't need a "strong" likelihood of success — but rather only a likelihood of success. There is an ordered difference between the two standards (with "strong likelihood" requiring more than "likelihood") even if it would be difficult to quantify that difference with precision.

101. **Answer (C) is the correct answer.** Ulla may obtain a preliminary injunction to enjoin Kronel from violating her privacy while the litigation is pending. She has filed her complaint and can show irreparable harm from Kronel's continued invasions of her privacy.

    Answer (A) is incorrect because the threat of harm is not imminent enough to warrant a temporary restraining order. While Kronel has violated her rights in the past, he has not committed any violation in the past few weeks, nor are there any facts showing a particularized threat in the upcoming week. Temporary relief only enjoins harm that is threatened before the time the adverse party can be fully and fairly heard in opposition at a hearing.

    Answer (B) is incorrect because the court would not order both of these at the same time. A temporary restraining order is a bridge to a preliminary injunction. A judge may order both types of relief in the same case, but would do so in sequence, not at the same time.

    Answer (D) is incorrect because at this initial stage of the litigation, Ulla will be unable to obtain a permanent injunction. Permanent relief is not available until the merits are resolved.

102. **Answer (B) the correct answer.** Because this is about money, Bunnik has a legal remedy — and it seems adequate. In the fact pattern, the plaintiff camouflages somewhat the true nature of her request by requesting an order requiring Venago to pay the provider of the temporary housing. But whether or not the payment runs through Bunnik's hands, it's still just money. That said, if Bunnik has no money, and will be evicted from temporary housing and live on the streets if Venago doesn't continue paying, then Bunnik may have the irreparable injury that is a prerequisite to injunctive relief. However, there is no hint of that situation here, especially since Bunnik's ownership of a "beautiful suburban house" may suggest that she has resources.

    Answer (A) is incorrect because Bunnik appears to have coverage unless the Earth Movement exclusion applies. The fact pattern instructs that the house was damaged by vibration, not by some natural force. Bunnik may or may not win this suit at trial, but at this stage, she seems likely (enough) to succeed.

    Answer (C) is incorrect because the balance of hardships tips in favor of granting preliminary relief. For Venago, paying for Bunnik's temporary housing is just another check for this "prominent insurer." By contrast, even if Bunnik has financial resources, it could be a burden to pay, month after month, thousands of dollars for temporary housing.

    Answer (D) is incorrect because it is not in the public interest to deny Bunnik coverage for the cost of her temporary housing. Defense counsel might argue that requiring Venago to pay is the sort of excessive behavior that raises insurance rates for all purchasers of home insurance. But plaintiff should prevail on this element, since it is in the public interest to err on the side of caution and protect a consumer who is already inconvenienced and suffering, rather than protect an insurance company.

ANSWERS • TOPIC 9: TEMPORARY AND PRELIMINARY INJUNCTIONS

103. **Answer (B) is the correct answer.** The black letter law states that the basic goal of a preliminary injunction is to preserve the status quo while the parties litigate the case. Determining the status quo is sometimes difficult when a party, like Stephan, has changed his behavior just prior to the initiation of the lawsuit. Courts thus look for the last uncontested or agreed upon status quo. Here, that last uncontested position would be Stephan selling snacks at the First and Main location where he worked for four years without university complaint.

Answer (A) is incorrect because it is overbroad in going beyond the scope of the alleged illegality of selling in the licensed library area. In addition, this injunction alters the status quo prior to the completion of litigation conclusively determining the legal rights of the parties.

Answers (C) and (D) are incorrect because neither of these orders would return the parties to the last uncontested status quo. Stephan could find some other location on campus that is not at Second and Elm (or that is more than x feet from the library yet not at First and Main). Placement of his cart there might also be a trespass; thus, an injunction with this scope may not adequately protect the university and is an invitation for more squabbling.

104. **Answer (B) is correct.** Federal Rule of Civil Procedure 65(c) requires that a plaintiff post an injunction bond prior to obtaining temporary or preliminary relief. (Many states have similar rules mandating injunction bonds for provisional relief.) The security must be "an amount that the court considers proper to pay the costs and damages sustained by any party found to have been wrongfully enjoined or restrained." Courts traditionally have considerable leeway in setting this amount, as equitable principles tend to reject hard formulae.

Answer (A) is incorrect because judges have broad discretion. And the exercise of discretion here would be informed by the fact that the state is not reliant on the bond to be made whole if the plaintiff loses its suit. Unlike, say, a defendant who is wrongfully enjoined from releasing a product into the marketplace (and must recoup the damages of that wrongful delay from the bond), *this* defendant will simply be able to collect the tax deficiency upon the conclusion of the litigation. Accordingly, a modest (or even nominal) bond might be enough to protect the state's interest here.

Answer (C) is incorrect because bonds are required by Federal Rule 65: "The court may issue a preliminary injunction or a temporary restraining order *only if* the movant gives security in an amount that the court considers proper to pay the costs and damages sustained" by a defendant who was enjoined until they ultimately prevailed in the litigation. To be sure, judges occasionally waive the requirement of a bond when it would be oppressive or unfair; but there is no allowance for that in the rule. Bonds have a pay-to-play component. Some view this as a bug in the system that provides for equitable relief, while others see it as a feature.

Answer (D) is incorrect. To be sure, Federal Rule 65 relieves the U.S. government from the requirement to give security. But on the stated facts, it is the plaintiff Indian tribes that are seeking the injunctive relief, and thus them (not the state government) that must post the bond.

Topic 10　　　　　　　　　　　　　　　　　　　　　　　Answers

Contempt

105. **Answer (D) is the correct answer** because the party has willfully engaged in contumacious behavior. To be clear, even a defendant involved in *civil* litigation may be found responsible for *criminal* contempt.

    Answer (A) is incorrect because contempt requires willful, intentional conduct, which is not established here by the accidental underpayment of money.

    Answer (B) is incorrect because, while the company is under an obligation generally to produce all relevant documents, in the absence of a specific court directive to produce the identified document, it is unlikely that a court would find the requisite willful intent necessary to establish a contempt violation. Under the stated circumstances, a court may instead impose a sanction under Fed. R. Civ. P. 37.

    Answer (C) is incorrect because the company is under no court order to adopt such polices. Although the company appears to have violated the law, punishment *for contempt* would be inappropriate.

106. **Answer (C) is the correct answer** because criminal contempt can trigger a fine and/or a jail term (and/or some other punishment).

    Answers (A) and (B) are incorrect because a court could order a fine, a jail term, or both of these punishments.

    Answer (D) is incorrect. To be sure, there is some validity in the sentiment that judges generally impose the minimum punishment necessary to achieve the desired result. But criminal contempt can lead to a punishment of a fine and/or a jail term as the judge deems appropriate.

107. **Answer (A) is correct** because the conduct dishonored the court and occurred in the presence of the judge. Even a modest fine is a *criminal* penalty when imposed under circumstances like these.

    Answer (B) is incorrect because the conduct occurred *directly* before the judge.

    Answer (C) is incorrect because Bunker is being punished for conduct that has already occurred. She has no opportunity to avoid or purge this punishment. That Bunker's punishment is a fine (as opposed to a jail term) does not make this a *civil* contempt. Bunker's contempt is *criminal,* no matter the type or magnitude of the punishment.

Answer (D) is incorrect because the court's authority is not limited to holding *parties* in contempt. Indeed, a court may hold a lawyer (or witness or juror or anyone in the courtroom) in contempt if they engage in contumacious willfully disobedient or disrespectful behavior.

108. **Answer (B) is correct** because criminal contempt requires a willful violation of a court order, and an order that is vague cannot be willfully violated.

    Answer (A) is incorrect because criminal contempt can be used to punish violations of consent decrees. A consent decree is an order of the court even though its terms were drafted (and agreed upon) by the parties. A party will often seek a consent decree (rather than merely sign a settlement agreement) to ensure that it can be enforced through the power of contempt.

    Answer (C) is incorrect because of limitations on a court's authority to hold someone in contempt. Criminal contempt requires the full range of criminal procedures such as the right to counsel, right to jury trial, right against self-incrimination, and proof beyond a reasonable doubt. Due process requires these procedures because of potential arbitrariness of a judge who is enforcing her own order against a violator. There is concern that a judge might be overly punitive simply because it is her own command, rather than that of the legislature or another judge, that has been disobeyed. In addition, the procedural safeguards address the potential abuse of power inherent in contempt where the traditional separation of powers is omitted and the judge embodies lawmaker, decisionmaker, and executioner in one. Due process will not tolerate a criminal sanction for violating the "spirit" of some mandate.

    Answer (D) is incorrect because bad faith is not the standard for holding someone in criminal contempt. Criminal contempt requires a willful violation of a specific court order.

109. **Answer (C) is the correct answer.** This is civil coercive contempt, because the defendant is able to purge the contempt remedy and avoid any consequence by complying with the court's order. She holds the "keys to the jail" in her pocket.

    Answer (A) is incorrect. Summary contempt is immediate punishment for a threat to the court's authority.

    Answer (B) is incorrect. Criminal contempt punishes the defendant for a past violation of an order with a fixed, determinate sentence. Here, McDonagal's sentence is indeterminate and designed to force future compliance.

    Answer (D) is incorrect. Civil compensatory contempt imposes a monetary fine for past harm caused (with the money paid to the harmed party).

110. **Answer (C) is the correct answer.** It appears that Sherman wasn't even invited to be heard before the punishment was imposed, much less receive the full range of criminal procedures (such as the right to counsel, right to jury trial, right against self-incrimination, and proof beyond a reasonable doubt) to which one is entitled before they can be held in criminal contempt.

    Answer (A) is incorrect because the finding of a willful violation must be found within the context of the full range of criminal procedural protections. The "no excuses" language in the order is no preemptive substitute for due process.

Answers (B) and (D) are incorrect because this is not an instance of civil coercive contempt. After day 90, Sherman does not have the ability to purge the contempt remedy; instead it is a fine for past behavior and thus is criminal contempt. The legal problem arises when the judge creates a hybrid contempt remedy, such as this one, that mixes characteristics of criminal and civil remedies thus threatening the legitimacy of the contempt remedy. Merely announcing the penalty in advance does not convert a criminal contempt into a civil contempt.

111. Defendants can challenge the validity of the injunction, arguing that the language was vague and imprecise, giving improper notice of expected conduct. They can establish that there was not a willful violation, or that they were unable to comply. Alternatively, they can seek a modification of the injunction to better fit the actual circumstances that the defendants find themselves in. Or defendants can seek to terminate the injunction based upon their good faith and substantial compliance over time.

112. **Answer (A) is the correct answer** because the court's power of summary contempt allows the judge to take measures to control the courtroom without further procedures.

    Answers (B) and (C) are incorrect because the procedures for (indirect) civil contempt are not required when the authority of the court is directly threatened.

    Answer (D) is incorrect because, when conduct appears in the presence of the court, the summary contempt power authorizes immediate action.

113. **Answer (C) is the correct answer** because both (A) and (B) are solid arguments. **Answer (A)** is a solid argument because, even when some contempt sanction is appropriate the sanction imposed can be challenged as an abuse of discretion. In fixing the amount of a fine, for example, the exercise of discretion requires a court to consider to the amount necessary to secure compliance, the contemnor's financial resources, the seriousness of the conduct, and the burden. **Answer (B)** may also be worth raising on appeal, since the assessment of a mounting fine when imposed upon defendants after the occurrence of the act becomes fixed and unavoidable and thus arguably constitutes criminal contempt. This argument channels *International Mine Workers v. Bagwell*, 512 U.S. 821 (1994), where the Court essentially reclassified as criminal contempt a series of fines that were nominally civil coercive. In *Bagwell*, however, the Court emphasized the complexity of the injunction, the importance of elaborate fact-finding, and the magnitude of the monetary penalty. The facts of this case are less compelling (than in *Bagwell*).

    Answer (D) is incorrect because the appellant could succeed on appeal by pursuing the arguments raised in Answer (A) and/or Answer (B).

114. **Answer (D) is the correct answer** because this is a classic case of civil compensatory contempt: Nabors is being compensated in an amount that corresponds with her loss caused by Hislop's contempt.

    Answer (A) is incorrect because this is not criminal contempt. Hislop is not being punished, so the protections of criminal procedure are unnecessary.

Answer (B) is incorrect because "good faith" is not a defense to civil compensatory contempt. Hislop's intentions would be probed coincident to a finding of criminal contempt, but that is not the situation here.

Answer (C) is incorrect because the collateral bar doctrine does not apply to findings of civil compensatory contempt. Generally speaking, the collateral bar doctrine applies to *criminal* contempt.

Topic 11 Answers

Unjust Enrichment

115. **Answer (A) is the correct answer.** A restitution theory of recovery does not apply here because there is no unjust enrichment to the defendant. Builder has not received a profit or gain unjustly at plaintiff's expense. The problem with the non-conforming building and the additional remodeling expenses involves a loss to Joe that is addressed by compensatory damages.

    Answer (B) is incorrect. Irreparable injury is a requirement for injunctive relief. If Joe had suffered irreparable injury, he would be able to seek equitable relief in the form of an injunction or equitable restitution (*i.e.*, constructive trust or equitable lien). However, those remedial options are not what Joe is seeking in this case nor has he established that damages or legal restitution are inadequate to redress his injury.

    Answer (C) is incorrect because if Joe wanted to punish Builder for the loss caused, Joe would seek punitive damages rather than restitution. In addition, punitive damages are not available for breach of contract and require the existence of a tort claim.

    Answer (D) is incorrect. Restitution is not based upon plaintiff's loss, but is focused on defendant's gain. If Joe wants money to compensate for his losses, he would seek compensatory damages.

116. **Answer (C) is the correct answer.** Landlord can sue in quasi-contract to obtain restitution for the Tenant's unauthorized use of the machine. Quasi-contract is a fictional theory that implies a contract at law as a basis for awarding monetary relief.

    Answer (A) is incorrect. Quantum meruit is a restitution theory seeking recovery for the value of a plaintiff's services unjustly conferred upon the defendant. Here, Landlord has not conferred a service upon the Tenant.

    Answer (B) is incorrect. Constructive trust is an equitable restitution theory that implies a fictional trust and holds the defendant accountable as a trustee for the benefits accrued from the wrongdoing. Constructive trust generally requires fraud and the use of the plaintiff's specific property. Here, there is no fraud or breach of trust involved in the dispute, and thus constructive trust would not be an appropriate theory.

    Answer (D) is incorrect. Rescission is a restitution theory that cancels the contract and returns the parties to their original pre-contract positions. Here, there is no actual contract regarding the use of the machine to cancel.

117. All of these measures are potential measurements of relief in restitution cases. The appropriateness of a measure depends upon which measurement best fits the facts and theory of the case and that which disgorges all of the benefit to the culpable defendant. Here, the operative theory of restitution is quasi-contract and contract measures generally look to an objective market measure of the worth of the item at issue. Thus, the market rental or purchase value of the machine would be a common default measure in this case. The market value of the entire machine best fits the facts of the case as Tenant converted the entire machine for its use. However, because plaintiff elected restitution instead of damages for the tort of conversion, a court would not limit him to a damages-like measure. In addition, the use of a market measure of a ten-year-old depreciated machine would not disgorge the full benefit from the culpable defendant who converted the machine. Thus, **Answers (A) and (B) are incorrect**. A profit measure that disgorges the benefit gained by the defendant from the machine would be more appropriate. The profits would be apportioned to disgorge only that measure of profits associated with the wrong, the **correct answer as indicated in Answer (C)**. Thus, the profits made from the design and marketing of the product indicated in **Answer (D) is incorrect** and would not be an appropriate measure.

118. Quantum meruit is a claim to recover the value of services rendered. It is a more specialized subset of the general claim of quasi-contract which is an implied at law contract for the value of the benefit gained by the defendant. Here, the more specific action of quantum meruit is appropriate for Artista to seek recovery of the value of her design services provided to the University. Thus, **Answers (A) and (B) are incorrect**. Under the majority rule, if she sues for quantum meruit for partial performance of a contract, she is not suing under the contract and thus the value of her services is not measured by the value of the contract ($5000). The objective value of her services can be measured by her actual cost of $9000 worth of actual services rendered. *See Boomer v. Muir*, 24 P.2d 570 (Cal. Ct. App. 1933). This is a situation of a "losing contract," where a party has entered into a contract that, if performed, would lose her money. By virtue of the cancellation of the contract and her partial performance, the plaintiff gains an opportunity to sue in restitution for the value of the services rendered under the theory that the design work was intended for University's benefit. Thus, the **best answer here is Answer (D)** that Artista can sue in quantum meruit for the $9000 and **Answer (C) is incorrect**. It should be noted that a few jurisdictions would limit Artista's recovery to the value of the contract ($5000) to preclude any windfall above the contract expectancy. A few other jurisdictions would measure her services by the contract value of $5000 and limit her to recovery of 90% ($4500) of that for her partial performance.

119. **Answer (B) is the correct answer.** In order for a unilateral mistake to be the basis for rescission, that mistake must be known or should have been known to the other side. Here, the mathematical error was Bionicle's unilateral mistake, but it was not known to Lego. Furthermore, the fact that Bionicle's bid was $25,000 lower than the other bids of $200,000 is insufficient to establish that Lego should have known of the mistake.

Answer (A) is incorrect because the fact that the mistake was made before the time of the bid is irrelevant to the availability of rescission.

ANSWERS · TOPIC 11: UNJUST ENRICHMENT

Answer (C) is incorrect because the facts do not establish the existence of a bilateral mistake since Lego was not aware of a mistake.

Answer (D) is incorrect because a unilateral mistake, alone, is not sufficient to qualify for rescission. The mistake must be known (or should have been known) to the other side.

120. **Answer (C) is the correct answer.** Unjust enrichment of the defendant is not established when the plaintiff volunteers the benefit. Here, Accountant volunteered his services, and thus the defendant's benefit was not unjustly obtained at the plaintiff's expense.

    Answer (A) is incorrect. The answer describes a recovery in quantum meruit for the value of the services provided by Accountant. However, the predicate basis of unjust enrichment is not established where the accountant has volunteered the services.

    Answer (B) is incorrect. Restitution is unavailable as indicated in **Answers (A) and (C)** because Accountant volunteered the services. In addition, this answer provides a measure of plaintiff's loss, which is a measure of compensatory damages rather than a measure of defendant's benefit.

    Answer (D) is incorrect because the neighbor did in fact receive a benefit in the form of the tax preparation services provided by Accountant.

121. **Answer (B) is the correct answer.** The doctrine of promissory estoppel provides that a promise reasonably expected to induce action and that does induce detrimental reliance is an enforceable promise limited to recovery of reliance damages. The promise by Almondia of "don't worry, we'll work things out" is a promise reasonably expected to induce action that did induce detrimental reliance in the extra costs incurred by Distributor.

    Answer (A) is incorrect. There is no implied-in-fact contract because the facts and circumstances here do not establish the existence of an actual contract upon which to base recovery. There was never a meeting of the minds as to the terms of the distributorship agreement.

    Answer (C) is incorrect. Unjust enrichment arises if there is a benefit to defendant. Here, there was no benefit resulting to Almondia from Distributors' additional workers and larger lease space.

    Answer (D) is incorrect. Quasi-contract is a restitution remedy when there is an unjust benefit retained by the defendant. As described in **Answer (C)**, no benefit accrued to Almondia here. However, in a few jurisdictions where promissory estoppel is not available, some courts might apply quasi-contract to address the inequity of plaintiff's performance done with the intention to benefit the defendant.

122. The restitution remedies of subrogation, indemnity, and contribution may all be involved in this case. These three restitution remedies are implicated by the involvement of three or more parties in the underlying dispute. The basis for restitution in all of these is the theory that one party has been unjustly enriched when its debt has been unfairly paid by another. Subrogation may be sought by Driver's insurance company to seek reimbursement for the med-

ical expenses paid from any monetary damages Driver might receive from the second negligent driver in the accident litigation. Driver might seek indemnification from its employer due to the Restaurant's promise to cover any legal problems related to the delivery policy. Indemnification provides for reimbursement when one person pays for the debt or liability of another. Indemnity here would mean that Restaurant would pay for any monies Driver would be ordered to pay in the underlying accident suit. Finally, contribution might be an applicable remedy between Driver and the second driver who were both liable in the underlying accident. Contribution is an action between two liable parties when one party has paid more than his fair share of the obligation.

123. **Answer (D) is the correct answer.** The fraud of the CEO creates a basis to rescind the contract. In addition, the unilateral mistake known to the CEO (that Insurance Co. mistakenly believed it was insuring a non-smoker) is an alternative basis upon which to seek rescission. Rescission then restores both parties to their pre-contract position. Thus, the insurance contract is cancelled, no payout is due, and Big Corporation is entitled to the return of the premiums it paid over the several months.

    Answer (A) is incorrect. Rescission is appropriate here due to the fraud of the CEO. However, both parties and not just Insurance Co. must be returned to their pre-contract position.

    Answer (B) is incorrect. Insurance Co. would be successful in its claim for restitution due to the fraud of the CEO, or alternatively due to the unilateral mistake that it was insuring a non-smoker that was known to the CEO on the other side of the bargain.

    Answer (C) is incorrect. This would be a proper measure of compensatory damages if Insurance Co. sued under the contract for its losses from the CEO's breach. However, the facts indicate that Insurance Co. is suing here in restitution, which is a more attractive remedy as it saves the company $3 million rather than accruing a few hundred dollars more in premiums due.

124. **Answer (D) is correct.** The facts of the check and its deposit into the bank account provide circumstantial evidence to establish that an actual contract was created between the parties. An implied-in-fact contract is not a restitution theory, but rather a theory to establish a contractual basis upon which to seek further legal or equitable relief.

    Answer (A) is incorrect. To rescind a contract, there must be fraud, duress, substantial breach of contract, mutual mistake of fact, or unilateral mistake known to the other side. While the substantial breach of contract would provide a basis to seek rescission here, the end result desired by Public Agency—the delivery of the computer screens—could not be obtained by rescission. Rescission would cancel the contract and restore the $20,000 payment to Public Agency.

    Answer (B) is incorrect. The facts indicate that there is no express contract proven by the evidence at trial either by evidence of a written agreement or evidence of an offer and acceptance.

Answer (C) is incorrect. Quasi-contract is an implied-in-law contract, a fictional analogy, used as a vehicle to award a remedy in the absence of any contractual or other legal basis for liability. This implication is not necessary here where the facts establish the existence of an actual contract upon which Public Agency can sue.

Topic 12 Answers

Equitable Restitution

125. **Answer (A) is the correct answer.** Quasi-contract is a legal restitution theory that is a contract implied at law to disgorge the defendant's unjust gain.

    Answer (B) is incorrect. A constructive trust is an equitable restitution claim that implies a fictionalized trust to disgorge the profit retained by the defendant at the plaintiff's expense.

    Answer (C) is incorrect. An equitable lien is an equitable restitution remedy that secures a debt owed to the plaintiff with the defendant's tangible property.

    Answer (D) is incorrect. An accounting of profits is an equitable restitution remedy that requires the defendant to account for and then disgorge the amount of profit unjustly gained by the defendant at the plaintiff's expense.

126. The hallmarks of equitable restitution are its historical origins, its tracing capacity, the possibility of an irreparable injury requirement, and the unavailability of a jury trial. It should be noted, however, that there is much inconsistency in the law with respect to the application of these rules. Equitable restitution includes those forms of restitution that historically developed in the courts of chancery. In England, restitution developed as specific writs in both courts of law and equity to address gaps in relief provided by other causes of action. The historical equitable restitution claims are constructive trust, equitable lien, and accounting of profits. Like other equitable remedies, equitable restitution does not include the right to a jury trial and may trigger the irreparable injury rule requiring that legal remedies are inadequate. Equitable relief also permits the plaintiff to "trace" the funds by following the money through changes in forms and ownership. This tracing enhances the valuation of the benefit and the ability to collect the funds through bankruptcy and other creditor situations.

127. **Answer (C) is the correct answer.** The general measure of restitution under a constructive trust remedy is the amount of profits and appreciation of those profits retained by the defendant. Here, the parents have benefited from the addition of a house to their farm land which caused an appreciation in value of $200,000 ($220,000 current value minus $20,000 original value of farm land). Winifred's marital share (50% as Winifred and Harry split marital property equally) of that appreciation is $100,000.

    Answer (A) is incorrect. The $22,000 is the value of Winifred's services put into the house and thus is a measure of quantum meruit.

Answer (B) is incorrect. The $85,000 represents Winifred's marital share of the financial investment in the home and would constitute a partial measurement of the debt owed to her under an equitable lien theory. However, it does not represent a measure of the profit gained by the parents.

Answer (D) is incorrect. The $107,000 represents the total of Winifred's financial and in-kind investments into the home, as indicated in the **Answer to Question 128**, below. This is an appropriate amount under an equitable lien theory which measures the amount of debt owed to the plaintiff from the benefit unjustly retained by the defendant.

128. **Answer (D) is the correct answer.** An equitable lien is measured by the amount of debt owed to the plaintiff from the unjust benefit gained by the defendant. Here, the defendant parents unjustly gained from Winifred's financial assistance (1/2 of $30,000 + $140,000 = $85,000) and construction services ($22,000) related to the house that total $107,000.

Answer (A) is incorrect. The $22,000 is the value of Winifred's services put into the house and thus is a measure of quantum meruit.

Answer (B) is incorrect. The $85,000 represents Winifred's marital share of the financial investment in the home, but constitutes only a partial measurement of the debt owed to her under an equitable lien theory.

Answer (C) is incorrect. The $100,000 represents Winifred's marital share of the total appreciation of the house gained by the parents. This measure of profit and appreciation is appropriately awarded under a constructive trust theory, as indicated in the **Answer to Question 127**, above.

129. **Answer (C) is the correct answer.** A constructive trust would disgorge all of the profits from Bonnie's fraudulent use of her mother-in-law's recipes. Constructive trust is available when the plaintiff originally owned the property at issue and when the defendant commits a wrong involving fraud or breach of a confidence. Both of these elements are satisfied in this scenario.

Answer (A) is incorrect. An equitable lien is a restitution remedy used to secure a debt owed to plaintiff with the tangible property of the defendant at issue. Here, the mother-in-law is not seeking repayment of a debt, but rather seeking to disgorge Bonnie's unjust gain.

Answer (B) is incorrect. Quasi-contract would imply a contract at law between the two women for Bonnie to use her mother-in-law's recipes in the book. The measure of the rental or purchase value of those recipes would not be the amount of Bonnie's total profits.

Answer (D) is incorrect. An accounting of profits remedy would disgorge the benefits unjustly gained by Bonnie at the expense of her mother-in-law, but allow her to retain any profit she derived from her own efforts. The facts here do not indicate that any of the profits were related to Bonnie's own efforts, and thus this remedial option is not appropriate.

130. **Answer (C) is the correct answer.** Bob would use an equitable lien theory to recover the debt owed to him for his improvements to Gretta's house in the amount of the money he loaned to her for the construction on the house.

Answer (A) is incorrect. Quantum meruit would allow Bob to recover the value of services provided. However, Bob did not provide any construction or remodeling services in this case.

Answer (B) is incorrect. A constructive trust remedy would be attractive to Bob in order to recover the appreciated value of the house ($70,000) due to his remodeling work. However, constructive trust is not available to Bob because Bob does not have a claim to ownership of the house or a severable interest in the house. Constructive trust requires the plaintiff to have a claim to ownership of the property over which the constructive trust will be imposed. Additionally, constructive trust generally requires a fraud-like wrong on the part of the defendant, and Gretta did nothing to defraud or breach a confidence with Bob.

Answer (D) is incorrect. Indemnification is available only when there is an agreement between the parties that one party will assume liability if the second is found liable to a third party. No such third party liability is at issue here.

131. The slavery reparations cases seek restitution in the form of monetary payments for the uncompensated labor of the slaves. A constructive trust theory has been used, arguing that the slave owners, and companies like banks and insurance companies that financed slavery, unjustly benefited from the labor of the slaves and held that profit in trust for the slave beneficiaries. A theory of equitable lien also works to seek monetary relief for the slaves' work to improve the value of other people's land. Where strict doctrinal rules of constructive trust fail, because the jurisdiction requires that the plaintiff demonstrate prior ownership of the property, equitable lien assists the slaves in seeking payment for the debt owed by the slave owners of the benefit conferred upon the farming and working of the owners' land. Plaintiffs have also used the legal restitution theories of quasi-contract and quantum meruit to obtain the value of the labor services provided by the slaves.

132. **Answer (C) is the correct answer.** Under an accounting of profits, a plaintiff is awarded only those profits attributed to the wrongful conduct. The plaintiff has the burden of proving the total amount of revenues, and the defendant has the burden of proving its costs and any profits generated from its own efforts rather than the wrong. Here, the $3 million in total revenues was offset by the $2 million in costs, and then further reduced by the $250,000 in profits attributed to the defendant's own lawful advertising actions, leaving $750,000 as the restitution measure of recovery.

Answer (A) is incorrect. Three million is the total amount of revenues earned by the defendant during the time of the wrong. It could be the measure of recovery under different facts if the defendant failed to prove any offsetting costs or lawful profits. The shared burden of the accounting for profits remedy gives this advantage to the plaintiff in not having to prove the precise amount of offsetting benefits, as this information is usually in the possession of the defendant.

Answer (B) is incorrect. One million is the amount of total profits ($3 million) offset by the defendant's costs of production ($2 million). It fails to take into account the profits earned by the lawful advertising conduct of the defendant ($250,000), which should not be awarded to the defendant.

Answer (D) is incorrect. The amount of Beerman's lost profits proven at trial was $0. However, the amount of plaintiff's loss is a compensatory measure, whereas restitution measures the amount of defendant's gain. The difference is important in cases like this one involving trademark infringement, where it is difficult to prove the losses to plaintiff, or where the defendant gains more than the plaintiff loses.

133. **Answer (B) is the correct answer.** Equitable restitution uses the tracing device to follow a plaintiff's funds through changes in form and ownership in order to restore the unjust gain to the plaintiff. Tracing thus allows the church to reach the funds in possession of a third party, because Betty is not a bona fide purchaser for value. Here, the original $200,000 of embezzled funds can be traced to the $100,000 cash given to Betty—the $50,000 purchase of the car now worth $30,000—and the $50,000 in stocks now worth $100,000.

    Answer (A) is incorrect. Tracing follows the funds through the changes in form, including appreciation and depreciation of the original amounts. Here, the original $100,000 given to Betty can be traced to a change in value of the appreciated stocks and the depreciated car.

    Answer (C) is incorrect. The amount of $150,000 would give the church the appreciated amount of the stocks ($100,000), but not properly trace the car to its current depreciated value.

    Answer (D) is incorrect. Of the original amount embezzled ($200,000), only $100,000 can be traced to Betty from LeMar's gift. Betty is not responsible for the total original amount embezzled that cannot be traced to her.

134. **Answer (B) is the correct answer.** An equitable lien will be awarded and secured by tangible property for the value of a debt owed by another for benefits unjustly conferred and secured by tangible property. Here, Jane owes a debt to Dick for his addition to her home measured by his financial investment and construction services. The security mechanism of the equitable lien allows Dick to foreclose on Jane's house if she does not pay him the amount owed.

    Answer (A) is incorrect. The value of Dick's services is an incomplete measure of the debt owed to Dick because it does not include the financial investment of $10,000 that he made in Jane's property.

    Answer (C) is incorrect. A constructive trust is measured by the amount of profits earned by the defendant and any appreciation (or depreciation). Jane received more benefit than the $10,000 in savings from the addition to her home and its appreciation ($140,000), though part of that appreciation is due to market forces.

    Answer (D) is incorrect. Dick will not be awarded a constructive trust in many jurisdictions because he does not have a claim to ownership of the home. Instead, courts will use an equitable lien as a restitution device to address the improvements made by a party to the property of another. The equitable lien measures the defendant's benefit by the amount of debt owed and not by the amount of profit obtained by the defendant. Thus, the appreciation of the house owned by Jane will not be awarded to Dick.

Topic 13   Answers

Declaratory Judgment

135. **Answer (D) is the correct answer** because all of the provided answers are relevant to the ripeness inquiry. A declaratory judgment action must be based on a real and substantial controversy, as opposed to a merely hypothetical set of facts. **Answer (A)** informs the relevancy inquiry in both positive and negative respects. That Devi is an accomplished businessperson makes it more likely that the business venture Prime fears is real; that Devi has never been in the outdoor advertising business makes the feared business venture seem less plausible. **Answer (B)** also has positive and negative effects on ripeness: the promissory note suggests that Devi is buying some asset (such as the billboards) from Oliver; but if no money has been paid, in fact, there may be no (serious) note or asset transfer. **Answer (C)** suggests ripeness, because Devi may be the new seller offering lower prices. Although none of Answers (A), (B), or (C) would alone establish ripeness, the call of the question asks only which facts would be relevant to the inquiry.

136. The question poses a false choice: Prime may seek a declaratory judgment *and* preliminary relief in one suit. The advantage of obtaining preliminary relief is that the defendant(s) will be ordered to do — or to not do — certain acts while the parties litigate, and that court order can be enforced through the power of contempt. By obtaining preliminary relief, Prime (1) creates leverage vis-à-vis the defendant(s) and (2) avoids suffering (additional) harm.

137. **Answer (D) is the correct answer** because the threat that Artemis will be arrested for leafletting is real and imminent. She has twice been warned by the police that she will be arrested, and Apollo's arrest concretizes the threat. And because all of these events occurred this month, Artemis has a strong claim that the time is right for the court to issue its declaration.

    Answer (A) is incorrect. Although Artemis did not participate in last weekend's leafletting, the controversy is still ripe. There are no further facts or actions that are necessary for Artemis to complete the controversy short of leafletting again, which would subject her to the penalty of arrest and jail time (like Apollo). This is exactly what the declaratory judgment seeks to avoid.

    Answer (B) is incorrect because it is neither the standard for — nor the goal of — declaratory relief. If Artemis wants an order against the police to cease and desist, she should choose an injunctive remedy.

    Answer (C) is incorrect because the dispute between Artemis and Rometown is adverse as both sides disagree about the concrete issue of the application of the criminal trespass statute to the definite conduct by Artemis of leafletting in Rometown. And the matter is ripe as described above.

138. **Answer (A) is the correct answer.** The question about "the premises" is legal and narrow, and its resolution would promote the resolution of the parties' dispute. Perch has formally triggered the appraisal process, so the issue is also ripe for determination.

Answer (B) is incorrect because this dispute is not hypothetical: the appraisal process has been initiated, and the appraiser needs to know what to value. Answer (B) would be correct if, say, Perch initiated a declaratory judgment action because he was curious about the meaning of "the premises" but was not, in fact, able to exercise the purchase option no matter the price.

Answer (C) is incorrect because questions of law are especially well-suited for declaratory relief.

Answer (D) is incorrect because declaratory relief is appropriate even if it does not *definitively resolve* the parties' dispute. Declaratory relief can be appropriate even where it clarifies or resolves an important question that would be useful to the parties. Answer (D) could be correct if, say, Sales and Perch had multiple, related, complex disputes regarding this transaction; under those circumstances, declaring the meaning of "the premises" would narrow the parties' dispute but not, as a practical matter, resolve it.

139. **Answer (B) is the correct answer.** The claim is not ripe because Paul has not attempted to return the coat. A court is not going to hypothesize about how the corporate policy might be applied by some presently-unknown sales rep to presently-unknown circumstances. Declaratory judgments resolve actual disputes, not hypothetical disputes.

Answer (A) is incorrect because there is no express substantiality requirement — even if this claim might be labeled by some as trivial.

Answer (C) is incorrect because Paul's likelihood of success on the merits is not the standard for obtaining declaratory relief.

Answer (D) is incorrect because even if this is a pure legal issue, the case is not ripe. To be sure, courts are more likely to allow declaratory judgments in matters that raise pure legal issues. But this alone is not enough.

140. **Answer (D) is the correct answer** because all of the provided answers are reasons that a declaratory judgment could be an attractive option. **Answer (A) is correct** because clarification of the parties' rights allow them to avoid losses (or penalties) they otherwise might incur by proceeding with questionable conduct in the absence of a declaration. **Answer (B) is correct** because civil rules can expedite resolution of declaratory judgment actions. **Answer (C) is correct** because litigants might choose a declaratory judgment in order to avoid acrimonious litigation and to preserve ongoing business relations as in the case of long-term contractual agreements.

141. **Answer (C) is the correct answer.** Although the plaintiff has an interest in having the statute declared unconstitutional, it is not obvious that the defendant (which is the Hospital, not the state) has an interest in defending the constitutionality of the statute. Indeed, it is possible that the Hospital doesn't like the statute either. A declaratory judgment is appropriate only where the interests are adverse.

Answer (A) is incorrect because the involuntary medical treatment is already underway and the more aggressive regimen is imminent.

Answer (B) is incorrect because declaratory relief could forestall the forthcoming round of treatment which is more aggressive. In a variation of this hypothetical where Pat is expected to receive more of the same treatment (rather than a round of more aggressive treatment, that is), then Answer (B) could be a correct answer. Under those circumstances, one could argue that declaratory relief wouldn't provide Pat with practical relief, because he has already been involuntarily medicated.

Answer (D) is incorrect because the constitutionality of a statute is a question of law.

142. **Answer (C) is the correct answer.** A court may deny declaratory relief when it is used merely for the purpose of procedural fencing — that is, when the declaratory action is filed in anticipation of the natural litigation so that the declaratory plaintiff can choose a favorable forum. If A1 filed the declaratory action before Gerson had even filed his suit, a court might question A1's motives for filing; such a declaratory action might also be unripe.

Answer (A) is incorrect. To be sure, an insurer's liability *may* be litigated as part of the state court action: Millenium could implead A1 as a third party defendant, for example. But impleaders are not mandatory. And litigating the insurer's liability in the underlying action is not necessary.

Answer (B) is incorrect because a declaratory judgement regarding coverage would appear to resolve the dispute between Millenium and A1 over who will pay for the state-court litigation.

Answer (D) is incorrect because the propriety of declaratory relief doesn't turn on the merits of the claim (for declaratory relief). If Gerson's state court claim expressly alleges that the shooter committed "assault" and/or "battery," then A1 has a greater likelihood of success on its claim that the insurance policy's exclusion exempts it from liability to Millenium. But even if Gerson's state court claim doesn't use those terms, A1 will still argue that the policy exclusion applies, and its claim (for declaratory relief), even if weaker on the merits, is no less appropriate for a declaratory judgment.

143. **Answer (C) is the correct answer.** The requested declaratory judgment will not terminate the uncertainty as to whether the insurance company must cover the loss or defend the teacher's lawsuit, because the declaration addresses only one of three charges against the teacher. Even if molestation were excluded from coverage, the other two charges might fall within the policy's coverage.

Answer (A) is incorrect. There is an actual controversy between the teacher and the insurance company. However, the discretionary standards still weigh against issuance of the declaration even though the mandatory bases for judicial power have been satisfied.

Answer (B) is incorrect because like **Answer (A)**, it addresses only the threshold mandatory bases for judicial power, rather than completing the analysis with a determination as to whether the court's discretion is proper.

Answer (D) is incorrect as there is no impermissible tactical advantage sought by the insurance company. It may use declaratory relief to seek a determination about coverage prior to the determination of the insured's loss.

144. **Answer (D) is the correct answer.** A court may deny declaratory relief when it is used merely for the purpose of procedural fencing—that is, when the declaratory action is filed in anticipation of the natural litigation so that the declaratory plaintiff can choose a favorable forum. On these facts, the natural litigation is *Datsun Motor Co. v. Old Datsun Car Parts* for trademark violation. Datsun Motor Co., as plaintiff, would choose the forum for that suit; it might choose a court in Detroit, Michigan, for example. By "immediately" filing its declaratory action in South Carolina, Old Datsun Car Parts appears to be trying to get a tactical advantage. This is not why the declaratory judgment action exists.

Answer (A) is incorrect. Although there is an actual controversy between these two companies regarding the use of the Datsun trademarks, the availability of the declaratory judgment is at the discretion of the judge. And Old Datsun Car Parts' use of the device is dubious here.

Answer (B) is incorrect because like Answer (A), it addresses only the threshold mandatory bases for judicial power, rather than completing the analysis with a determination as to whether the court's discretion is proper.

Answer (C) is incorrect because a declaratory judgment about the trademarks *would* resolve the uncertainty that fuels the parties' dispute.

145. **Answer (C) is the correct answer** because it falls in the "sweet spot" between times that are either too short or too long. Declaratory plaintiffs who file promptly at the outset of a dispute are criticized for seeking a tactical advantage: rather than allowing the natural litigation to proceed in due course, they are using a declaratory suit to steal the forum (from the natural plaintiff). Declaratory plaintiffs who wait too long to file their suit, however, risk a different criticism: if the natural plaintiff still hasn't filed suit, then declaratory relief seems unnecessary (and therefore inappropriate). Although there is nothing especially appropriate about the period "six to twelve months," it is the best of the provided options.

Answers (A) and (B) are incorrect because these periods are too short. Declaratory relief will be denied because Old Gremlin Car Parts appears to be trying to seize a tactical advantage.

Answer (D) is incorrect because two years or more is too long. If Gremlin Motor Co. has allowed Old Gremlin Car Parts to misuse it trademarks for so long, the former's threats of a lawsuit ring ever-more hollow. And if Gremlin Motor Co. is never going to sue, there is no uncertainty to justify the discretionary exercise of declaratory relief.

Topic 14   Answers

Remedial Defenses

146. **Answer (B) is the correct answer.** Casey might use unconscionability as a defense based on the procedural unfairness in the creation of the contract. Unconscionability prohibits the enforcement of an oppressive contract when either the terms or the formation of the contract are substantially unfair. Here, the cancellation terms of the contract and the legal representation on only one side suggest unfairness in the formation of the contract.

    Answer (A) is incorrect. Waiver is a defense that applies when the plaintiff tries to assert a right that, through words or conduct, it has relinquished. Unless Radia has done something (beyond the stated facts) that would suggest a waiver of her right to cancel the contract, Casey should not assert this defense.

    Answer (C) is incorrect. Laches is a defense that bars claims because of the tardiness of their assertion. But Radia is no slacker.

    Answer (D) is incorrect. To be sure, most equitable defenses are designed to prevent various types of unfairness. But "unfairness" is not itself a defense.

147. **Answer (C) is the correct answer.** *In pari delicto* and unclean hands both relate to a plaintiff's wrongdoing or misconduct. *In pari delicto* is a defense meaning "in equal fault." Unclean hands is an equitable defense derived from the legal maxim that "he who comes into equity must come with clean hands." Unclean hands applies to misconduct that is connected with the controversy at issue in the case. *In pari delicto* applies when the plaintiff's misconduct is closely connected with the controversy and is equal to or greater than that of the defendant. *In pari delicto* applies in a subset of cases that might otherwise fall within the broader framework of unclean hands.

    Answer (A) is incorrect because codification of the plaintiff's cause of action is not the proper inquiry.

    Answer (B) is incorrect because neither of the defenses makes fine distinctions between illegal and wrongful conduct.

    Answer (D) is incorrect. To be sure, both defenses are designed to prevent plaintiffs from misusing the judicial system by asserting rights that are in some sense tainted by the plaintiffs' prior misconduct. But formally (even if not in practice), there are three differences: First, unclean hands is available only to claims for equitable relief, while *in pari delicto* is more broadly applicable. Second, the *in pari delicto* defense demands that the plaintiff's misconduct cause the harm for which it is suing; the unclean hands defense demands that the plaintiff engage in misconduct that is related to the claim. And third, the *in pari delicto* defense insists that the plaintiff contribute to its harm in equal or greater measure than the defendant's misconduct; the unclean hands doctrine bars relief based on plaintiff's related misconduct without regard to the defendant's behavior.

148. **Answer (A) is the correct answer.** The Center could argue that estoppel bars the landlord's eviction remedy because it detrimentally relied on the landlord's prior inconsistent statement. Estoppel prevents a party from changing positions when the adverse party has justifiably relied upon a prior position. Here, the Center relied on the landlord's first statement that she "understood" the need for the fence. Thus the landlord is prevented from changing that position to say that the fence now constitutes a basis for eviction.

    Answer (B) is incorrect. Laches is a remedial defense related to a party's unreasonable delay in the case. It would be difficult for the Center to argue that four weeks was an unreasonable amount of time for the landlord to wait before taking legal action based upon the fence.

    Answer (C) is incorrect. Unclean hands is a remedial defense based upon the plaintiff's misconduct (that is related to the plaintiff's claim). The landlord has not engaged in any misconduct. His expressed understanding of the Center's need for the fence is not fraudulent or wrongful.

    Answer (D) is incorrect. There was no oppression in the process or the substance of the original lease agreement that could form the basis for an unconscionability argument about the substantial unfairness of enforcing the contract.

149. **Answer (B) is the correct answer.** If Medal Jeans acquired the mark through fraud or misconduct, then those unclean hands will thwart its effort to enforce that mark in this litigation. Although "provid[ing] varying accounts of how it acquired the trademark" is not necessarily evidence of fraud or misconduct, it hints at a viable unclean hands defense.

    Answer (A) is incorrect because losing a different trademark infringement suit is not evidence of misconduct.

    Answers (C) and (D) are incorrect because they refer to Medal Sport's actions. The defendant Medal Sport is invoking the unclean hands defense, so it is the plaintiff Medal Jeans's hands that will be examined.

150. **Answer (B) is the correct answer.** Courts will apply the statute of limitations to the legal claim and the doctrine of laches to the equitable claim.

    Answer (A) is incorrect because the equitable defense of laches applies to the equitable claim. To be sure, courts often invoke statutes of limitations as analogues when evaluating the reasonableness of an equitable plaintiff's delay. But these are guideposts or benchmarks—not constraints—on the discretionary exercise of equity.

    Answer (C) is incorrect because it inverts the roles of the legal and equitable defenses.

Answer (D) is incorrect because it would undermine the important role of statutes of limitation. Legislative efforts to condition claims cannot be overrun merely by invoking the court's equity jurisdiction.

151. **Answer (C) is the correct answer.** Rufus's misconduct of trespass from the roof overhang could bar his request for equitable relief. His trespass is probably sufficiently egregious to satisfy that first element of the unclean hands defense. But Natalie will also need to establish that Rufus's misconduct is sufficiently *related* to this claim. In this regard, it is not enough that Rufus is himself a trespasser now complaining of trespass. Natalie will argue that the two events are related because of their similarity and because of their proximity in time and space. Like most equitable doctrines, the unclean hands defense is somewhat vague by design, allowing courts discretion to determine when misconduct is sufficiently related to bar equitable relief.

Answer (A) is incorrect because *in pari delicto* requires that the plaintiff's misconduct be a substantial cause of the defendant's breach. On the given facts we have no reason to believe that Natalie is trespassing because Rufus's trespassing roof prevents her from locating the pool anywhere else.

Answer (B) is incorrect. Waiver is the relinquishment of a known right. There are no facts to suggest that Rufus gave up his right to the property or otherwise approved the encroachment of the swimming pool.

Answer (D) is incorrect. The laches defense bars an equitable claim if the plaintiff has unreasonably delayed the assertion of its rights. But Rufus appears to be acting very promptly, since Natalie is still building the pool at the time of the suit. The delay of "two years" in the fact pattern is not Rufus's (the plaintiff's) delay in asserting his right, but rather the time that has passed since Rufus trespassed on Natalie's property.

152. **Answer (B) is the correct answer** because Gakh installed his motor home approximately one year ago. The neighbors could have filed their claim then, but waited until "recently" to file this action. If Gakh is to prevail on his laches defense, he will need to persuade the judge that one year is an unreasonable delay in asserting this claim.

Answer (A) is incorrect because the neighbors didn't have this cause of action when Gakh purchased the land (eleven years ago). The claim accrued only when he installed the prohibited mobile home.

Answer (C) is incorrect. The neighbors made "gestures" for approximately six months, and have been quiet for another six months, but Gakh has been violating the restrictive covenants for one year, not six months.

Answer (D) is incorrect because the neighbors could have filed suit one year ago, but didn't. The fact that they have threatened to sue and made other efforts to get Gakh to behave does not change the fact of their delay. In fact, those efforts clarify the delay, because there is no question that the neighbors were aware of this claim.

153. **Answer (C) is the correct answer.** Gakh will suffer great prejudice because his family will be evicted: the kids will be disrupted from school, this family of five will need to live somewhere, etc. Critically, if the neighbors had more promptly asserted their right—when they said they were going to sue, for example—then only Gakh would have been evicted and his family would not have suffered. Gakh's family moved to the property two months ago, which is four months after the neighbors' threats and gestures had stopped.

Answer (A) is incorrect because this is not an expenditure that Gakh suffered because of (or even during) the neighbors' delay. Put another way, Gakh would have suffered this $50,000 loss even if the neighbors had sued immediately to enforce the restrictive covenants.

Answer (B) is incorrect because, like Answer (A) this is an injury that Gakh would have suffered even if the neighbors had sued the day after he moved in. The mobile home will be damaged by the removal no matter when the removal happened (or happens). This prejudice is not traceable to the neighbors' delay in asserting their claim.

Answer (D) is incorrect because Answers (A) and (B) are incorrect. The prejudice necessary to sustain the defense of laches is prejudice that is attributable to the *timing* of the assertion of the plaintiff's claim. Ask yourself: how would defendant's position be different if plaintiff had asserted their claim then rather than now?

Topic 15   Answers

Attorney Fees

154. **Answer (D) is the correct answer.** Under the "American Rule," a prevailing party is not entitled to recover its attorney fees from the losing party. Rather, each party pays its own fees. An exception to the American Rule exists when a party acts in bad faith. However, generally, this exception applies only when a party acts in bad faith during its conduct of the litigation or when the party acts in bad faith in instituting the litigation. A party's conduct that gives rise to the substantive claim does not create liability for attorney fees. Thus, Simpson will not be liable for attorney fees based on Simpson's reasons for breaching the contract.

Answers (A), (B) and (C) are incorrect because these answers explore possible states of mind that Simpson had when she breached. But as already explained above, Simpson's then-state of mind is irrelevant to the question of attorney fees.

155. **Answer (B) is the correct answer.** When a lawyer recovers a common fund that will benefit claimants other than the lawyer's own client, the lawyer is entitled to recover her reasonable attorney fees from the common fund. Here, the settlement fund will benefit all class members who were wrongfully denied reimbursement for the professional licensing fees. Thus, Pilot is entitled to recover attorney fees from the settlement fund under the common fund exception to the American Rule.

Answer (A) is incorrect. First, Because Pilot did not win a verdict (but instead merely settled the case favorably), she may not be a "prevailing party" under some laws. But second, even prevailing parties are not automatically entitled to recover attorney fees. Even a prevailing party must invoke some exception to the "American Rule."

Answer (C) is incorrect. Even if a class member elects not to file a proof of claim and collect a portion of the settlement fund, the class member has received a benefit, because the class member was entitled to present a claim and receive a portion of the fund if the class member so elected.

Answer (D) is incorrect. Under the common fund exception, the prevailing plaintiff can recover her reasonable attorney fees.

156. **Answer (B) is the correct answer.** A plaintiff who prevails at trial is eligible—perhaps even likely—to receive an award of attorney fees. But defendants are usually treated differently—even though statutes like this one don't distinguish between prevailing plaintiffs and prevailing defendants. The rationale for plaintiffs' recovery is that litigation costs are a significant obstacle to victims who wish to bring suit. If plaintiffs were forced to pay prevailing defendants' fees, this exposure would chill the litigation that the statute is trying to incentivize.

Accordingly, defendants often cannot receive fees unless the plaintiff's claim was frivolous, unreasonable, or without foundation.

Answer (A) is incorrect because it is too definitive. A court might interpret this as a two-way fee-shifting statute. Or a particular defendant might prevail because the plaintiff's claim was frivolous, unreasonable, or without foundation.

Answers (C) and (D) are incorrect because they are too sanguine about the defendant's prospects. As stated above, courts are less inclined to award attorney fees to prevailing defendants. Even if a court interprets this statute as a two-way fee-shift, appreciate that the court "may" but is not obligated to award attorney fees under the quoted statute.

157. **Answer (A) is the correct answer** because courts generally enforce fee-shifting provisions in contracts.

    Answer (B) is incorrect because it matters only that Landers prevailed; it doesn't matter whether she was awarded legal and/or equitable relief.

    Answer (C) is incorrect because Tenneson's good faith in the course of litigation does not excuse his contractual obligation to pay if he loses.

    Answer (D) is incorrect. To be sure, the American Rule requires each party to pay his or her own attorney fees. However, parties may shift the obligation to pay such fees by contract, and courts will enforce those agreements provided they are not contrary to law or public policy.

158. **Answer (C) is the correct answer.** The contract includes a one-way fee-shifting provision that benefits only the landlord, not the tenant. But courts may view this as against public policy and impute a reciprocal provision to benefit the other side. That is the likely situation here where a landlord and a tenant may not have equal bargaining power and sophistication.

    Answer (A) is incorrect because this is not a two-way fee-shifting provision. The fact pattern describes a fee-shift that benefits only the landlord. Accordingly, this is a one-way fee shift.

    Answer (B) is incorrect because, if the court enforces the contract as written, Lavoie is not entitled to recover her attorney fees. Only the landlord has that contractual right.

    Answer (D) is incorrect because this is not a two-way fee-shifting provision. Moreover, if this were a two-way fee-shifting provision, courts would likely enforce it, because courts generally enforce fee-shifting provisions in contracts.

159. **Answer (C) is the correct answer.** This buyer prevailed on two of its seven claims for breach, and recovered less than one-tenth of the damages it sought. Under such circumstances, courts typically try to identify the portion of the attorney fees that produced the favorable result(s), and award a reasonable fee (only) for this apportioned work.

    Answer (A) is incorrect because it would overcompensate the prevailing party. A fee-shifting provision will not reward this plaintiff for its unsuccessful pursuit of certain claims. Moreover, even if plaintiff prevailed on all of its claims and recovered all its sought damages, the contract permits recovery only of "reasonable" fees, which are not necessarily the litigant's actual fees.

Answer (B) is incorrect because it would overcompensate the prevailing party. Again, a fee-shifting provision will not reward this plaintiff for its unsuccessful pursuit of certain claims.

Answer (D) is incorrect because a damages award of $125,000 is not trivial. To be sure, a court will discount plaintiff's award—perhaps even to the amount of zero—in light of its relative success. But the court will undertake that analysis with the approach described in Answer (C).

160. **Answer (D) is correct.** In determining the reasonableness of a fee award, a court will consider numerous factors, including the time and labor required to litigate the claims; the novelty of the claims and the difficulty of the issues raised in the suit (**Answer (A)**); the skill required to prepare the case; the loss of other employment opportunities as a result of the case; the customary fee; time limitations imposed by the case or client; the success obtained; the expertise of the attorney; the "undesirability" of the case; the nature and length of the attorney-client relationship (**Answer (C)**); and awards in similar cases (**Answer (B)**).

161. **Answer (C) is the correct answer.** In *Marek v. Chesny*, 473 U.S. 1 (1985), the Supreme Court held that when a prevailing plaintiff in a civil rights action recovers less at trial than the plaintiff would have recovered under a valid offer of judgment, Federal Rule of Civil Procedure 68 precludes the prevailing plaintiff from recovering any *post-offer* attorney fees.

Answer (A) is incorrect. In *Marek*, the Supreme Court held that a defendant need not specify separately which portion of an offer of judgment is in satisfaction of costs and attorney fees.

Answer (B) is incorrect. In *Marek*, the Supreme Court held that a plaintiff could not combine post-offer costs with the judgment awarded at trial in determining whether the award at trial exceeded the offer of judgment.

Answer (D) is incorrect. In *Marek*, the Supreme Court recognized that a prevailing plaintiff who recovers less at trial than the plaintiff would have recovered under the offer of judgment is still a prevailing plaintiff and, hence, entitled to recover the plaintiff's *pre-offer* attorney fees.

Topic 16   Answers

Right to Jury Trial

162. **Answer (A) is the correct answer.** For a state common-law claim in state court, only the state constitution can confer the right to a jury trial.

Answers (B) and (C) are incorrect because the Supreme Court has consistently held that the Seventh Amendment is not incorporated into the Fourteenth Amendment and, thus, is not applicable to state court proceedings.

Answer (D) is incorrect because the right to a jury trial belongs to both plaintiffs and defendants. When there is a right to a jury trial, either party may invoke it.

163. **Answer (A) is the correct answer** because the Seventh Amendment preserves the right to a jury trial in a common-law action where the value in controversy exceeds $20. A state law claim for negligence is a paradigmatic example of such an action.

Answers (B) and (C) are incorrect because these are not suits at common law within the meaning of the Seventh Amendment. To be sure, the Seventh Amendment preserves "rights" not merely "actions" that existed in 1791. Although some claims under federal law are sufficiently analogous to those preserved rights, these are not examples. Further, the plaintiff in **Answer (B)** is seeking only equitable relief.

Answer (D) is incorrect because only Answer (A) exemplifies a situation where the jury trial right is preserved by the Seventh Amendment.

164. **Answer (B) is the correct answer.** Allowing the jury to resolve the claim for damages respects the importance of the Seventh Amendment. Allowing the judge to resolve the equitable claim respects the difference between law and equity; there were no juries in equity.

Answer (A) is incorrect because judges — not juries — typically exercise the powers of the courts of equity.

Answer (C) is incorrect because it inverts the order of decision-making. The primacy of the Seventh Amendment requires that the jury's resolution of the legal issues guide the judge's resolution of the equitable issues.

Answer (D) is incorrect. To be sure, the equitable clean-up doctrine once allowed federal courts to resolve the legal and equitable claims under certain circumstances. (And it is still allowed in some state courts.) But since *Beacon Theatres, Inc. v. Westover*, 359 U.S. 500 (1959), the Seventh Amendment has required federal courts to allow a jury to try the legal claims first. And Adams filed this case in federal court.

165. **Answer (C) is the correct answer.** In *Chauffers, Teamsters & Helpers, Local No. 391 v. Terry*, 494 U.S. 558 (1990), the Supreme Court established a two-step analysis to determine whether a party has a right to a jury trial under the Seventh Amendment. The court first determines whether the claim, or one analogous to it, would have been deemed legal or equitable in Eighteenth Century England before the merger of law and equity. Thus, **Answer (A)** provides information that would assist the court in its Seventh Amendment inquiry. Second, the court examines the remedy sought and determines whether it is legal or equitable in nature. (This second prong of the test tends to be given more weight than the first.) Accordingly, **Answer (B)** provides useful information.

Answer (D) is incorrect because the Seventh Amendment is a constitutional mandate that supersedes congressional legislation. Moreover, in the absence of relevant statutory *text*, reliance on legislative history could be especially dubious.

166. **Answer (A) is the correct answer.** If Congress provides a statutory right to a jury trial, then the right exists. No further inquiry is necessary.

Answers (B) and (C) are incorrect because the Seventh Amendment analysis is unnecessary when Congress establishes the right by statute. Whether the Seventh Amendment *also* guarantees the right to a jury trial for this claim is a moot question.

Answer (D) is incorrect. To be sure, a federal constitutional mandate supersedes a legislative enactment. But the Seventh Amendment operates as a one-way ratchet: it *confers* the right to a jury trial in certain circumstances. But it doesn't negate the right to a jury trial in all other circumstances. Accordingly, if a congressional statute creates a jury trial right, then the Seventh Amendment is irrelevant.

Practice Final Exam: Answers

Answers

Practice Final Exam

167. **Answer (A) is the correct answer.** When a seller has wrongfully failed to deliver goods, UCC § 2-712 allows a buyer to "cover" by purchasing substitute goods and to recover from the seller as damages the difference between the cost of cover and the contract price. However, the buyer's failure to cover does not preclude the buyer from recovering damages. Instead, under the UCC § 2-713(a), a buyer is entitled to recover as damages the difference between the market price and the contract price. Here, Sally wrongfully failed to deliver her used car. Bradford has failed to cover. However, Bradford is entitled to recover damages under § 2-713(a). Bradford's damages will be measured as the difference between the market price of $2000 and the contract price of $1500. Thus, Bradford will be entitled to recover $500. This result is found in **Answer (A)**, **making Answer (A) the correct answer** and **Answers (B), (C), and (D) incorrect answers.**

168. There are several advantages to seeking declaratory relief rather than an injunction. Both provide a preventive remedy that can avoid harm. Declarations however are easier to obtain because they do not require that irreparable injury or the inadequacy of damages be proven. Declaratory judgments are often placed on a shorter procedural timetable in court and thus a client can obtain relief more quickly. Declaratory judgments also have the strategic advantage of preserving ongoing business relations between parties because, unlike injunctions, they do not carry the threat of contempt. Declaratory judgments also provide for supplemental or further relief in the event that the defendant does not voluntarily comply with the court's determination of the appropriate legal rights.

169. **Answer (B) is the correct answer.** To recover damages for future expenses, an injured plaintiff must show that it is more likely than not that she will incur the future expenses. Here, because only a small number of people develop future vision problems and because Plaintiff has not shown any signs of developing future problems, Plaintiff will not be able to show that it is more likely than not that she will incur future medical expenses related to the treatment of any recurring vision problems. Hence, damages for Plaintiff's future medical expenses are too speculative.

   Answer (A) is incorrect. Plaintiff will be able to recover the reasonable value of the surgery as long as she shows it was reasonably necessary. Because the surgery restored her vision and posed only a small risk of complications, Plaintiff will be able to show that the surgery was reasonably necessary.

Answer (C) is incorrect. Under the collateral source rule, the payments from her employer are considered benefits that are collateral to the defendant. Thus, the defendant cannot offset these benefits against Plaintiff's harm.

Answer (D) is incorrect. Plaintiff cannot recover damages for medical expenses related to the treatment of future vision problems because Plaintiff cannot demonstrate that she more likely than not will suffer from future vision problems.

170. **Answer (D) is the correct answer.** Larry's own subjective fears, in the absence of any other conduct by Slime, are insufficient to establish a real threat of harm upon which the court can act. An injunction must be necessary to prevent harm, and no such threat of harm is shown here.

    Answer (A) is incorrect because the facts do not demonstrate Slime's propensity to commit a legal harm. Slime's general reputation is insufficient to establish his propensity to commit the particular harm of failing to produce documents in this case.

    Answer (B) is incorrect. While the scope of an injunction must match the scope of the harm, scope is a legal matter determined after the necessity of an injunction is established. The necessity of an injunction due to a real threat of imminent harm is not shown here.

    Answer (C) is incorrect. Slime's failure to produce documents would constitute irreparable injury since damages would be insufficient to replace the loss of documents valuable to prosecuting and resolving the case. However, necessity of an injunction must be shown in addition to irreparable injury. For the reasons stated above regarding **Answers (B) and (C)**, such legal necessity is not demonstrated here.

171. **Answer (A) is the correct answer.** Money damages were available at law as a remedy for breach of contract. Thus, a right to a jury trial will attach if Baker seeks money damages.

    Answer (B) is incorrect. Although breach of contract was a claim recognized by common law courts, specific performance was available as a remedy only in equity. The right to a jury trial will not attach if either a claim was not cognizable at common law or the remedy sought was not available in common law courts. Because specific performance is an equitable remedy, no right to a jury trial attaches.

    Answer (C) is incorrect. Only money damages will entitle Baker to a jury trial. Specific performance is an equitable remedy to which no right to a jury trial attaches.

    Answer (D) is incorrect. Baker will be entitled to a jury trial if Baker seeks money damages.

172. **Answer (D) is the correct answer.** Courts generally will not order specific performance of personal service contracts because it would impose difficult burdens of supervision on the court to monitor the quality of the employment and the relationship with the employer. Thus, the burden on the court from enforcing this injunction and the public policy weighing in favor of free competition in the employment market weigh against the granting of specific

performance. The general policy against specifically enforcing employment contracts and requiring personal servitude is implicated less in a case like this one where the employee, rather than the employer, seeks to enforce the contract.

Answer (A) is incorrect because detrimental reliance is irrelevant to the question asked and is not a basis for qualifying for an injunction.

Answer (B) is incorrect. Although Mr. Clean's contract is unique given the fact of a "once-in-a-lifetime" opportunity in a personalized, family business, the public policy against specific performance of employment contracts weighs against the issuance of the injunction.

Answer (C) is incorrect because the facts suggest that Mr. Clean cannot find another job as the contract is for a "once-in-a-lifetime" opportunity. If Mr. Clean were able to find another job, then the job would not be unique, and specific performance would be inappropriate.

173. An attorney for the successful plaintiffs would first seek preventive injunctive measures to stop the harm. Such preventive measures would order the state to stop sexually assaulting and harassing female inmates and to stop the cruel and unusual conditions of confinement. The plaintiffs would also seek to correct or reverse the existing conditions with reparative injunctive relief that would require the provision of adequate medical care, the establishment of sanitary conditions, and corrective action against the perpetrators of harassment. Due to the severity of the infractions and the personal invasions, the plaintiffs would also seek prophylactic measures designed to install preventive, cautionary steps that would aim to avert future harm. Such prophylactic measures could include the establishment of standards of care for the medical treatment, environmental standards for the temperature and cleanliness of the prison, policy measures against sexual harassment and assault, training and education of employees regarding sexual harassment, the establishment of a grievance process for inmates, and the development of employee sanctions for violations of the policy.

174. Porter's counsel has made a per diem argument. A per diem argument is a suggestion to the jury during closing argument that the jury calculate a plaintiff's pain and suffering damages by determining what amount of damages would be appropriate compensation for each day of pain and suffering then multiplying that amount by the number of days that the plaintiff will incur the pain and suffering. Many jurisdictions permit plaintiff's counsel to make such per diem arguments. However, some jurisdictions have rejected per diem arguments. Jurisdictions that reject per diem arguments do so on the ground that they are unduly prejudicial to defendants for several reasons. First, the per diem figure suggested by counsel is not evidence, but rather argument of counsel. The per diem argument, thus, invites the jury to calculate damages based on argument rather than evidence. Second, the per diem argument unfairly assumes that pain is constant, uniform and continuous during the injured plaintiff's life. This may not be the case. Because of the reasons, the jury may be misled by the per diem argument. Defense counsel in the problem could raise an objection to the per diem argument by Porter's counsel on these grounds.

175. **Answer (D) is the correct answer.** Homeowner would prefer rescission to cancel the contract for the sale of the house and return to the pre-contact position by being reimbursed for the costs of moving and expert investigation. The seller's fraud and substantial breach of contract in delivering a non-habitable home is a sufficient basis for rescission.

Answer (A) is incorrect. The facts indicate that Homeowner is seeking a restitutionary remedy, but implied-in-fact contract is not a theory of restitution. The finding of an implied-in-fact contract establishes the existence of an actual contract upon which further legal or equitable relief can be awarded. Here, Homeowner does not seek compensation for losses in the amount of the diminution in market value of the home; instead, Homeowner wants to cancel the contract.

Answer (B) is incorrect. There is no need to imply a contract at law when an express contract exists between the parties for the sale of the house.

Answer (C) is incorrect. Quantum meruit is an implied-in-law contract for the value of services. Homeowner is not seeking monetary payment for any services, and thus quantum meruit is inapplicable here.

176. **Answer (D) is the correct answer.** For a preliminary injunction, the plaintiffs must show harm to themselves during the trial that cannot later be remedied with monetary damages. Here, the district court found that damages would be adequate, thus negating the existence of irreparable harm.

Answer (A) is incorrect because the court expressly held that the plaintiffs do not have a likelihood of success because the legal question is close.

Answer (B) is incorrect. Harm to the plaintiffs alone is insufficient to establish irreparable injury necessary for preliminary relief. Instead, the plaintiffs must show harm during the litigation that cannot later be addressed by monetary damages. As discussed above in **Answer (D)**, that irreparable injury cannot be shown here.

Answer (C) is incorrect. Preliminary relief can be denied where the burden to the defendant is greater than the irreparable harm to the plaintiff. However, the facts given do not suggest any particular undue hardship to the city.

177. **Answer (C) is the correct answer.** The court can award the attorney fees as a measure of civil compensatory contempt imposed after the civil hearing of which defendant had notice and an opportunity to appear.

Answer (A) is incorrect because the determinate jail sentence is a criminal contempt penalty imposed for the attorney's past failure to appear without the full panoply of criminal procedural protections including the right to counsel, right against self-incrimination, and proof beyond a reasonable doubt.

Answer (B) is incorrect because the fine would be a criminal contempt measure that could not be imposed in the absence of full criminal procedures.

Answer (D) is incorrect because this is not a situation of frivolous conduct during litigation but rather a direct violation of a court's order to appear for trial.

178. **Answer (A) is the correct answer.** To be liable for punitive damages, unlike liability for an intentional tort, a defendant must intend not only the conduct but also must intend to cause harm. Here, because the casino patron intended to touch the dealer, he may be liable for an intentional tort. However, because he was jubilant over a big win, the patron likely did not intend to cause harm to the dealer. Therefore, the patron would not be liable for punitive damages.

Answer (B) is incorrect. Here, because the law student was disappointed with her grade, she likely intended to harm the professor and, thus, acted with the requisite bad state of mind. Additionally, because she caused serious physical injuries, her conduct rises to the requisite level of serious misconduct.

Answer (C) is incorrect. Although punitive damages are not appropriate in contract cases, punitive damages may be awarded if the misconduct constituting a breach of contract also constitutes an independent tort. Here, if the repair person knowingly misrepresented the time required for performance to induce the customer to enter into the contract, the misrepresentation would constitute both a breach of contract and the independent tort of fraud. Fraudulent conduct will support an award of punitive damages.

Answer (D) is incorrect. As discussed above, an award of punitive damages would not be appropriate in the case described in **Answer (A)**.

179. **Answer (C) is the correct answer.** To qualify for a constructive trust in many jurisdictions, a defendant's wrongdoing must involve a fraud or breach of some type of trust, confidence, or fiduciary duty. While Father has not fulfilled his promise of a gift to Daughter, he has not engaged in the type of fraud or breach of confidence which is the necessary predicate for a constructive trust.

Answer (A) is incorrect. To qualify for a constructive trust in many jurisdictions, a defendant 1) must engage in wrongdoing that involves a breach of trust, and 2) plaintiff must have originally owned the property at issue. Both of these requirements are missing here where Father has always owned the business property and has not engaged in fraud or breach of confidence.

Answer (B) is incorrect. According to the facts, Daughter has not made any improvements to the Father's business property, nor has Daughter provided any other service or benefit to Father for which a debt would be owed.

Answer (D) is incorrect. Equitable lien is a restitution remedy that awards payment for a debt owed and secures that debt with the tangible property that is the subject of the dispute. Here, there is tangible property available with which to secure an equitable lien in the form of the Father's business property that is the basis of the dispute.

180. **Answer (D) is the correct answer.** Generally, medical expenses between the time of injury and death, pain and suffering, and lost wages are all items of compensable damages in a survival action such as the one brought by Victor's Representative. However, most jurisdictions limit recovery for pain and suffering to recovery for only conscious pain and suffering. Here, because Victor never regained consciousness after his injury, he could have no conscious pain and suffering. Thus, his Estate will not be entitled to recover damages for pain and suffering. Additionally, most jurisdictions cut off recovery for lost wages at death. Thus, Victor's Estate will not be entitled to recover damages for lost wages over his entire natural worklife span. As such, Victor's Estate can recover damages only for the medical expenses Victor incurred between the time of injury and his death. **This result is found in Answer (D), making Answer (D) the correct answer and Answers (A), (B) and (C) incorrect.**

181. **Answer (A) is the correct answer.** Most jurisdictions allow the next-of-kin of a decedent to maintain an action for wrongful death against the tortfeasor who caused the decedent's death. Additionally, most jurisdictions allow the next-of-kin to recover damages for both their economic and noneconomic losses. These damages include damages for loss of financial support and services provided by the decedent as well as the loss of the decedent's society and companionship. However, a few jurisdictions limit recovery to damages for the next-of-kin's economic losses only. Here, because Dan wrongfully caused Victor's death, Victor's Beneficiaries can maintain an action for wrongful death and recover damages both for their loss of financial support from Victor and their loss of his companionship. **This result is found in Answer (A), making Answer (A) the correct answer and Answers (B), (C) and (D) incorrect.**

182. **Answer (C) is the correct answer.** If the seller does not resell the goods or resells the goods in a manner that does not conform with the UCC, the seller is not precluded from recovery. Instead, the seller may recover the difference between the contract price and the market price at the time and place for tender. Here, Sampson did not resell the trucks in accordance with the UCC. However, Sampson is not precluded from recovery. Instead, Sampson can recover the difference between the contract price of $7500 per truck and the market price of $7000 per truck, or $500 per truck.

Answer (A) is incorrect. A seller is not entitled to recover the purchase price from a breaching buyer unless (1) the buyer accepts the goods; (2) the goods are damaged after the risk of loss has passed to the buyer; or (3) the goods cannot be resold through reasonable efforts. Here, Bivens has not accepted the trucks, nor have the trucks been damaged. Further, Sampson was able to resell the trucks, suggesting that the trucks were not so unique that they could not be resold. Thus, Sampson is not entitled to recover the price.

Answer (B) is incorrect. When a buyer rejects conforming goods, UCC § 2-703 permits the seller to resell the goods and recover the difference between the contract price and the resale price. If the seller elects to resell the goods, the seller must do so in a commercially reasonable manner, and if the seller resells the goods at a private sale, the seller must give the breaching buyer notice of the seller's intent to resell the goods. Here, Sampson attempted to resell the trucks. However, Sampson resold the trucks at a private sale but failed to give Bivens notice of the resale. Moreover, the discrepancy between the market price of $7000 and the resale price of $3000 might indicate that Sampson did not sell the trucks in a commercially reasonable manner. Thus, Sampson cannot recover the difference between the contract price of $7500 per truck and the resale price of $3000 per truck, or $4500 per truck.

Answer (D) is incorrect. If a nonbreaching seller fails to resell the goods or resells the goods in a manner that does not conform with the UCC, the seller is not precluded from recovery. Instead, the seller may recover the difference between the contract price and the market price at the time and place for tender.

183. **Answer (B) is the correct answer.** There is no showing that the protestors have violated or are likely to violate any law. There was no past illegal behavior nor any planned action that in and of itself is illegal. The protestors have a right under the First Amendment to free speech.

Answer (A) is incorrect. The notice here was adequate as the police delivered a copy of the motion for temporary relief to the protest leaders. Even though actual notice is not required, it was obtained in this case upon personal delivery.

Answer (C) is incorrect. The imminence factor requiring close proximity in time of the alleged threat is satisfied here by the scheduled timing of the protest next week. It is not the timing, but rather the absence of a threatened harm that disqualifies the temporary injunction here.

Answer (D) is incorrect. *Ex parte* hearings in which only one party appears before the judge are constitutional under Due Process.

184. **Answer (B) is the correct answer.** Civil compensatory contempt is a monetary fine assessed to compensate a party for costs incurred as a result of the opposing party's violation of a court order. Here, the monetary award compensates Smith for the costs Smith incurred as a result of Clintex's violation of the court order. Civil contempt requires the opportunity to be heard, and the court provided that opportunity to Clintex.

Answer (A) is incorrect. The fine here for the past violation is not fixed as an arbitrary penalty, but instead is measured precisely by the amount of loss caused by the defendant.

Answer (C) is incorrect because the court provided the proper procedures of notice and an opportunity to be heard. The procedures are required as part of the process of awarding contempt, but are not necessarily required prior to the court's ruling.

Answer (D) is incorrect. The fine is not a criminal contempt remedy as discussed with respect to **Answer (A)**. If it were criminal contempt, the procedures used by the court would be insufficient to sustain the award.

185. **Answer (B) is the correct answer.** Patterson is entitled to recover the cost to repair the car if repairs are both economically and physically feasible. Courts differ in the manner in which they measure economic feasibility. However, one measure is the pre-tort value of the car.

Answer (A) is incorrect. Repairs must be both physically and economically feasible.

Answer (C) is incorrect. Most courts reject the cost to repair when it exceeds either the diminution in value or the pre-tort value of the car regardless of the owner's reasons for repairing the car.

Answer (D) is incorrect. Patterson is entitled to recover the cost to repair the car as long as the repairs are physically and economically feasible. Economic feasibility will be measured by either the pre-tort value of the car or the diminution in value to the car as a result of the accident.

186. **Answer (D) is the correct answer.** There is an imminent threat to the testing company from the use of its secret testing questions within the next ten days that the court could prevent. In addition, the company would seek a preliminary injunction to bar the use of the test questions while the litigation is pending.

    Answer (A) is incorrect because it is incomplete. The company can obtain a temporary injunction, but it can also seek preliminary relief.

    Answer (B) is incorrect because it is incomplete. The company can obtain preliminary relief, but it can also request a temporary injunction.

    Answer (C) is incorrect because a party cannot seek a permanent injunction until the completion of trial. Here, trial is not scheduled for eight more months and thus it is not the appropriate time to seek permanent relief.

187. Under UCC § 2-709 a seller is entitled to recover price for goods identified to the contract that the seller is unable to resell through reasonable efforts. Here, Super Tees completed 100 t-shirts that are identified to the contract with Beasely. Super Tees will be unable to resell the t-shirts because they commemorate Beasely's graduation. Thus, Super Tees will be entitled to recover the price of $400 ($4.00 per shirt × 100 completed shirts). Super Tees also will be entitled to recover its lost profits for the remaining 100 t-shirts. UCC § 2-704 allows a seller that has not completed manufacture of the contract goods prior to the breach to cease manufacturing if to do so would be commercially reasonable. Here, Super Tees acted reasonably in ceasing production because no market appears to exist for the commemorative t-shirts. When a seller ceases production, market and resale differential damages will be inadequate. The measures envision the resale and the market price of finished goods. Thus, such a "components seller" is entitled to lost profits under § 2-708(2). Here, because Super Tees ceased production of the remaining 100 t-shirts, it has no finished goods. Accordingly, it is entitled to lost profits. Under UCC § 2-708(2), lost profits are measured as the seller's profits including reasonable overhead plus due allowance for costs reasonably incurred and less any payments or proceeds on resale. Profit is measured as the contract price less the seller's production costs. Here, Super Tee's anticipated profit was $2.50 per shirt or $250 (($4.00 contract price − $1.00 cost of shirt − $0.30 cost of ink − $.020 cost of overhead) × 100 shirts). Super Tees is entitled to recover $20 cost of overhead ($0.20 × 100 shirts). Super Tees also is entitled to recover costs it has reasonably incurred. Here, Super Tees already has paid $100 for the 100 t-shirts ($1.00 per shirt × 100 shirts) and $30 for the ink ($0.30 per shirt × 100 shirts). Assuming, Super Tees acted reasonably in pur-

chasing the blank t-shirts and ink, it will be entitled to recover these costs as well. Super Tees' recovery will be reduced by any proceeds it received on resale of the components. Here, Super Tees was able to sell the blank t-shirts for $50 ($0.50 per shirt × 100 shirts). Finally, Super Tees is entitled to recover any incidental damages it incurred in mitigating its loss. Here, Super Tees had to pay $10 ($0.10 per shirt × 100 shirts) to ship the blank t-shirts to the new purchaser. Thus, Super Tees' recovery will be $760 ($400 (price for completed t-shirts) + $250 (profit on unfinished t-shirts) + $20 (overhead attributable to unfinished t-shirts) + $130 (costs incurred for blank t-shirts and ink) – $50 (profit earned on resale of blank t-shirts) + $10 (incidental damages for shipping blank t-shirts)). This result is found in **Answer (B), making Answer (B) the correct answer and Answers (A), (C) and (D) incorrect answers.**

188. **Answer (B) is the correct answer.** Generally, the trier of fact determines whether to impose punitive damages and in what amount. Thus, if a jury is the trier of the fact, the jury determines whether and in what amount to impose punitive damages. Further, the imposition of punitive damages is always discretionary. Even if the jury determines that the defendant acted with the requisite state of mind to be liable for punitive damages, the jury in its discretion may choose not to impose punitive damages on the defendant. Thus, here, even if the jury determines that Davidson acted intentionally and, thus, could be liable for punitive damages, the jury may, but need not, impose punitive damages.

    Answer (A) is incorrect. The imposition of punitive damages is always discretionary. The jury is never required to impose punitive damages.

    Answer (C) is incorrect. Generally, the trier of fact determines whether to impose punitive damages and in what amount. Thus, if a jury is the trier of the fact, the jury determines whether and in what amount to impose punitive damages.

    Answer (D) is incorrect. If Davidson acted intentionally, punitive damages would be appropriate.

189. **Answer (A) is the correct answer.** The defendant Billy may assert the defense of waiver arguing that Bobby unilaterally relinquished his right to sue for breach of contract by going through with the sale even though his roommate told him of the lack of value in the cards. His father's statement establishes knowledge on Bobby's part regarding his right to a contract as warranted.

    Answer (B) is incorrect. Estoppel would be a defense barring Bobby from changing legal positions regarding the validity of the contract. He first acceded to the value of the contract despite the knowledge from this father, but now seeks to change that position. However, estoppel requires detrimental reliance on the part of Billy, and there are no facts to establish such detrimental reliance.

    Answer (C) is incorrect because estoppel is not a valid defense as explained in Answer (B) above.

Answer (D) is incorrect because the unconscionability defense is not available to Billy, but rather may be a defense for *Bobby* to consider. Unconscionability is a defense regarding oppressiveness in the creation or content of the contract. The defense would likely fail even as raised by Bobby because his roommate provided the notice and counsel necessary to counter any unfair bargaining power.

190. By excluding evidence of cost-of-living increases to wages but using a market discount rate, Judge Grumpy treated inflation inconsistently. Judge Grumpy refused to recognize that Plaintiff's future earnings would increase due to inflation. However, because a market interest rate reflects anticipated inflation, Judge Grumpy reduced her present award on the theory that she would earn more on her investment over time based on inflation. As such, Plaintiff may be undercompensated.

191. **Answer (B) is the correct answer.** Courts will issue injunctions where the irreparable injury to the plaintiff outweighs any undue hardship to the defendant. Here, the serious physical and emotional harm to Mrs. Small is intangible harm that cannot adequately be remedied after the fact with damages. While damages could be computed for her harm, the public policy preference is to avoid physical harm to individuals by preventing its occurrence. While Big, Bad and Boom may have some undue hardship in the form of financial loss from relocation or adaptation of its manufacturing process, that hardship does not outweigh the harm to the plaintiff.

Answer (A) is incorrect. Significant economic waste to a defendant is a basis upon which a court may deny the plaintiff its injunction. The facts here are close to the line of establishing undue hardship in possibly requiring Big, Bad, and Boom to go out of business. However, it is also likely that the injunction will merely impose some financial costs upon Big, Bad and Boom as it relocates or adapts its manufacturing process to avoid pollution. The possible economic waste does not rise to the level courts have required in cases of physical and medical harm to people.

Answer (C) is incorrect. The public interest is one factor relevant to the court's balancing test for an injunction. However, there is no absolute policy in favor of commercial interests, especially where they interfere with individual rights, as in this case.

Answer (D) is incorrect because the plaintiff's desire for an injunction, standing alone, is insufficient basis on which to award an injunction.

192. **Answer (B) is the correct answer.** The case presents a definite, adverse, ripe controversy that is not altered by the plaintiff's request for a declaration rather than an injunction. *See Nashville v. Wallace*, 288 U.S. 249 (1933) (the classic case on state power to issue declaratory judgments).

Answer (A) is incorrect because there is an actual controversy. In addition, the language of "case or controversy" indicates a conclusion about the related, but distinct, concept of constitutional judicial power rather than the required threshold for declaratory judgments.

Answer (C) is incorrect because the claimant does not seek an advisory opinion that is hypothetical, but instead challenges a specific tax law and its application to the company.

Answer (D) is incorrect because if the legal question were hypothetical, the court would not have judicial power to issue declaratory relief.

193. **Answer (D) is the correct answer.** An accounting of profits would be a proper restitutionary remedy to address the unjust benefit gained by Big Films in appropriating the writer's story for its film. An accounting of profits remedy is measured by the amount of profit derived by the defendant from the wrong. The accounting measure offsets the total revenues made by the defendant ($65 million) with production costs ($5 million) and any profits related to the defendant's own efforts ($30 million from star Devine).

    Answer (A) is incorrect. This is a measure of the plaintiff's loss, the payment she would have received from Big Films but for the wrong. However, restitution disgorges the defendant's gain, which is often greater than plaintiff's loss.

    Answer (B) is incorrect. The $65 million in total revenues made by the defendant is the measure of an accounting remedy only where the defendant fails to show offsetting costs or disassociated profits. Here, Big Films has established an offset of $35 million from the production costs and profits associated with the star power of Devine.

    Answer (C) is incorrect. The $60 million offsets the total revenues made by defendants minus its production costs. However, it fails to subtract out the amount of profits made by the defendants' own efforts of securing a famous star.

194. **Answer (D) is the correct answer.** Because the land cannot be restored to productive agricultural use, the damage to the land is permanent. When damage to land is permanent, the landowner is entitled to recover the diminution in value to the land as a result of the damage.

    Answer (A) is incorrect. Farmer Brown will not be entitled to recover the cost to remove the chemicals because the damage is permanent. The chemicals are not harmful to humans. Thus, the only use the chemicals prevent is an agricultural use. Removing the chemicals will not restore the land to agricultural use.

    Answer (B) is incorrect. The damage to the land is permanent rather than temporary because removing the chemicals will not restore the land for agricultural use. Because the damage is permanent, Farmer Brown is not entitled to recover the cost to restore the land.

    Answer (C) is incorrect. Even though the land is permanently damaged, Farmer Brown is not entitled to recover the full pre-contamination market value of the land because the land retains some productive uses after the contamination and, hence, retains some market value.

195. **Answer (A) is the correct answer.** Farmer Brown is entitled to recover the lost profits on the crops as measured by the market value of the lost crops less the expenses saved in growing and harvesting the crops.

    Answer (B) is incorrect. Awarding the full market value of the crops would overcompensate Farmer Brown because Farmer Brown has been saved the expense of growing and harvesting the crops.

Answer (C) is incorrect. The damage to the land and the damage to the crops are two distinct injuries. Thus, Farmer Brown can recover for both.

Answer (D) is incorrect. Farmer Brown can recover for lost crops as long as Farmer Brown can provide a reasonable basis for estimating the amount of crops lost and the value of those crops.

196. **Answer (A) is the correct answer** because the court correctly sought to coerce future compliance with the injunction by assessing a daily fine which the defendants could avoid or purge by compliance with the order. *See International Workers Union v. Bagwell*, 512 U.S. 821 (1994).

    Answer (B) is incorrect because the order is structured as a valid coercive contempt remedy as indicated above, and the court provided the required process of notice and an opportunity to be heard.

    Answer (C) is incorrect because a criminal contempt remedy would have been a fixed fine of a set amount for past violations that could not be avoided by defendants, rather than the indeterminate designation of a future, per day amount.

    Answer (D) is incorrect because it does not describe what the court attempted to do here. The answer would have fit if the court had attempted a criminal contempt remedy to punish the defendants for a past violation, but failed to use sufficient criminal procedures mandated by the U.S. Constitution such as trial by jury, proof beyond a reasonable doubt, the right to counsel, and the right against self-incrimination.

197. In *State Farm v. Campbell*, 538 U.S. 408 (2003), the Supreme Court recognized that a punitive award that was more than 9 times greater than the compensatory award such as the award in this case was constitutionally suspect. However, the Court refused to create a bright line rule prohibiting such awards and recognized that such awards might be merited in some cases. Here, Plimpton could argue that a large punitive award was necessary to deter Big Brother because Big Brother was aware of previous similar misconduct and took no steps to prevent it. Likewise, Plimpton could argue that a large punitive award was necessary because Big Brother's conduct, while reprehensible, caused little economic harm. As such, a large punitive award was necessary to provide an incentive for victims to bring suit against Big Brother and, hence, to deter the misconduct. Big Brother could argue that such a large award is unjustified in this case because it is duplicative of the plaintiff's compensatory award. As in *State Farm*, the compensatory award here is sizeable and the bulk of the award is to compensate for non-economic losses such as emotional distress. In *State Farm*, the Court recognized that under such circumstances, much of the emotional distress for which the plaintiff is compensated is caused by the outrage and humiliation that the plaintiff suffered as a result of the defendant's action. Punitive damages also are imposed to condemn the defendant for causing such outrage and humiliation. In such cases, then, the compensatory award already contains a punitive element.

ANSWERS · PRACTICE FINAL EXAM

198. Laches and the statute of limitations both relate to delay in the plaintiff's pursuit of a remedy through litigation. Laches originated as an equitable defense and includes any delay during the course of litigation. The statute of limitations is a statutorily created defense that pertains only to the delay in initially commencing the action. In addition, laches requires prejudice to the defendant, whereas the statute of limitations is an absolute time bar regardless of the impact or lack of harm to the defendant. Finally, the statute of limitations prescribes a specific time in which an action has to be commenced whereas laches is flexible and focuses on the unreasonableness of the plaintiff's delay.

199. **Answer (C) is the correct answer.** Fashion Mavens' substantial breach of refusing to pay royalties for the use of the software as agreed in the contract is a sufficient basis upon which to seek rescission of the contract.

    Answer (A) is incorrect. Proof of the inadequacy of legal damages is a required element in seeking equitable remedies. Rescission developed in both law and equity and thus inadequacy is not always required to qualify for relief. Moreover, an independent basis to qualify for the rescission remedy is first required (substantial breach, mistake, fraud, emergency) prior to consideration of whether rescission is an appropriate remedy over damages.

    Answer (B) is incorrect. Mistake, either bilateral or unilateral known to the other side, can constitute a legal basis for rescission. However, the facts do not indicate that the failure to pay the royalties was a result of mistake.

    Answer (D) is incorrect. If a court were to imply a contract at law, it would be using the restitutionary remedy of quasi-contract to award a restitution remedy. Quasi-contract is a separate restitutionary remedy distinct from rescission, and thus does not constitute a legal basis upon which to seek rescission.

200. **Answer (C) is the correct answer.** The measure of restitution for rescission seeks to return both parties to the status quo ante, the position they were in prior to the contract. To restore Software to its original position, it must disgorge the $60,000 received under the contract. To restore Fashion Mavens to its position, it must return the profits obtained by use of the software purchased under the contract. However, the law apportions the profits to require the return only of the profits obtained unjustly under the contract. The amount of profits Fashion Maven earned by its own efforts of marketing and consulting are not disgorged. *See, e.g., Earthinfo Inc. v. Hydrosphere Resource Consultants*, 900 P.2d 113 (Colo. 1995).

    Answer (A) is incorrect. Fashion Mavens does not have to disgorge the entire amount of its profits, but only the portion of the profits obtained unjustly by the use of software now required to be "returned" under the rescinded contract.

Answer (B) is incorrect. While this answer correctly describes the apportionment of profits, it fails to return Software to its original position by requiring the offsetting disgorgement of the return of the initial contract payment.

Answer (D) is incorrect. Monetary remedies measured by the amount of a plaintiff's loss are not restitution measures, but rather are measures of compensatory damages. Since Software is not seeking damages, this is an incorrect measure for restitution.

201. **Answer (B) is the correct answer.** If Insured prevails on either the bad faith or the breach of contract claim, Insured will be entitled to recover the attorney fees incurred in the client litigation as compensatory damages because the attorney fees were what Insured bargained for under the insurance contract and lost when Massive Mutual refused to defend client's lawsuit.

    Answer (A) is incorrect. If Insured prevails on the breach of contract claim only, he will be entitled to recover only those attorney fees he incurred in defending client's lawsuit because those were the attorney fees that he was promised under the insurance contract. Like any other attorney fees incurred in vindicating a party's contract rights, the attorney fees incurred in prosecuting the claims against Massive Mutual will be governed by the American Rule. Note that if Insured had prevailed on the bad faith claim as well as the breach of contract claim, many jurisdictions would allow Insured to recover all of his attorney fees, including those incurred in prosecuting the bad faith claim.

    Answer (C) is incorrect. The attorney fees that Insured incurs in bringing his breach of contract action against Massive Mutual are like the attorney fees incurred by any other party that brings a breach of contract action. Under the American Rule, such attorney fees are not recoverable unless the insurance contract expressly provides for recovery of attorney fees. However, if Insured had prevailed on the bad faith claim as well as the breach of contract claim, many jurisdictions would allow Insured to recover all of his attorney fees, including those incurred in prosecuting the bad faith claim, as an exception to the American Rule.

    Answer (D) is incorrect. Insured is entitled to recover the attorney fees he incurred in defending against client's claim.

202. **Answer (D) is the correct answer.** An equitable lien is an appropriate restitutionary remedy when a third party has made improvements to the property of another. The amount of debt owed to the church would be measured by the benefit gained by the Landlord in the amount of financial and construction investments into the building.

    Answer (A) is incorrect. Constructive trust is generally not available as a remedy when the defendant has not engaged in a fraud or breach of confidence and where the property at issue was not originally owned by the plaintiff. Both of these predicate requirements are absent in this scenario.

Answer (B) is incorrect. An accounting of profits disgorges the profits gained by the defendant from its wrongdoing. Here, Landlord has not engaged in an illegal act or wrongdoing, but merely has retained the benefit conferred by the church on the assumption that it would be the eventual owner of the building.

Answer (C) is incorrect. Quantum meruit is not an equitable restitution theory, but instead is a legal device.

203. Most jurisdictions recognize an implied condition in every attorney-client contract that allows a client to discharge her attorney at any time with or without cause. Thus, Parker has not breached the retainer agreement by discharging Anderson. However, most jurisdictions also allow an attorney to recover the reasonable value of her services in quantum meruit when a client discharges the attorney before completion of the representation. In some jurisdictions, this right to quantum meruit is subject to two conditions. First, if the retainer agreement conditions the attorney's right to receive a fee on some condition such as the client's recovery, then the attorney has no right to quantum meruit recovery unless and until that contingency occurs. Second, an attorney cannot recover more in quantum meruit than she would have recovered under the retainer agreement. Here, the retainer agreement between Parker and Anderson conditioned Anderson's right to receive a fee on Parker's obtaining a judgment or settlement. That contingency has occurred because Baker settled the case for Parker. Thus, Anderson is entitled to recover the reasonable value of services rendered to Parker. However, Anderson's recovery may be capped at $165,000 or 33% of the $500,000 settlement because that is the amount to which Anderson would have been entitled had the retainer agreement been performed.

204. **Answer (D) is the correct answer** because the moving party is attempting to use declaratory relief for the tactical advantage of evading the applicable time limits.

Answer (A) is incorrect because a declaration about the relative rights of the two parties with respect to the particular building permit at issue would terminate the uncertainty between those parties.

Answer (B) is incorrect because the controversy is ripe as the building permit has been denied and thus there are no further actions or facts which must occur before it would be the right time for the court to intervene in the dispute.

Answer (C) is incorrect because the Contractor presents a definite and concrete issue regarding its particular building permit and the actual reasons for denial.

205. **Answer (A) is the correct answer.** Unclean hands prohibits a plaintiff from coming into court to request equitable relief when it has engaged in misconduct. The misconduct must connect generally to the facts of the case, but not necessarily be directly related to the underlying claim. The plaintiff's misrepresentation in naming its product is related to the underlying trademark dispute sufficiently to bar it from seeking a remedy. A court will not adjudicate a dispute between two wrongdoers.

Answer (B) is incorrect. Defendant is being sued for trademark infringement. Any other potential liability of the defendant is not relevant to the availability of remedial defenses between the parties in this case.

Answer (C) is incorrect. The *defendant's* misconduct is not relevant to the plaintiff's claim for relief in this case. The defendant's misconduct could be relevant, under different circumstances, as a response to a counter-defense of the plaintiff or as a defense for the plaintiff against a counter-claim of the defendant.

Answer (D) is incorrect. *In pari delicto* would bar Big Fig's claim if it was at equal fault in the underlying trademark infringement at issue in the case.

206. **Answer (D) is correct.** In *Alyeska Pipeline Service Co. v. Wilderness Society*, 421 U.S. 240 (1975), the Supreme Court refused to recognize a public policy exception to the American Rule. Instead, the Court held that a prevailing party can recover its attorney fees only if the case fits into one of the pre-existing common law exceptions to the American Rule, including the common fund doctrine. However, the Court also recognized that the common fund exception does not apply when the plaintiff realizes only a generalized social benefit. Instead, the plaintiff's case must generate a common fund to which an easily identified class of claimants has an undisputed and ascertainable claim. Here, Do-Right's claim raises important public policy issues, and the resolution of Do-Right's claims will affect future permit applications. However, under *Alyeska*, these are merely generalized social benefits that do not create a determinative common fund to which an indentifiable class of claimants has an ascertainable claim. Thus, Do-Right is not entitled to recover his attorney fees. **This result is found in Answer (D), making Answer (D) the correct answer and Answers (A), (B) and (C) incorrect.**

207. **Answer (C) is the correct answer.** When a seller delivers non-conforming goods, the buyer is entitled to recover the difference between the value of the goods as accepted and the value of the goods had the goods been delivered in the condition warranted by the seller under UCC § 2-714. Under UCC § 2-715, a buyer also can recover consequential damages such as lost profits, if those losses were foreseeable and unavoidable. Under the UCC, consequential damages are foreseeable when the seller had reason to know of the particular needs of buyer that caused the consequential loss at the time of contracting. The UCC also requires the buyer to take reasonable steps through cover or otherwise to prevent the loss. If the loss occurs despite the buyer's reasonable efforts, the buyer can recover damages for the loss. Here, Specialty Products delivered a non-conforming press. Thus, Manufacturer is entitled to recover the difference between the value of the press as delivered and the value of the press as contracted for. At the time of contracting, Manufacturer informed Specialty Products that it needed the press to manufacture widgets that it intended to sell. Thus, Manufacturer's lost profits from the sale of widgets were foreseeable to Specialty Products. Finally, Manufacturer took prompt steps to repair the press. Thus, Manufacturer is entitled to recover its lost profits as well as the difference in value damages. This result is found in **Answer (C), making Answer (C) the correct answer and Answers (A), (B) and (D) incorrect answers.**

208. **Answer (D) is the correct answer.** Damages are adequate here to replace Surfer Dude's loss. Where a legal remedy is adequate to return the plaintiff to his rightful position, the equitable remedy will be denied. Damages here will be measured by the difference in the contract price minus the market price of the wax ($6.00 − $5.00 = $1.00 × 100 cans = $100).

    Answer (A) is incorrect because the surfer wax is not unique, as demonstrated by the market availability of a second brand of wax. The plaintiff's personal preference for a good, standing alone, is insufficient to establish the uniqueness or lack of fungibility of the good.

    Answer (B) is incorrect because the additional cost of the replacement goods is relevant to the calculation of damages, and does not dictate the availability of equitable relief.

    Answer (C) is incorrect because the contract for the sale of specified goods does not impose any additional burden of supervision or monitoring on the court. Where such a burden on the court does exist, courts will deny specific performance.

209. **Answer (C) is the correct answer.** Modification of the injunction is appropriate due to the changed factual circumstances of Joe's continued violation of the order. Prophylactic relief which goes beyond the legal harm to address the facilitators of harm is appropriate where the defendant has exhibited a history of similar illegal conduct. The order to stay 25 feet away from the castle is a prophylactic measure designed to provide an additional precaution against Joe's continued violation of Princess' privacy.

    Answer (A) is incorrect because Joe's failure to comply with the prior injunction is a significant change in circumstances since the time of the prior order.

    Answer (B) is incorrect because factually, Joe did not comply with the order in substance or in good faith. Additionally, the existence of a defendant's good faith compliance is a basis for seeking termination, rather than modification, of injunctive relief.

    Answer (D) is incorrect because the modification would be too broad in scope by going beyond the harm or the contributors of that harm and unduly burdening Joe's First Amendment right to report the news on public figures like Princess. Modification of the prior injunction is appropriate, but that modification must be tailored to the scope of the changed circumstances.

210. Potter has two possible claims against Tyson. First, Potter can pursue the legal theory of conversion because Tyson stole the painting. Under this theory, Potter will be entitled to recover the $5000 fair market value of the painting at the time of conversion. Second, Potter can pursue the restitutionary theory of "waiver of the tort and suit in assumpsit." This theory implies a fictitious agency relationship between Potter and Tyson such that Tyson would be deemed to hold the painting for Potter's benefit and to have sold the painting on Potter's behalf. Under this theory, Potter would be entitled to recover the $1 million that Tyson received from the sale of the painting. In this case, Potter would want to waive the tort and sue in assumpsit because this theory would yield a greater recovery for Potter.

Model Student Answer to Practice Essay Question One

The government bears the burden of proof on its motion for a preliminary injunction, and the statute doesn't modify the traditional four-part test. Thus, the government will have to establish the following:

1. That it is likely to succeed on the merits;

2. It will suffer imminent irreparable harm in the absence of a preliminary injunction;

3. The harm to it in the absence of an injunction outweighs any harm to SK Tax and Keefe if an injunction issues; and

4. The injunction is consistent with the public interest.

Likelihood of Success on the Merits.

Section 26000 of the Code requires "systematic" problems, and a sample of twelve tax returns is insubstantial both in absolute terms and relative to the defendant's business, since it's less than 0.1% of their 10,000+ returns. Moreover, while the returns contain errors, these findings are based on "informal audits." Tentative findings like this cast some doubt on what proof the government will have at trial. Further, the statute requires "reckless" or "intentional" conduct (or fraud), not merely negligence; can the government meet this higher standard? The errors on *these* returns may also pertain to matters that a tax preparer cannot reasonably be expected to verify or audit in this limited and discrete transaction (for which he is compensated approximately $1000). And finally, he seems to have been in business for several years without incident (as far as we know) until now.

However, there are several facts in the fact pattern which suggest that the government is reasonably likely to succeed at trial. Most importantly, twelve returns prepared by SK Tax contained false statements—which is 100% of the sample. And affidavits from those taxpayers blame SK Tax. Moreover, Keefe personally prepared ten of these returns. Even Keefe admits that errors were made. And his lack of formal training in tax preparation—plus his disavowal of tax expertise—make it more likely that he violated § 26000. Keefe's business has the markers of the shady business model that this statute targets.

Irreparable Harm

The *government* is not exactly facing imminent irreparable harm because it can always prosecute claims against the defendant (and the taxpayers) after they file their dubious returns. These returns are only about money—and the government's lost revenue can be calculated with precision after the fact.

However, this statute empowers the government to obtain injunctive relief to protect vulnerable taxpayers from unscrupulous tax preparation businesses. *Taxpayers* will face imminent, irreparable harm if the court does not issue a preliminary injunction. Without a preliminary injunction, thousands more taxpayers will file returns containing errors and misstatements, subjecting them to civil and criminal punishment. Because the court will not be able to try this case for at least 12 months, at least one tax cycle will pass before the court can resolve this case on the merits. Further, because SK Tax has prepared 10,000 tax returns over the past four years, it is likely that SK Tax will prepare thousands of tax returns in one tax season. As such, thousands of taxpayers will face the risk of civil and criminal punishment while the litigation is pending if the court does not issue a preliminary injunction.

Harm to taxpayers cannot be remedied after a trial on the merits. And although the harm to the government might be recouped (at least theoretically) from SK Tax after trial, Congress passed this statute authorizing equitable relief to prevent injuries just like ours here.

Balance of Hardships

If the preliminary injunction is granted, the defendant will be enjoined from operating the taxpayer preparation business for approximately twelve months (until there is a trial and a final judgment). Keefe seems to have the entrepreneurial gene that would allow him to find some other way to make money.

Yet a judge is likely to perceive Keefe's hardship as substantial. The sought injunction would prevent an existing chain of stores from doing business. Keefe will surely default on fifteen leases since a tax preparation store is unlikely to be repurposed. He presumably will need to lay off his fifteen employees (without any assurance of rehiring the people he has trained). And he will be deprived of his livelihood without any "formal degrees" to fall back on. We lack details about his living situation and family, but the collateral damage of being unable to work is obvious and is potentially catastrophic. It also bears mention that this injunction would be disturbing the status quo, rather than preserving it, as paradigmatic injunctions would do.

That being said, a court is likely to conclude that the potential harm to the government and taxpayers, including the specter of criminal liability, outweighs the financial consequences to SK Tax and Keefe. This seems particularly likely in light of the fact that SK Tax and Keefe have targeted their conduct at financially vulnerable individuals. Even if these individuals are only liable for financial penalties that can ultimately be recouped from SK Tax and Keefe, the financial consequences of having to pay penalties upfront and seek redress from SK Tax and Keefe are likely significant enough to outweigh the consequences to SK Tax and Keefe if they are temporarily enjoined.

Public Interest

This business prepares tax returns in fifteen communities for low-income individuals who qualify for tax credits. Yet it appears also that he charges them 7x the going rate for filing a 1040 tax return and encourages them to file false returns that subjects them to civil and criminal penalties. Again, the injunction may be seen as protecting this vulnerable population rather than depriving them of a service provider.

To be sure, some landlords, vendors, and other members of the "public" will suffer if the injunction is granted. But the broader public also has an interest in shutting down deceitful businesses — and even in enforcing the tax laws. The public interest is not served by allowing a crooked business to facilitate tax evasion.

Model Student Answer to Practice Essay Question Two

The Award of $130,000

The $130,000 appears to be a valid civil compensatory award, provided $100 per computer is the fair market value of the licensing fee. DG, or any other entity, is expected to pay for licenses for intellectual property work that it uses but does not own. Here, the court ruled that the intellectual property in use (even the Contrafite derivative version) are the property of Pocket who should be fairly compensated for it. DG's intent is irrelevant.

DG has been using infringing software for 13 months since it stopped paying the licensing fee it agreed to in its contract with Pocket. Damages must be clearly proven here for the $130,000 to be valid. If the $100 per computer is considered a fair market value fee for the software/intellectual property, then the $130,000 would be the appropriate compensatory damages here. However, if the market value is somehow proven to be instead, say, $60 per computer, per the original licensing agreement between DG and Pocket, then the extra $40 per computer during this duration should be considered punitive. For sure, the $60 per computer portion of the fee should be valid compensatory damages and should most likely not need to be appealed. The extra $40 might also be compensatory, if the $60 charge under the original agreement represented a discount off the (full $100) fair market value.

If the extra $40 is not, in fact, compensatory, then that amount is punitive and could not be imposed without all of the protections of criminal contempt, including intent, proof beyond a reasonable doubt, etc. If all of the protections of criminal law were not afforded DG in the first hearing staying the injunction, then 40% of this $130,000 is improper and should be vacated on appeal.

The Award of $50,000

This sanction was imposed presumably because DG failed to comply with the court's order to develop a replacement software within the allotted time. This is an indirect criminal contempt order that requires a right to a jury trial and all the protections of criminal procedure. Because this was imposed at a "status conference," I doubt that this was processed as a criminal contempt proceeding—prosecuted by the state in an appropriate evidentiary hearing, with proof beyond a reasonable doubt, and so forth. Moreover, in a proper proceeding, the argument that it was impossible for DG to comply would be a valid defense.

This error is immediately appealable.

The Award of $775,000

Although this is the largest of the three awards, it is the least appealable. This is civil coercive contempt. The monthly fine is analogous to sitting in jail until one is compelled to comply. DG had the keys to the jail in its pocket in the sense that it could have avoided any/all of this sanction by complying and installing replacement software. Someone facing civil compensatory contempt is still entitled to all the protections of *civil* procedure—just not the enhanced protections of criminal protection. Provided DG received these, the $775,000 award may be a valid civil coercive contempt sanction.

To be sure, DG could argue that, like *International Workers Union v. Bagwell*, 512 U.S. 821 (1994), this case involves a "complex" injunction involving a substantial penalty where the need for elaborate fact finding warrants the protections of *criminal* contempt. But this seems unlikely. This case seems to involve only the simple (not complex) issue of whether DG had new software installed. And the $775,000 penalty is not nearly as substantial as the tens of millions of dollars imposed by the court in *Bagwell*. That leaves only the argument that the escalating nature of these fines makes them *punitive* rather than merely coercive, and/or the broader argument that civil coercive contempt should be limited to its paradigm situation where the defendant sits in jail until she complies.

Index

Topic	Question
Accounting of profits	132, 193, 199, 200, 202
Attorney fees	5, 114, 154–161, 177, 184, 201, 203, 206
Backpay	1, 3, 4, 5
Certainty	8, 46
Collateral source rule	42
Comparative fault	12, 45
Compensatory damages	6, 7–63, 167, 169, 171, 174, 180, 181, 182, 185, 187, 190, 194, 195, 207, 208, 210
Contract damages	7, 8, 17–33, 115, 167, 171, 182, 187, 207, 208
Damages for bodily injury	15–16, 34–51, 169, 174, 180, 181, 190
Property damages	52–63, 185, 194, 195, 210
Tort damages	15–16, 34–51, 52–63, 64–72, 167, 174, 180, 181, 185, 190, 194, 195, 210
Consent decree	108
Consequential damages	10, 11, 207
Constructive trust	1, 125, 127, 129, 130, 131, 133, 134 179, 202
Contempt	93, 105–114, 177, 184, 196
Cover	18
Declaratory judgment	93, 135–145, 168, 192, 204
Defenses	146–153, 189, 198, 203, 205
Discount to present value	37, 39, 190
Double recoveries	6, 44
Due process	97, 108, 110, 183, 184

Topic	Question
Emotional distress	47
Employment remedies	3–5
Equitable lien	125, 128, 129, 130, 134, 179, 202
Equity	1–6, 83, 125, 126, 171
Estoppel	148, 189
Expectancy	8
Fed. R. Civ. Proc. 65	95–97, 104
Fluctuating value	54
Foreseeability	21
Incidental damages	19, 26
Indemnity	122
Imminent harm	77, 79, 82, 170, 183
Injunction	73–104, 170, 172, 173, 176, 186, 191, 208, 209
Qualifications	73–83, 170, 172, 176, 183, 186, 191, 208, 209
Types	84–104, 136, 173, 186
Injunction bond	104
Insurance "write off"	42
Interlocutory relief	99
See also Preliminary Injunction, Temporary Injunction	
Irreparable injury	99, 102, 115, 140, 170, 172, 176, 191
Jury trial right	1, 3–4, 83, 162–166, 171
Laches	146, 148, 150–153, 198
Land sale contracts	31, 32, 33
Liquidated damages	30
Loss of consortium	44, 45, 181
Loss of use	10, 53
Lost earning capacity	35, 36, 38
Lost profits	8, 11, 21, 23, 27, 29, 63, 187, 195, 207
Lost wages	10, 37, 38, 39, 44, 169, 180

Topic	Question
Market value	52–54, 60, 62
Measurement of damages	17, 18, 20, 22, 24–25, 27–29, 33, 41, 52, 58, 59–61, 167, 182, 194, 195, 210
Medical expenses	10, 34, 41, 42, 169
Mineral rights	62
Mitigation	12, 13, 14, 43, 167, 207
Modification of injunction	92, 205, 209
Non-economic (non-pecuniary) damages	40, 47, 51, 181
Pain and suffering damages	37, 43, 44, 47, 51, 174, 180
Per diem arguments	174
Personal value	56, 57, 185, 194
Post-judgment interest	16
Pre-judgment interest	15
Preliminary injunction	94–104, 136, 176, 186
Preventive injunction	82, 84–87
Promissory estoppel	121
Prophylactic injunction	84–87, 90, 173, 209
Punitive damages	64–72, 178, 188, 197
Quantum meruit	118, 175, 202, 203
Quasi-contract	116, 124, 125, 175
Reliance damages	8
Remittitur	51, 197
Reparative injunction	84–87, 173
Repair costs	7, 52, 58, 59, 185, 194
Replacement costs	61
Replevin	1
Rescission	116, 119, 123, 124, 175, 199, 200
Restatement (Second) of Contracts	7, 30
Restatement (Second) of Torts	10, 59

Topic	Question
Restitution	115–134, 175, 179, 193, 202, 210
Equitable restitution	125–134, 179, 193, 202
Restitution in contract	31–32, 175, 202, 210
Sentimental value	57
Special damages	10
Specific performance	1, 6, 75–76, 80, 171, 172, 208
Structural injunction	84, 86, 89–90
Subrogation	122
Temporary injunction	94–104, 183, 186
Termination of injunction	92, 95
Unclean hands	147–149, 151, 205
Unconscionability	146, 148, 189
Uniform Commercial Code	17–29, 167, 182, 187, 207
Unjust enrichment	115–124, 175, 179, 193. 199, 200, 202, 203, 210
Volume seller	27
Waiver	146, 151, 189
Wrongful death	48–49, 180, 181